The Holy One of Israel

The Holy One of Israel

Studies in the Book of Isaiah

JOHN N. OSWALT

CASCADE *Books* • Eugene, Oregon

THE HOLY ONE OF ISRAEL
Studies in the Book of Isaiah

Copyright © 2014 John N. Oswalt. All rights reserved. Except for brief quotations in critical publications or reviews, no part of this book may be reproduced in any manner without prior written permission from the publisher. Write: Permissions. Wipf and Stock Publishers, 199 W. 8th Ave., Suite 3, Eugene, OR 97401.

Scripture quotations are the author's own, unless specified.

Scripture quotations marked NIV are taken from the *Holy Bible, New International Version*,® copyright © 1973, 1978, 1984 by International Bible Society. Used by permission of Zondervan Publishing House. All rights reserved.

Scripture quotations marked NLT are taken from the *Holy Bible,* New Living Translation, copyright ©1996, 2004 . Used by permission of Tyndale House Publishers, Inc., Wheaton, IL 60189. All rights reserved.

Scripture quotations taken from the New American Standard Bible®, Copyright © 1960, 1962, 1963, 1968, 1971, 1972, 1973, 1975, 1977, 1995 by The Lockman Foundation. Used by permission.

Cascade Books
An Imprint of Wipf and Stock Publishers
199 W. 8th Ave., Suite 3
Eugene, OR 97401

www.wipfandstock.com

ISBN 13: 978-1-59752-659-3

Cataloging-in-Publication data:

Oswalt, John.

    The Holy One of Israel : studies in the book of Isaiah / John N. Oswalt.

    xii + 162 p. ; 23 cm.

    ISBN 13: 978-1-59752-659-3

    1. Bible. Isaiah—Criticism, interpretation etc. 2. Bible. Isaiah—Theology. I. Title.

BS1515.52 O88 2014

Manufactured in the U.S.A.

Contents

Acknowledgments | vii
List of Abbreviations | ix
Preface | xi

1. The Kerygmatic Structure of the Book of Isaiah | 1
2. The Book of Isaiah: A Short Course in Biblical Theology | 16
3. Judgment and Hope: The Full-Orbed Gospel | 28
4. Holiness in the Book of Isaiah | 41
5. Righteousness in Isaiah: A Study of the Function of Chapters 56–66 in the Present Structure of the Book | 59
6. Isaiah 40–66: Addressed to People during and after the Exile | 73
7. The Mission of Israel to the Nations: Micah and Isaiah | 88
8. The Nations in Isaiah: Friend or Foe; Servant or Partner? | 94
9. God's Determination to Save His People | 106
10. The Significance of the ᶜ*almah* Prophecy in the Context of Isaiah 7–12 | 121
11. Isaiah 24–27: Songs in the Night | 134
12. Isaiah 52:13—53:12: Servant of All | 141
13. Isaiah 60–62: The Glory of the Lord | 152

Acknowledgments

The author and publisher gratefully acknowledge the cooperation of the following journals and publishers in granting permission for republication of these essays in revised form.

Chapter 1: "The Kerygmatic Structure of the Book of Isaiah" is a revised version of an essay that first appeared in *Go to the Land I Will Show You: Studies in Honor of Dwight W. Young*, edited by Joseph Coleson and Victor H. Matthews, 143–57. Winona Lake, IN: Eisenbrauns, 1996.

Chapter 2: "The Book of Isaiah: A Short Course on Biblical Theology" is a revised version of an essay that first appeared in *New Biblical Dictionary of Biblical Theology*, edited by T. Desmond Alexander and Brian S. Rosner, 217–23. Leicester, UK: Inter-Varsity Press, 2000.

Chapter 3: "Judgment and Hope: The Full-Orbed Gospel" first appeared in *Trinity Journal* 17 (1996) 191–202.

Chapter 4: "Holiness in the Book of Isaiah" is a heavily revised version of articles that appeared in *The Herald* 87/3 (1975) 16–18; 87/5 (1975) 16–18; 88/1 (1975) 19–20; 88/3 (1976) 14–15, 18; 88/5 (1976) 12–13, 24.

Chapter 5: "Righteousness in Isaiah: A Study of the Function of Chapters 56–66 in the Present Structure of the Book" first appeared in *Writing and Reading the Scroll of Isaiah: Studies of an Interpretive Tradition*, edited by Craig C. Broyles and Craig A. Evans, 1:177–91. VTSup 70. Leiden: Brill, 1997.

Chapter 6: "Who Were the Addressees of Isaiah 40–66?" first appeared in *Bibliotheca Sacra* 169 (Jan–Mar 2012) 33–47.

Chapter 7: "The Mission of Israel to the Nations" first appeared in *Through no Fault of Their Own: The Fate of Those Who Have Never Heard*, edited by William V. Crockett and James G. Sigountos, 85–96. Grand Rapids: Baker, 1991.

Chapter 8: "The Nations in Isaiah: Friend or Foe; Servant or Partner?" first appeared in *Bulletin for Biblical Research* 16/1 (2006) 41–51.

Chapter 9: "God's Determination to Save His People" first appeared in *Review and Expositor* 88 (1991) 153–65.

Chapter 10: "The Significance of the ʿ*almah* Prophecy in the Context of Isaiah 7–12" first appeared in *The Criswell Theological Review* 6 (1993) 223–35.

Chapter 11: "Isaiah 24–27: Songs in the Night" first appeared in *Calvin Theological Journal* 40 (2005) 76–84.

Chapter 12: "Isaiah 52:13—53:12: Servant of All" first appeared in *Calvin Theological Journal* 40 (2005) 85–94.

Chapter 13: "Isaiah 60–62: The Glory of the Lord" first appeared in *Calvin Theological Journal* 40 (2005) 95–103

Abbreviations

AOAT	Alter Orient und Altes Testament
AUSS	*Andrews University Seminary Studies*
BWANT	Beiträge zur Wissenschaft vom Alten und Neuen Testament
BZAW	Beihefte zur *Zeitschrift für die alttestestamentliches Wissenschaft*
CB	Cambridge Bible
CBQ	Catholic Biblical Quarterly
FOTL	Forms of the Old Testament Literature
IB	*Interpreter's Bible*
Int	*Interpretation*
JBL	*Journal of Biblical Literature*
JETS	*Journal of the Evangelical Theological Society*
JSOT	*Journal of the Study of the Old Testament*
JSOTSup	Journal of the Study of the Old Testament Supplement Series
LQ	*Literary Quarterly*
LXX	Septuagint
MT	Masoretic Text
NAC	New American Commentary
NASB	New American Standard Bible
NCBC	New Century Bible Commentary
NKJV	New King James Version
NLT	New Living Translation
NIV	New International Version

Abbreviations

NICOT	New International Commentary on the Old Testament
OTL	Old Testament Library
RSV	Revised Standard Version
SJT	*Scottish Journal of Theology*
TWAT	*Theologisches Wörterbuch zum Alten Ttestament.* 14 vols. Edited by G. Johannes Botterweck and Helmer Ringren. Stuttgart: Kohlhammer, 1970–1994
TynBul	*Tyndale Bulletin*
VT	*Vetus Testamentum*
VTSup	Supplement to Vetus Testamentum
WBC	Word Biblical Commentary

Preface

IN THE FALL OF 1973 I received a telephone call that changed the course of my life. The call was from Professor R. K. Harrison, editor of the New International Critical Commentary on the Old Testament. He was calling to invite me to write two volumes on the Book of Isaiah for the New International Commentary on the Old Testament. I was happy to be able to accept the invitation and did so with alacrity, little understanding all that would be involved in completing the project. The second volume finally appeared in 1998, after Professor Harrison had died. Then I had the opportunity to write the Isaiah volume in the *New International Version Application Commentary*, which appeared in 2003. Between these two projects I have spent some 30 years of my life with the great, bottomless well of truth, beauty, and inspiration that is this book of the Bible. Looking back, I can hardly believe that I have had this privilege, nor can I think of a more rewarding way to have spent the better part of my professional life. Thanks be to God.

Along the way, I have had the opportunity to write a number of articles in journals and chapters in books on the book of Isaiah as a whole, or some aspect of it. These materials have necessarily been scattered in various places, and I have often wished that they could be collected in some single volume. So when I proposed such a volume to Wipf and Stock Publishers, and they responded positively, I was very pleased. That is the volume you now have in hand.

The chapters in the book are arranged in something of a descending order, that is from more general treatments of the book as a whole and how I see the parts contributing to the whole, to studies of themes, such as holiness, righteousness, the nations, etc., and finally to treatments of specific segments. Some of the articles are more popular and some are more scholarly. Because each of the chapters first appeared separately, there is some overlapping. I apologize for this in advance, but hope that the repetition will at least serve to fully elucidate how I understand the book to be structured.

In all cases, you will see repeatedly that I understand the book to be a theological unity, a conviction that is happily more acceptable today than it would have been 50 years ago.

It is a pleasant duty for me to thank all who have had a part in bringing this work to completion, including original editors who either invited submissions or accepted them, colleagues who read drafts and made helpful comments, and assistants who typed and re-typed manuscripts. Particularly for the present book, I want to thank Sarah McQueen who has put into electronic form several of the articles and chapters which were not originally in that form. Her duties at the Francis Asbury Society have not specifically included such work, but she has undertaken it with generosity and a warm spirit, and I am very grateful. I also wish to extend thanks to the editorial staff at Wipf and Stock who have been unfailingly helpful. Finally, as with everything I write, I thank Karen, "the wife of my youth" who has given herself to me, making all this work possible, and worthwhile.

1

The Kerygmatic Structure of the Book of Isaiah[1]

IN HIS BOOK *The Formation of Isaiah 40–55*, Roy Melugin concludes that, while Isaiah 40–55 is composed of originally independent discourses, they have not been arranged in a chance or haphazard manner. Rather, they have been put in this order because of the specific message that the author or editor wished to communicate.[2] Melugin uses the New Testament Greek term *kerygma* 'message' to define this organizing principle.

It is my conviction that this conclusion applies to the book as a whole, not merely to the portion often labeled Deutero-Isaiah. Whatever we may conclude about the date and authorship of the various parts of the book, it is not now in its present form because of chance or because of such mechanical matters as word similarities. Rather, the various components are in their present shape and organization because of the theological points that the author(s) and/or editor(s) were trying to communicate.

Fortunately, the older position that chapters 40–55 and 56–66 were composed as independent books without any necessary dependence on Isaianic writings preceding them has mostly faded away.[3] I say "fortunately"

---

1. This is a revised form of a chapter which first appeared in *Go to the Land I Will Show You: Studies in Honor of Dwight W. Young*, eds. J. Coleson and V. H. Matthews (Winona Lake, IN: Eisenbrauns, 1996) 143–157, and appears here by permission

2. Roy F. Melugin, *The Formation of Isaiah 40–55*, BZAW 141 (Berlin: de Gruyter, 1976) 175.

3. For an example of the older position, see Otto Eissfeldt, *The Old Testament: An Introduction*, tr. P. R. Ackroyd (Oxford: Blackwell, 1965) 304, 332–46.

because such a position stems more from the early enthusiasm for source criticism, which sought to find independent sources behind every document, than it does from an attempt to understand the present book.[4]

An interim attempt to explain the phenomenon of the present book was the school hypothesis. This theory saw the present unit as the result of a school of prophets who were committed to studying and transmitting the Isaian corpus. Eventually, new books were written by members of the school, which, while still independent of First Isaiah (and later, Second Isaiah), nonetheless show the influence of the great eighth-century prophet's thought and outlook. Ultimately, other members of the school combined their colleagues' work with that of the master.[5] However, as Clements and others have recently noted, the existence of such a school is both unprecedented and unattested.[6] There is no evidence in support of the hypothesis except the present form of the book, which gave rise to the hypothesis in the first place and which can be better explained in other ways.

Recently, a number of studies showing the interdependence of the various sections of the book have appeared.[7] First Isaiah is not ignorant of Second Isaiah or even Third Isaiah. This observation is not new, but whereas it used to be said that these passages were insertions from the second or third Isaianic "sources," it is now argued that First Isaiah *in its present form* reflects a thoroughgoing impact of the ideas of the last twenty-seven chapters.[8] Furthermore, it is asserted that these last chapters were never meant to stand alone but were written in the full knowledge of the earlier work(s)

---

4. Eissfeldt dismisses the entire question of the origin of the present book in less than a page (ibid., 345–46).

5. William L. Holladay, *Isaiah, Scroll of a Prophetic Heritage* (New York: Pilgrim, 1987) 18. This book is an excellent example of the atomistic tendencies in critical studies that have reduced the book of Isaiah, and others, to collections of often artificially and accidentally collected phrases and sentences.

6. R. E. Clements, "The Unity of the Book of Isaiah," *Int* 36 (1982) 119.

7. P. R. Ackroyd, "Interpretation of the Babylonian Exile: A Study of 2 Kings 20, Isaiah 38–39," *SJT* 27 (1974) 329–52; Walter Brueggemann, "Unity and Dynamic in the Isaiah Tradition," *JSOT* 29 (1984) 89–107; Brevard S. Childs, *Introduction to the Old Testament as Scripture* (Philadelphia: Fortress, 1979) 216–25; R. E. Clements, "Unity," 117–29; Clements, "Beyond Tradition-History: Deutero-Isaianic Development of First Isaiah's Themes," *JSOT* 31 (1985) 95–113; Rolf Rendtorff, "Zur Komposition des Buches Jesaja," *VT* 34 (1984) 295–320; Christopher Seitz, "Isaiah 1–66; Making Sense of the Whole," in *Reading and Preaching the Book of Isaiah*, ed. C. R. Seitz (Philadelphia: Fortress, 1988) 105–26.

8. Seitz, "Isaiah 1–66," 113–14. See also H. G. M. Williamson, *The Book Called Isaiah* (Oxford: Clarendon, 1994) in which the author maintains that the present chapters 1–55 are largely the work of "Deutero-Isaiah," who was moved by the work of "Proto-Isaiah" to edit and supplement the work of that earlier prophet in the light of the exile.

and with the intent of bringing the ideas found there to their full development.[9] The implications of these findings for date and composition have been profound. Many now argue that the present book is the product of a thoroughgoing revision that took place sometime during the fifth century B.C.E. At that time the materials was ordered and reordered in such a way as to give a theological unity to the whole.[10] However one may receive this last suggestion, the new recognition of the wholeness of the book can only be greeted with enthusiasm. The dissection and fragmentation of one of the great pieces of world literature, not to mention one of the great pieces of theological reflection, has been nothing less than scandalous.

Scholars have identified several indications of the literary unity of the present book. Some of these relate to terms and concepts, such as, for instance, the even distribution of the phrase "the Holy One of Israel" throughout the book (twelve occurrences in chapters 1–39; thirteen in chapters 40–55).[11] Clements has also noted the recurrence of the theme of "deaf and blind," especially in relationship to Israel, in the various segments of the book (6:9-10; 35:5-6, 7; 42:18-20; 43:8; 50:4-5; 55:2-3; see also 63:17).[12] Rendtorff has pointed out the presence of "comfort," a leading idea in chapters 40–52, at such key junctures as 12:1 and 61:2.[13] The importance of redeemed Zion is another concept that is found throughout (1:27; 4:5; 12:6; 28:16; 29:8; 30:19; 33:20; 34:8; 35:10; 40:9; 46:13; 51:3, 11, 16; 52:1-2, 8; 59:20; 60:14; 61:3; 62:11; 66:8).[14] It has also been observed that the hymnic portions of 40–48 closely resemble the preexilic psalms (as do the similar portions of chapters 1–39).[15] Two other concepts worth mentioning are "wait" (8:17; 25:9; 26:8; 33:2; 40:31; 42:4; 49:23; 51:5; 59:9, 11; 60:9; 64:4) and rebellion (1:2, 20, 23, 28; 24:20; 30:1, 9; 36:5; 43:27; 44:22; 50:1, 5; 53:5, 8, 12; 57:4; 58:1; 59:12-13, 20; 63:10; 65:2; 66:24).

---

9. Rendtorff, "Komposition des Buches Jesaja," 320.

10. For example, see John D. W. Watts, *Isaiah 1–33*, WBC 24 (Waco, TX: Word, 1985).

11. J. J. M. Roberts, "Isaiah in Old Testament Theology," *Int* 36 (1982) 131–33; "The Holy One" with reference to God occurs a total of 35 times, 18 in 1–39 and 17 in 40–66. As noted above, 25 of these are "the Holy One of Israel," one is "the Holy One of Jacob," 3 times it occurs with a pronoun referring to Israel, and 6 times it stands alone (3 in 6:3).

12. Clements, "Unity of the Book of Isaiah," 125.

13. Rendtorff, "Komposition des Buches Jesaja," 298–99.

14. Ibid., 305–9.

15. Claus Westermann, *Isaiah 40–66*, trans. D. M. G. Stalker, OTL (Philadelphia: Westminster, 1969) 56, 59.

But beneath and around these hints of the unity of the book is a conceptual unity that gives shape and substance to what must otherwise remain somewhat ephemeral. By this I mean that, lacking a central theological concern and purpose, the presence of these repeated terms and concepts proves little. But if such a concern can be identified, then these elements become confirmatory evidence and take their places as component parts of a larger whole.

Melugin's phrase *kerygmatic structure* is a happy one for Isaiah, I believe. For without question, Isaiah is a kerygmatic book. It might be urged that all of the prophets are kerygmatic in their strong emphasis upon proclamation of both judgment and salvation. But Isaiah is more so. From the opening verse to the last, the book resounds with calls to hear, to attend, to deal with, to take action. The prophet is depicted as proclaiming a message that demands response. Moreover, it is a message of good news, not only, as is especially the case, in chapters 40–55, but long before that. The message to Ahaz, though not received as such, was intended to be good news: "God is with us; we need not fear Rezin and Pekah" (7:4–10). But even before that, the announcement of salvation is clearly an integral part of the introduction (chapters 1–5), not only in chapter 1 (vv. 16–19, 26–27), but also in 2:1–5 and 4:2–6. Moreover, that note of hope caps each succeeding segment (chapters 6–12 end with chapters 11–12; chapters 13–24 are followed by chapters 25–27; chapters 28–35 close with chapters 32–35, etc.). All this is brought to a climax in chapters 60–66, which, without denying the people's inability to save themselves (63:1–65:7), nevertheless insist upon the absolute triumph of the grace of God.[16] Thus, if the message of any book has a claim to the term "kerygmatic," Isaiah's does.

But what precisely is the message of Isaiah? When we look to the first five chapters of the book, which most scholars, regardless of their convictions on authorship, believe were written to introduce the present book, two aspects are likely to catch the reader's eye. The first is the dramatic interchange between light and dark, judgment and hope. The judgment passages are almost unremittingly dark, from the bitter injunction to turn away from useless, dying humanity in 2:22, to the call for the howling winds of battle to destroy a nation so far gone as to call evil good (5:20, 26–30). Against this backdrop, the hope passages are almost unbelievably bright. They speak of a nation clean and pure, sheltering beneath a benevolent God (4:2–6), to whom all the nations will come to hear how the Creator intended them to

---

16. As one more element in all of this, remember that the prophet's name is *yešaʿyahû*—'Yahweh saves.'

live (2:1–5).¹⁷ The sense of contrast between these emphases is heightened by the way in which they are alternated with each other. After chapter 1, which is largely judgmental, except for two brief rays of light (vv. 18–19, 26–27), comes hope in 2:1–5. But then we return to judgment in 2:6–4:1. This is followed by hope again (4:2–6), which gives way yet again to the judgment that closes the segment (5:1–30).

The second aspect that will impress the reader in these introductory chapters is the shocking abruptness with which these interchanges occur. There are no transitions whatsoever from judgment to hope, or back again—this in a book that is noted for such smooth transitions that scholars cannot agree in given cases whether the transitional statement is to be interpreted with the previous segment or with the following one.¹⁸ Yet here there are no transitions, and we must ask why. Surely it will not do to posit a construction by mechanical means (e.g., similar words in two otherwise unrelated pieces) or by chance. This would be as if to say that one motif follows another in Beethoven's Fifth Symphony because both happen to have been written in the same key, or because the one happened to fall from a student's composition book at the moment the master was in need of another phrase. No, the abrupt juxtaposition of these kinds of ideas, whatever their ultimate source, not once, but twice, in these opening chapters, whether done by author or editor, must be seen as an indication of intent.¹⁹ Furthermore, the inclusion of the prophet's call only after these introductory chapters must be taken into account

What does the structure and content of these chapters say about the kerygmatic intent of the book, about the way in which the author or editor wishes us to read the book? Without question it speaks about the inescapability of divine retribution. This is clear both by the way chapter 1 concludes and by the way chapter 5 concludes the introduction, Whatever the distant future may hold, it is *through* judgment, not around it, Whatever

---

17. Calling the Mountain of the Lord the highest mountain of the world is a figurative way of calling him the Creator.

18. Some of the debated transitional passages are 1:9; 2:5; 6:1–13; 9:1[2]; 17:9; 30:18; 32:5; 44:6–8; 45:23, etc.

19. While I insist that this kind of structuring is indicative of intent, I am cautious regarding hypotheses that depend on identifying elaborate structures, such as chiastic parallelism, extending over several chapters or even over the whole book. Too often these proposals seem to me to depend on misusing some of the data sooner or later. They also do not seem to take enough account of the way the motifs of the book appear and reappear. Thus, it is possible to create any number of these "structures," each one plausible and each one differing from the rest. An example in point is John Goldingay's "The Arrangement of Isaiah 41–45," VT 29 (1979) 289-99. On the other hand, see the proposal in chapter 13 below.

the ultimate destiny of Israel and Judah, their immediate destiny is one of destruction.

But against this bleak backdrop stands another certainty equally as real, one whose absolute nature is not mitigated in any sense by the certainty of destruction. This certainty is the realization of the Exodus promises: God's people will be holy, as he is, experiencing his continual guidance and protection (4:2–6; cf. Exod 19:3–6; Num 9:15–18). Whatever may come upon the nation in retribution for their rebellion (chapter 1), their pride (2:6–4:1), and their corruption of moral truth (5:1–30), God's promises will not fail.

But to what purpose are those promises? Was the covenant with Israel merely a fiat of divine love, one manifestation of that eternal Tao that reveals itself to other cultures in other ways? Hardly! The placement of 2:1–5 could not be more telling. The God of Israel is the *only* manifestation of the Tao, and his law was given to the Israelites so that it might be transmitted to the entire world. They cannot perform this function if they are filthy and blood-stained, but cleansing and holiness are not ends in themselves, either. Rather, they are necessary conditions if the ultimate end of the promises—worldwide acknowledgment of the God of Abraham, Isaac, and Jacob—is to be attained.[20] Furthermore, this acknowledgment is expected to result in a rule of peace and equity (see also 9:5–6 [6–7]; 11:3–9; 25:6–9; 42:1–4).

Thus, the opening chapters of Isaiah tell us how we are intended to read the book. We are intended to see that as sure as destruction is apart from some radical and continuing change of moral direction (1:16–20), restoration is equally sure. But restoration is for a purpose, the purpose of revealing God to the world and drawing the world to him.

Investigation of the placement and distinctive content of chapter 6 confirms this judgment. The central focus of this chapter is the revelation of God in his moral perfection and in his world-filling glory. God must be known, both in his own essential character and in his relationship to the world. But this revelation can only be destructive to sinful humanity. Thus, Isaiah's response to the experience is not that he is limited, or finite, or even

---

20. Controversy continues to rage over whether Isaiah is "truly" universalistic. See Harry M. Orlinsky, *Studies in the Second Part of the Book of Isaiah*, VTSup 14 (Leiden: Brill, 1967) 97–117. But unless conjectural emendation is resorted to and offending parts are excised, it seems to me beyond any qualification that the present book teaches that the God of Jerusalem is the sole God of the world and that the whole world must eventually come to him in submission, either voluntary or coerced. (Along with this passage, see 19:23–25; 25:6–8; 45:5–6; 66:18–19.) Whether this end is envisioned as resulting from Jewish "missionary" activity or simply as a result of God's activity on behalf of his people may be argued. But I do not think that the nature of the expected outcome can be disputed. See chapters 8 and 9 below.

mortal, but that he is unclean and so cannot exist in God's presence. This parallels the judgment passages in chapters 1–5. Alongside the Holy One of Israel (1:4; 5:19, 24; cf. 6:3) the hubris of humanity (1:31; 2:7–8, 11, 17) that fuels our rebellions (1:2–4, 3:9) would be laughable if it were not so hideous.

It is very significant that it is his lips and the lips of his countrymen that the prophet recognizes to be unclean. What else can this signify but the sense that the glory of God demands to be declared, but cannot be, either by the prophet to his people, or by his people to the world, because of a fundamental uncleanness of their lives? Thus, the experience of cleansing—a gracious act on the part of God, both unbidden and undeserved—is immediately followed by the commission to speak. Cleansing is not for its own sake, but for the purpose of communication. But communication cannot take place until cleansing, a cleansing by fire (cf. 4:4), has taken place.

Thus chapter 6 is in its present place in the book to answer the questions raised by the shocking oscillations of chapters 1–5, As the reader careens back and forth between grimmest judgment and highest hope, he or she must ask, "But how can this Israel, proud, rebellious, corrupt, become that Israel, clean, holy, displaying the truth for which all hunger?" Chapter 6 provides the answer. When the nation of unclean lips has shared the experience of the man of unclean lips, they can declare to the world the glory he has declared to them. Thus, chapter 6 is not merely the call of the prophet; it is the call of the nation.

This equation (cleansing is for declaration) emerges with special clarity again in chapters 40–48. It is present in the intervening chapters, as will be seen below, but in more muted ways In chapters 40–48 Israel is in the position of Isaiah in 6:5. They are undone. Their fundamental uncleanness has delivered them over to destruction and they, like him, can see no other possible outcome than dissolution and disappearance. But completely unexpectedly, as unexpected as the seraph's words after the coal had seared Isaiah's lips, comes the announcement of forgiveness, cleansing, and commission (40:1–11).[21] The captive Judeans will be restored; far from being cast off, they are called God's chosen servants.[22] What will these servants do? In chapters 40–48 (with the exception of 42:1–9, on which see below), they do nothing. They are strictly recipients of the unmerited grace of God.

---

21. The MT makes it plain that Jerusalem is the messenger of good news, not the recipient, in 40:9. Note the similarities between chapter 6 and 40:1–11. But 40:1–11 is not an independent call narrative. It assumes chapter 6 and builds on it. See Seitz, "Isaiah 1–66," 109.

22. Almost certainly the sense of "servants" in these passages is that of performers of religious service. This is the equivalent of holy priesthood in Exod 19:6. See Pss 100:2; 102:23[22]; 134:1–2; 135:1–2.

But by receiving that grace they become the vehicle whereby God will demonstrate to the world that he alone, the deity of little, defeated Jerusalem, is deity of the whole world.

The point just made needs to be emphasized, and this can be accomplished by comparison with Ezekiel 34–48, There too the message of gracious, undeserved restoration is declared. But there, except for one brief though important passage (36:16–36), the stress is solely upon the return and its blessed character. Here in Isaiah the emphasis is quite different. Here the point of Ezekiel 36:16–36 is expanded to the entire section. Virtually all of chapters 40–48 is given over to a discussion of what the restoration of Israel will demonstrate to the nations about God. Israel, without doing anything but receiving God's cleansing grace (40:2; 41:10; 44:1–5; 46:12–13; 48:9–11), will not only be the evidence to prove that God alone is God (41:25–29; 43:8–13; 44:6–8; 48:14–15), but also the evidence to cause the nations to come to Jerusalem in acknowledgement of him (45:14, 22–25).

The final section, chapters 60–66, confirms this understanding of the *kerygma* of the book. Although it is not as widely agreed that this section was written as a conclusion to the book as it is that chapters 1–5 were written as an introduction,[23] nevertheless, there is something of a concluding emphasis. The opening verses (60:1–3) make the point and set the tone. The glory of God has risen on Israel and its brightness will draw all nations to that dawning.[24] Thus, the promises of chapters 1–5 are realized. It is sometimes urged that the picture here is not of co-religionists or converts but of captives.[25] Surely this element is present (e.g., 60:11–12, 14; 61:5; 63:6; 64:2), but it is by no means the only or even the dominant note. The light to the nations concept not only opens the segment, as just pointed out, but also closes it (66:18–19, 23). Jews will travel the world over to proclaim the glory (cf. 6:3; 40:5–6) of God with the result that the dispersed Jews will be sent home in triumph as an offering to the Lord, and all will join in worshiping him. Nor is this emphasis merely confined to the opening and closing of the section, important as that is. It also appears within the segment at 61:9, 11 and 62:2. The point of these verses is, to be sure, not that the Jews

---

23. The uncertainty largely stems from the failure of these chapters to summarize the themes of the preceding chapters quite as completely as one might expect in a purposefully written conclusion. Also, it seems to introduce a certain amount of new material (especially in 63:1—65:7).

24. For those who believe that this is more than empty rhetoric, the coming of Christ, in whom the glory of God dwelt bodily (John 1:14) and because of whom all the nations have come to Jerusalem, fulfills the meaning of this passage precisely.

25. So Orlinsky, *Second Part*, 36. For a comprehensive treatment of this question, see chapters 8 and 9 below.

The Kerygmatic Structure of the Book of Isaiah

will proselytize the nations. But what they will do is entirely consistent with 2:1–5 and 43:8–13; the nations will be moved to acknowledge God's lordship and saviorhood when they see how he has redeemed and purified his people.

In the light of the foregoing observations, a strong case can be made that the kerygmatic message of the book centers on Israel's servanthood. To be sure, this actual terminology is only prominent in chapters 40–55. But as I have tried to show, the sense in which servanthood is used there, especially in 40–48, is precisely the same as the sense of chapters 1–6 and 60–66. It is as the chosen are graciously redeemed from their just judgment that the world will come to acknowledge God. It is as Israel accepts its role as servant of God that this goal, elucidated at the beginning of the book, reemphasized in the middle, and reiterated at the end, could be achieved.

With this realization in mind, we can now look at the rest of the book and see to what extent other sections complement and develop this theme. In chapters 7–39 the nations, and Israel's relation to them, is the special focus. The great question is: will Israel trust the nations to insure its future, or will it trust God? The historical sections, chapters 7–12 and 36–39, stand at either end as mirror images of each other.

In chapters 7–12 Israel refuses to trust God in the face of Rezin's and Pekah's threats. Instead of being a light to the nations, demonstrating to them God's trustworthiness, Israel turns for its hope to the very kingdoms of humanity it was to have led to God. As a result, Isaiah has to tell Ahaz that Assyria (whom Ahaz has trusted in place of God) will turn on him and destroy Israel. But the true test of God's trustworthiness, Isaiah then says, is that in spite of all this rebellion, God will graciously reestablish the house of David, restore his people from captivity, and establish his universal kingdom. It is when the people will have reaped the just results of their foolish choices and yet have received God's totally unmerited deliverance that they will be able to cry, "I will trust and not be afraid" (12:2). Furthermore, it is out of this deliverance that they will declare to the nations the exalted name and glorious deeds of the Holy One of Israel (12:4–6).

Chapters 36–39 move in the opposite direction, At the outset, the response is one of trust. The predicted outcome of Ahaz's choice is at hand—the Assyrian lion is clawing the door, the flood is up to the chin. Should Hezekiah surrender? God's answer through Isaiah is, "No, trust me" (37:6–7, 22–35). Hezekiah does trust God and the army of the mightiest nation in the world is destroyed. In place of the lack of trust in chapters 7 and 8, here is a clear manifestation of a lesson learned and of the validity of that lesson, But whereas the lack of trust and consequent destruction in 7:1–10:4 became a basis for a proclamation of eventual salvation in 10:5—11:16, here the movement is in the opposite direction. Chapter 39 concludes with a prophecy of destruction at the hands of the Babylonians. What is happening? Two significant points need to be made. First, chapters 38 and 39, which detail Hezekiah's mortality and fallibility, make it painfully clear that he is not the promised Messiah of 9:5–6 [6–7] and 11:1–5. The miraculous deliverance might make it appear so, but he is not. For the ultimate confirmation of the truth that God is with us (7:14), that he is trustworthy, we must look to another. Our trust is in God, not in any expression of human perfectibility.

The second point that these chapters make relates directly to what we are identifying as a dominant motif of the book. According to 39:1, the reason the Babylonian envoys visited Jerusalem was because they had heard of Hezekiah's recovery from his illness. In other words, this was the time to perform the task of 12:1–6: to declare to the world the wondrous name and the glorious deeds of God, to announce absolute and unreserved trust of him. In fact, Hezekiah failed to do so. Instead of magnifying God, he magnified himself (cf. Num 20:10–12). Trust is a way of life, not a one-time or a two-time declaration, and Hezekiah typifies the short-term trust of the nation that would eventually result in its own destruction. Thus, we may argue that both chapters 7–12 and 36–39 are governed by the concerns we have already identified: the witness of redeemed servant Israel, both pivoting around the theme of trusting the nations or trusting God. Chapters 7–12 move from negative to positive while chapters 36–39 move from positive to negative. In so doing each sets the stage for what is to follow.[26]

Chapters 7–12, with their promise that God will deliver from the nations, raise the question of whether he can really do this. Chapters 13–35 insist that he can and use several literary structures to make the point. Chapters 13–23 consist of oracles against the nations which assert that all nations, not only Israel, are accountable to God. When God desires to restore his people, he can be trusted to do so, for no nation can stand in his way. Chapters 24–27 insist that all history, not merely Israel's, is under the dominion of God.[27] Chapters 28–33 use the examples of contemporary history to show the folly of the alliances a craven and corrupt court is advocating and conclude with the promise that the True King who will give right counsel is coming. Finally, the entire section is concluded by chapters

---

26. Chapters 36–39 are also a fitting conclusion to chapters 7–39 because they confirm what Isaiah had prophesied and show that he was right when he declared that God could be trusted. For further discussion of these points see my *The Book of Isaiah, Chapters 1–39*, NICOT (Grand Rapids: Eerdmans, 1986) 627–98.

27. As noted above, it is in 25:6–8 that the redemption of all people on "this mountain" (cf. 2:2–3; 66:20) is declared. History will culminate in redemption for all who will submit.

34–35, which sum up the options in graphic form: turning the world into a desert if we refuse to trust God (chapter 34); and having God turn our desert into a garden if we will turn back to him and trust him in the end (chapter 35).

Thus we can say that, within the larger movement of the book, chapters 7–39 establish the basis for servanthood. That basis is trust in the sovereign grace of the only God. Unless one can trust ones master, servanthood can only be compelled and will always fall short of what it might be. Furthermore, the division also illustrates the fundamental problem that was first exposed in chapters 1–5: the idolatrous tendency of human pride to deify human glory and accomplishment, putting our trust in what is temporal, mortal, and fallible, instead of in the transcendent Creator to whom Israel's eventual deliverance would bear witness.

Chapters 36–39, while concluding the earlier division, also point the way to what follows. This is not merely in the more superficial sense of predicting the coming exile, but on a deeper, more ideological level.[28] Again, a question is raised that falls to the next section to answer, That question is, "Who is the Deliverer?" If indeed Hezekiah is representative of his people in the short-term nature of his trust, who will be the ideal king of chapters 9 and 11? If Hezekiah is not Immanuel, then who is?

Furthermore, these chapters raise another question that calls for an answer in this book. Isaiah has insisted in the most absolute of terms that this God is God of the whole world, able to deliver any who trust in him from any threat. This had certainly seemed true in the case of Assyria. But now the prophet says that God will not deliver Jerusalem from Babylon. Does this not call into question the whole theme of the book? How can the people of God testify to the world about the complete trustworthiness and absolute incomparability of Yahweh of Jerusalem if they are captives in Babylon? As chapters 1–39 are now structured, it is impossible for chapter 39 to be the conclusion of the book. It would not be a conclusion, but a negation of all that the book claimed.

In fact, chapters 40–66 are a necessary part of the message that was introduced in chapters 1–6. They show that the new situation after 586 B.C. will not negate what was said in chapters 7–39. God is so far from being overcome by the new historical situation that he can use the new situation to do something previously unheard of—deliver a captive people from exile. The new situation will provide an even better platform for demonstrating to the nations that the God worshiped on Mt. Zion is indeed their God, the

---

28. See Ackroyd, "Interpretation of the Babylonian Exile," for additional reflection on this topic.

only God. Furthermore, it is in this context that the completely unmerited grace of God can provide motivation for service. The stunning word that the Babylonian captivity did not mean abandonment by God was exactly what was needed to move the Judeans to put into actual practice the trust that had been so clearly taught in chapters 7–39.

But what about the deliverer? If not Hezekiah, then who? Is Cyrus the promised Messiah? Beyond this, chapters 40–48 raise their own question. How can sinful Israel become servant Israel? How can the nation of unclean lips be made the bearer of God's truth? Is it merely the fires of judgment that will take care of the problem? Or is something more at stake? Here we must consider the role of the "suffering servant." Undoubtedly, this is the single most controversial issue in the book. Literally hundreds of books and articles have been written on the topic in the last century alone. Thus, it is impossible even to offer a complete review of the alternatives here, much less solve the problem. We can only ask readers to consider again the evidence that two different servants are discussed between 41:8 and 54:17. The identity of the one servant is quite unmistakable: it is the nation of Israel. In all those instances where the nation is unquestionably referred to, the servant is described as being insensitive and fearful but encouraged with the promised benefits of servanthood. His role is to be a witness to grace.

But there are other references in which the identity of the servant is not obvious, and in these (42:1–9; 49:1–12; 50:4–11; 52:13—53:12) the servant's vocation is to bring justice and salvation to the earth (42:1–4; 49:6), light to the nations (42:6; 49:6; 50:10–11), and deliverance to the people, i.e., Jacob (42:6; 49:5–6; 53:4–9). The dominant characteristics of this servant are humility, uncertainty, being misunderstood, and pain (42:2; 49:4, 7; 50:4–6; 53:1–9). All of this is so enigmatic that Duhm proposed that these so-called "Servant Songs" were not a part of the original chapters 40–55.[29] Although this judgment was initially widely accepted, it has held less and less sway in recent years. In part this is so because there has been no unanimity about the origin of the songs or their function, either in their original format or after having been edited into the present structure.[30] The figures most often identified as this "suffering servant"—the nation, Cyrus, the prophet himself, or some other figure—all have one or more problems in the above descriptions that must be explained away.

---

29. B. Duhm, *Das Buch Jesaia*, HAT 3/1(Göttingen: Vandenhoeck & Ruprecht, 1892) 311–13.

30. James Muilenburg, "Isaiah, Chapters 40–66," in *IB*, vol. 5 (Nashville: Abingdon, 1956) 406–8, argued that the "Servant Songs" were an integral part of chapters 40–55. T. N. D. Mettinger, *A Farewell to the Servant Songs: A Critical Examination of an Exegetical Axiom* (Lund: Gleerup, 1983), has argued forcefully for the same conclusion.

The point that I would like to make here is that an examination of the material in chapters 49–55, where three of these four passages occur, shows a major emphasis on the means and the fact of deliverance (note the repetition of "the arm of the Lord": 51:5, 9; 52:1; 53:1; cf. also 59:1). Gone are the disputations with the gods of 40–48 in which the possibility of deliverance from Babylon was established. Here the issue revolves around Israel's sin and God's willingness to deliver in spite of that previous condition. Two different atmospheres can be identified. In chapters 49–52, deliverance is being anticipated and Jerusalem is being encouraged to believe it can happen. In chapters 54–55, there is a lyrical call to participate in a deliverance proleptically seen as having already occurred. It can hardly be accidental that the segment that falls between these two is 52:13—53:12. What all of this indicates is that whoever this servant is, he is equated with the means by which Israel's servanthood is made possible. In chapters 40–48, the means is Cyrus, except in 42:1–9, where the servant is described in terms like those ascribed to the Messiah in chapter 11. The servant described in chapters 49–53 does not resemble Cyrus in any degree. This suggests that the deliverance the Israelites require is more than simply from Babylonian captivity. That the problem is Israel's sin is intimated in 50:1 and 51:1–3, 7. This is confirmed by the repeated references to suffering for sin, iniquity, and transgression in 53:5–12.

In sum, I would argue that chapters 49–55 deal with the deliverance from captivity to the *nations* and from what prompted that captivity, as was first predicted in 4:2–6 and followed up on in 11:10–16. Israel's witness to the nations depended on the evidence of God's power and his faithfulness. The identity of Cyrus is perfectly clear, but the identity of the other deliverer seems almost purposely enigmatic. Nevertheless, the *function* of this person seems clear: he offers himself in order to deliver from that which Cyrus cannot. It seems a telling comment that chapter 55, just prior to its mention of the nation's being a witness to the peoples and calling the nations together because of God's glory given to them (vv. 4–5) refers to the everlasting covenant with David. Is this an identification of the suffering servant with the Davidic Messiah? So it would seem. Thus chapters 49–55 tell us that the ultimate means of Israel's servanthood is the self-giving of the servant who is the ideal Israel (49:3).

The section of the book remaining to be discussed is chapters 56–59. Here we are reminded again that deliverance from Babylonian captivity does not automatically constitute one a servant of God. Unless there has also been a deliverance from sin to righteousness, from transgression to faithfulness, one is no better than a foreigner or a eunuch. In fact, foreigners and eunuchs can be very effective servants of God, if they will live in ways that are consistent with God's character (56:3–8). Birthright and physical characteristics no longer define acceptability, Behavior is now the only criterion (57:3–4, 11–13). Thus, there is here an indication that the outreach to the nations that was forecast in 2:1–5 is already at work in the community. The segment closes with the admission by the prophet on behalf of the people that they are unable to do right or to bring justice in and of themselves (59:9–15a). Unless God delivers them by himself and imparts his spirit to them, they will be unable to speak the message of judgment and deliverance (59:15b–21).[31]

I have argued that the single most dominating theme of the present book of Isaiah, the one that gives shape to the message of the book and thus to the book itself, is that of servanthood. But it is a particular approach to servanthood. Israel is called to be the means whereby the understanding of God that it has received—that the God of Jerusalem is the sole Lord of History, the only Judge and only Savior—should become known to the whole world. This is only possible by means of an accurate knowledge of God and a life that is an accurate reflection of his character. Chapters 1–6 lay down these basic ideas. Chapters 7–39 reveal to the servants the essential trustworthiness of Yahweh and show that there is nothing and no one else who is worthy of such trust. They also reinforce the ideas of God's absolute sovereignty and his utter righteousness. The glory of humanity, as seen in the great nations of the earth, is as nothing in comparison to the Lord's. If Israel is to fulfill its function of servanthood, learning the lesson of God's trustworthiness is essential.

Chapters 40–48 demonstrate God's election of the Israelites and explain how their deliverance from political oppression will be the evidence of God's uniqueness. These evidences of underserved love will provide the motivation for servanthood. Chapters 49–55 address the problem of the means of servanthood. There is a deeper obstruction to servanthood than bondage or oppression. What shall be done about the sin that put them into bondage in the first place? Here it is the servant who becomes the Arm of the Lord to set them free.

---

31. In Oswalt, *The Book of Isaiah, Chapters 40–66*, 461–65, I argue that chapters 56–66 are arranged chiastically with 61:1–3 being the climax. See also chapter 13 below. Thus the point of chapters 56–59 is the same as that of 63–66, but in reverse order: Yahweh's purpose is that all peoples, whether foreigners or eunuchs (56:1–8) should "see his glory" (66:19) and "worship before" him" (66:23). But his light cannot shine out of Israel to the world because of their unrighteous lives (56:9–59:15a; 63:7–65:16). In order for that to change the Divine Warrior (59:15a–21; 63:1–6) must come and defeat their sin. Who is that Divine Warrior? He is none other than the One anointed by the Spirit to preach Good News, delivering them from their captivity (61:1–3).

The Kerygmatic Structure of the Book of Isaiah

It might be expected that Isaiah's message is completed with the great hymn of salvation in chapter 55. But it is precisely because of the nature of the message that the book cannot end there. The Judeans must not be permitted to believe that their servanthood is carried out merely because they have experienced the hand of salvation from the bondage of the past. Their mission to the nations will fail if there are no clear evidences of God's unique character in the changed lives of his servants. Thus, one of the recurring themes of chapters 56–66 is the inability of humans to live the life of God, but the divine ability to do in them what they cannot do in themselves. God will make of them a light to the nations. If chapters 49–55 deal with the work of God *for* his servants, these chapters focus upon his work *in* his servants, all to the end that, because of his glory (6:3; 35:2; 60:1, 9, 19; 66:18–19) shining in them, the whole world might come to recognize God as the only God (60:3; 60:19).

The book of Isaiah, in a way almost unparalleled in any other biblical book, reveals a complete picture of God: sovereignty, creativity, purposefulness, trustworthiness, faithfulness, justice, grace, holiness, glory, and patience. Surely the book's purpose is to declare Yahweh's uniqueness and to call people in every age to experience his deliverance and to share in the task of demonstrating his uniqueness to the watching world.

2

The Book of Isaiah
A Short Course on Biblical Theology[1]

INTRODUCTION

ALTHOUGH IT IS SURELY coincidence that the number of chapters in the present book of Isaiah corresponds exactly to the number of books in the Christian Bible, it is still true that there is no other single book in either testament which comprehends the whole of Biblical theology so completely as does the book of Isaiah. Here we find the terrifying holiness of God depicted as clearly as it is anywhere in the Old Testament. But we also find the unchanging grace of God depicted as clearly as it is anywhere in the New Testament. Thus, in many ways the book of Isaiah offers a summary of Biblical theology.

THEOLOGY OF THE BOOK AS A WHOLE

Recent studies of the book of Isaiah have rediscovered its thematic unity. Earlier work, dominated by hypotheses of multiple authorship, tended not to see the complex interplay of themes which is a special characteristic of this book. Such themes as judgment and hope, blindness and deafness, rebellion and trust, or even highways and trees, not to mention such an obvious one as "The Holy One of Israel," have been utilized throughout the

---

1. This is a slightly revised version of an article that first appeared in the *New Biblical Dictionary of Biblical Theology,* eds. T. D. Alexander and B. S. Rosner (Leicester, UK: Inter-Varsity Press, 2000) 217–23, and is used here by permission.

book to tie the various units together. Clearly, the parts of the final form of the book have been structured in the light of the whole.

Chapters 1–6

In the present form of the book, chapters 1–5 function as an introduction. As such, they paint in strong relief the contrast between the rebellion and corruption of Judah and Israel in Isaiah's own day (1:1–31; 2:6–4:1; 5:1–30) and the future holiness and blessedness which the nation would enjoy (2:1–5; 4:2–6). One of the chief marks of this rebellion is the tendency to glorify humanity at the expense of God. But such folly can only result in the humiliation of humanity, for only God's glory fills the earth. Nevertheless, God will not be content to leave his people in their humiliation. But this raises a question. How can the promised holiness and blessedness replace rebellion and corruption? Chapters 1–5 do not answer it.

In fact, chapter 6 provides the answer, and this explains why the prophet's call is only narrated after the five preceding chapters. Just as the man of unclean lips had to abandon all hope before receiving a fiery cleansing, so too must the nation. In many ways the rest of the book is an outworking of the components of Isaiah's experience on a national scale. Just as Isaiah needed to see both God and himself correctly (6:1–4), so did the nation (chaps. 7–39). Just as Isaiah needed to receive the fiery, but ultimately gracious cleansing of God (6:5–7), so did the nation (chaps. 40–55). And just as Isaiah needed to receive God's commission (6:8–13), so did the nation (chaps. 56–66).

Chapters 7–39

The vision of God and of themselves which is found in chapters 7–39 chiefly revolves around the question of trust (see below). Judah is called to trust God and to be delivered from the nations. Thus she will be in a position to demonstrate God's unique glory to them. But instead, she is inclined to be impressed by human glory and to trust the nations instead of God. As a result, she will be captured and destroyed by the very nations she trusted. Nevertheless, God is so trustworthy that even after Judah has brought upon herself the results of her own failure to trust, God will still offer himself to her.

These ideas are represented in an A–B–A structure. Chapters 7–12 (A) tell about Ahaz's refusal to trust God and the immediately tragic and yet ultimately hopeful results of that choice. Chapters 13–35 (B) show in detail why it is folly to trust the nations rather than God. The nations are all under God's judgment, both in the near term (chaps. 13–23) and in the long term (24–27). Only woe lies ahead for those who rush to ally themselves with the nations and refuse to wait for God who is the true King of the universe (chaps. 28–33). The stark nature of the alternatives is summed up in chaps 34 (negative) and 35 (positive). In chapters 36–39 (A') Ahaz' son Hezekiah is given the test of trust again. Will he succeed where his father failed? Has he learned the lessons contained in the intervening chapters? The answer is both yes and no, for although he trusts God to deliver him from the Assyrians and experiences a mighty confirmation of God's trustworthiness, he also succumbs to the temptation to parade his wealth and power before the visiting Babylonians. Thus, the previous section is brought to an end, and the stage is set for the following section which will address issues raised by the Babylonian captivity.

Chapters 40–55

Chapters 40–55 are addressed to a people in despair. They are asking whether history has not made a mockery of all the previous fine words about trusting God. Has not God been defeated by the Babylonian gods, or if not by them, by his people's sins? Isaiah's response to these questions is twofold. First, God demonstrates that he alone is God (see Uniqueness of God below). He does this by showing that the gods are not really independent of the world, that they did not create it and cannot say what will become of it. He is the sole creator and he is able to do new things as he wishes. Second, God declares that he will use Israel to be the evidence of all this. He is no more defeated by Israel's sin than he is by the Babylonian gods. Far from being cast off, the Israelites are his chosen servants who will declare his glory to the world.

But sinful Israel cannot automatically become servant Israel. Just as Isaiah's lips were made clean, so the nation must be cleansed. Mere return from exile will not automatically produce different behavior. Already in chapter 42 this issue begins to be addressed, for there another servant makes a brief appearance. In language very much like that used to describe the coming king in chapters 9, 11, 16, and 31–32 it is said this servant will "bring justice to the nations" (42:1, 3–4) and will be "a covenant to the people" (42:6) "to open the eyes of the blind [Israel]" (v. 7). This is surely not the nation healing itself. This conclusion becomes even surer in chapters 49–55 where the idea is put forward that God will find a way of reconciling himself to his people and of restoring them to fellowship. Here the unidentified servant comes into much sharper relief and it is clear he is not Israel personified. Instead of being rebellious and corrupt, this servant is obedient and pure-hearted. Instead of being self-protective, this servant is self-surrendering for the sake of others. The climactic treatment of this servant is found in the enigmatic 52:13—53:12. Here he suffers and dies for the sin and rebellion of people the prophet calls "us." This section is immediately followed in chapters 54–55 by lyrical invitations to Israel to come and receive restoration and cleansing. Clearly the substitutionary suffering of the servant in 52:13—53:12 is the operative element making this invitation possible.

Chapters 56–66

After the lyrical tone of chapters 54–55, chapters 56–66 come as something of a dash of cold water. In language very reminiscent of chapters 1–39, the people are challenged to *do* righteousness. This seems very different from chapters 40–55 where they were invited to *experience* the righteousness of God (his deliverance) which was made available to them freely. Now they are told in no uncertain terms that obedient foreigners and eunuchs are more pleasing to God than pure-bred Judeans who pride themselves on their worship practices. These Judeans are quoted as saying that they are unable to do justice no matter how hard they try, and God responds that he himself will come in the person of a Divine Warrior who will do in them what they cannot. The result is that Israel will become a light to the nations through whom the Spirit-anointed Messiah can declare his good news to the whole world.

Two ideas are clearly highlighted. On the one hand, merely being among the chosen people does not make one a servant of God; obedience is the irreplaceable evidence. But on the other, no one dare think that obedience is merely a result of human effort. It is the divine ability that makes obedience possible.

KEY THEMES

Judgment and Hope

If there is a single dominant theme in the book it is this one. It is present in chapter 1 and in chapter 66 and in some form in every chapter in between. It is even more dominant than the almost breath-taking understanding of God. While the understanding of God does underlie judgment and hope it does not itself provide the structure of the book, whereas judgment and hope do.

The distinctive vision of the book is in the way in which judgment and hope are intertwined. The Israelites and Judeans thought, as many moderns do, that judgment and hope are contrasting elements. But Isaiah shows that they are complementary. This appears in the macro-structure of the book where chapters 1–39 might be said to focus on judgment while chapters 40–66 focus on hope. But when these two larger sections are examined more closely, it is clear that the general observation is only generally true. For there is a great deal of hope in 1–39 and there is a great deal of judgment in 40–66. The interdependence of the two themes is already apparent in chapter 1 and in the rest of the introductory unit. Judgment is seen as a foregone conclusion. God announces that he will rid himself of his adversaries and take vengeance on his enemies, who are immediately identified as his people (1:24–25). But what is the purpose of these acts of judgment? It is not destruction, but purging, with the result that once again the city will be called the city of righteousness, the faithful city (1:26). Hope for Judah is not to be found in the avoidance of judgment, but precisely in it. If they could somehow escape the fire, then in their present condition, there would be no hope that they could ever become what they were designed to be (cf. 6:9–10). As noted above, this seems to be the significance of the interchange between the announcements of judgment and the declarations of hope which appears in chapters 1–5. Judgment cannot be avoided, but that should not be a source of despair. It is through the "spirit of judgment and the spirit of burning" (4:4) that Zion can experience the presence of God in which the Exodus was intended to issue.

The same point may be seen in chapter 6, where a devastating experience of uncleanness before God is not intended to result in dissolution, but in cleansing and calling. In chapters 7–12, it is through the failure of the house of David and the concomitant destruction of the land at the hands of the Mesopotamians (7:13–25), that Immanuel will be revealed and the new age will be inaugurated by the budding of the stump of Jesse (11:1). Even the judgment of the nations (13–23) is intended to eventuate in all nations having the veil of death removed forever (25:8). And if the foolish advisors of the Judean monarchy bring the nation to the point of being nothing more than a tattered flag waving on a hilltop (30:17), it is in order that all God's blessings, especially the blessing of the true king, might come to his people (30:18–26; 32:1–8).

If chapters 1–39 are not unmitigated judgment, neither are chapters 40–66 unmitigated hope. In particular, chapters 56–66 pronounce judgment on anyone who would think that the gracious salvation of God presented in chapters 40–55 is simply a result of election and that therefore righteousness is not necessary as a response to that salvation. Strong words are spoken against such an attitude, and judgment is announced against any who persist in it (57:9–14; 58:1–59:15a; 63:10–6 5:16; 66:3–4, 14–17).

But judgment is not restricted to chapters 56–66. Even in chapters 40–55, which speak so lyrically about God's deliverance, unbelief is repeatedly denounced. Judgment is pronounced on those who refuse to believe that judgment is meant to issue in hope and have succumbed to despair (42:18–25; 43:25–28; 45:9–19; 46:8–13; 48:1–19; 50:1–3, 10–11; 51:12–16)!

The Uniqueness of God

Perhaps more than any other book in the canon, Isaiah insists on the uniqueness of God. This theme is especially prominent in chapters 40–48, where it is in particular focus in the insistence that the Babylonian gods can do nothing to prevent the restoration of Judah and Jerusalem. But it is not restricted to that section. Already in chapter 2 we find the thought that the Lord is God of all nations, not just Judah, and that it his Torah by which all nations will be judged (vv. 1–4). Later in that chapter it is asserted that all humanity and the idols made in the image of humans will be humiliated before the sole glory of the Lord (vv. 6–22). All the nations are seen as subservient to his call in 5:26–30. But it is clear that the defining expression of God's uniqueness came to the prophet in his call experience. The triple "Holy, holy, holy" is an assertion that God is supremely, uniquely holy. He alone is qualified to carry this description. He alone is truly other than this world, truly transcendent. The gods are not holy at all. They are made of wood and stone, covered with precious metal by some human craftsman (cf. 2:8–9, 20; 17:7–8; 31:7; 40:18–20; 44:6–20). How can those things be called holy? Thus it is no accident that the favorite appellation of God in this book (twenty-six times out of a total of 31 in the OT) is "The Holy One of Israel (including the one occ. of "The Holy One Jacob)." The God of Israel is the uniquely holy one.

These ideas are furthered in 13–23, where all nations are depicted as falling under the judgment of God. They are not merely his tools, subject to his purposes, they are also accountable to him, to be judged by his standards. And in the end, it is this God alone who will bring history to its appointed end in which the nations will find either healing or final destruction (chaps. 24–25, cf. also 34).

The implications of these assertions are made explicit in chapters 40–48, which directly face the challenge to Israel's faith mounted by the exile. It would appear that God had been defeated by the Babylonian gods. In response God calls them into court and challenges them to prove they are gods (cf. 43:8–13). The evidence which God specifies is very significant. He calls upon the gods to explain the former things and the latter things. This shows a very sophisticated understanding of the philosophy of paganism. Because the gods are part of the ceaseless cycles of the cosmos, there is no past or future. Neither can they explain the purpose nor the destiny of the cosmos. This identity with the cosmos is devastatingly exampled in the fact of idolatry where a "god" is nothing other than an expensively decorated block of wood (e.g., 44:9–20). But God "sits above the circle of the earth" in absolute transcendence. He is the sole creator, the one who brought the cosmos into existence for a good purpose. Not only can he explain the purpose and meaning of existence, he knows the future before it occurs and can do things which have never occurred before. Only a divine being who was separate from the cosmos could do such a thing. He alone can say, "I am."

Trust

Trust is the particular theme of chapters 7–39, but it underlies other parts of the book as well. Unless the people of Israel will entrust their future to God and let him demonstrate his unique creatorhood and saviorhood through them, their mission to the world can never be worked out.

The initial challenge to trust God comes to Ahaz (7:1–7), but the king has already decided to put his hope in Assyria, as 2 Kings 16:7–9 tells us. Isaiah declares that by doing this Ahaz has delivered his nation up to destruction at Assyria's hand. Nevertheless, God will demonstrate his genuine trustworthiness by bringing Assyria under judgment, restoring his people from captivity and bringing a true son of David to rule Judah and Jerusalem. The response of the people is to "trust, and not be afraid" (12:2). As mentioned above, chapters 13–35 provide lessons in trust, demonstrating the folly of trusting the nations of the world. They are all under judgment and will all prove helpless against superior forces. God alone can be trusted in all circumstances (26:3–6). When we humans have made a desert out of our worlds through our insistence on meeting our needs for ourselves, God will still remain trustworthy and will bring those who "wait" for him out of the desert into a garden (chaps. 34–35).

The way in which trust is treated in chapters 36–39 is very important. After Hezekiah's deliverance from the military enemy in 36–37 and his deliverance from the enemy of illness in 38, it is very surprising to see him succumbing to the enemy of pride in 39. Thus, whereas Ahaz' refusal to trust in chapter 7 ended in hope in chapter 12, here Hezekiah's trust ends in judgment. The section seems to be saying two things: trust is a way of life, and hope is not in the perfectibility of any human. Thus, the reader is prepared for the next section of the book: first, the trustworthiness of God has been amply demonstrated, and second, it has been made quite clear that Hezekiah is not "Immanuel."

Creation

Probably no Old Testament book outside of Genesis treats creation so fully as Isaiah does. Here in chapters 40–48 particularly, the prophet argues that since the Lord alone is the creator of the universe, he alone directs history, and he alone is the savior. So it is insisted that God made the world without assistance or counsel (40:12–14; 44:23). He is the creator of the whole earth (40:28), and in it Israel is a special creation (43:8). Everything that exists is ultimately the work of God; no one else can take credit for the origination of anything (44:5–7). Unlike the pagan "creation" stories, where all things originate in material chaos and where humanity is an afterthought, Isaiah insists that God spoke the world into existence purposely for human inhabitation (45:18–19). Because the gods have been made by human ingenuity, they must be carried by their worshippers (46:1–2). But God, the Maker, carries his worshippers (46:3–9). Because God is the creator, he can do new things, things never heard of before (48:6–7).

Salvation

Like many of the other themes in the book, the treatment of salvation is remarkably full-orbed. The concept is directly related to the nature of the problem. If the problem is rebellion, self-exaltation, injustice, alienation, and resultant devastation, then the solution must deal with all of these. Furthermore, there are both physical and spiritual ramifications of the problem. Thus, a full solution must address both. Salvation must produce persons who trustfully submit to God, believing him to supply all their needs. It must result in reconciliation between God and humans and between humans and humans. It must mean deliverance from bondage of every sort, physical and spiritual alike. It must mean forgiveness and cleansing. It must produce persons who are committed to all of the justice prescribed in their covenant with God. It must issue in a glad desire to declare the glory, the uniqueness, and the saviorhood of God to all the world.

The basis for this salvation is found in the trustworthiness of God: even when his people have turned their backs on him and trusted in the empty glory of the nations, he will not turn his back on them. Instead he reaches out to comfort them in the tragedies which have justly befallen them, and declares to them that their sin is forgiven and they are restored to his favor. The means of the forgiveness and the restoration are twofold. On the one hand, the fires of judgment themselves are cleansing if they will be received as such and not allowed to destroy faith in the one who sent them. But beyond that, the question must be raised, can fire atone for sin? No, it cannot. Leviticus is clear: only a life can atone for sin. Thus we find the ideal Servant giving his life for the transgression of the people. He is the reaffirmation of the covenant of God to them, and the means of their healing. How this could be possible is not explained in Isaiah, but it made perfect sense to the first Christians to think that God himself was in the servant accomplishing these things.

Messiah-servant

From the outset of the book it is clear that corrupt leadership is one of the chief causes of the failure of Israel to be the obedient people they were called to be (1:10, 23). The issue is made more explicit in chapter 7 where Ahaz and the house of David are accused of lack of faith (7:2, 13). These ideas are repeated several more times in the succeeding chapters (see 22:15–19, e.g.). But they are given special prominence is chapters 28–33. Priests and prophets are drunk, both literally and figuratively (28:7–13; 29:9–10), and the princes are those worst of sinners, scoffers, who mock the truth and cynically plan to save themselves when the worst comes (28:14–19; 29:15–16). But the problem is not only with Israelite leadership, it is with any human ruler who exalts himself against God, as chapter 14 so graphically shows.

It is against this backdrop that Isaiah depicts another kind of leader, one who will rule in the actual righteousness and justice which the ancient Near Eastern kings often pretended to bring (1:26; 9:7; 11:4–5; 16:5; 32:1–8). He would be of the tribe of Jesse (11:1) and the house of David (9:7; 16:5), and yet somehow he would be all that his predecessors in that line had failed to be. He would do what they had only promised to do, to the extent that his kingdom would be without warfare, danger, evil or oppression (9:4–5, 7; 11:1–9 [cf. 65:17–25, where it is explicitly God who creates this kingdom]; 32:1–8. That kingdom would have no end (9:7), because he would be the evidence of God's presence with his people, even being called "Wonderful

Counselor, Mighty God, Everlasting Father, Prince of Peace" (9:6). The reader or hearer of these words may well ask who such a person could be?

Perhaps it is to be Hezekiah, Ahaz' son who learned the lesson of God's trustworthiness which his father would never learn. Could he not be the son born to the "virgin," the one upon whose shoulder government would rest? Whatever else chapters 38–39 exist to do, they exist to destroy that idea once and for all. Hezekiah is mortal (38). He may be given an additional 15 years, but at the end he will die and his rule with him. Furthermore, Hezekiah is tragically fallible (39). He is as prone as the next man to parade his wealth and power, to depend in the end upon his own achievements. Thus, Isaiah is signaling to us that the one he has described is not Hezekiah and that we must look farther if we are to find him.

But is the Messiah to be found in chapters 40–66? Many scholars would say not. The kingly descriptions just seen do not seem to appear. On the other hand there is an anointed one spoken of in 61:1. He is anointed by the Lord to announce the salvation of God to the world, and to do those things which will make it possible for the people to be called "trees of righteousness" (61:3). This reference to righteousness recalls that promise of the king in 11:1–5 and elsewhere in chapters 1–39. This in turn calls attention to that description of the servant in 42:1 and 49:6 where he is said to bring justice to the nations and God's deliverance to the ends of the earth.

But if this is the same person as the one promised in the earlier chapters, why is there such a complete absence of royal imagery? First of all, it must be said that the point of the humility of the messianic figure is surely emphasized in chapters 1–39. The answer to the arrogance of Assyria and the stubbornness of the Judean court is a baby! Throughout chapters 7–12 children are seen as the signs of God's promised kingdom. In chapter 11 the point is made that the coming King will not rule by means of the obvious trappings of power, but in the power of righteousness. In chapter 32 the same point is emphasized. The power will not be of compulsion, but of attraction. Note also that one of the functions of the coming king will be to give sight to the blind and hearing to the deaf (32:3–4) as in 61:2–3.

Thus, the messianic figures in the two parts of the book are not contradictory, but complementary. The king will be the servant and the servant will be the king. This paradox underlines one of the key points in the book: only God is high and lifted up. To exalt humanity against him is to be utterly humiliated. But one of the chief marks of God's high holiness is in his delight to dwell with the lowly and the contrite (57:15). God's power is not so much in his ability to smash the wicked as it is in his ability to take all the wickedness of the earth into himself and give back love. Only One who has utterly abandoned himself in service to God and his people can dare to take the crown upon his head.

ISAIAH IN THE NEW TESTAMENT

Along with the books of Psalms and Deuteronomy, the book of Isaiah is a favorite among New Testament authors. It has been calculated that it is alluded to or quoted more than 115 times. While some the supposed allusions may be questioned, fifty-eight of the occurrences are direct quotes. In these fifty-eight, forty-one different verses or passages are represented. The most frequent of these passages is 6:9–10, which appears in five different places (Matt 3:14–15; Mark 4:12; Luke 8:10; John 12:40; Acts 28:26–27). Clearly the apostles saw a parallel between Isaiah's experience and theirs in which the preaching of the Good News seemed actually to turn people away. Isaiah 8:14 is used in the same way in Rom 9:33 and 1 Pet 2:8 to explain why so many of the Jews stumbled over Christ. In this regard it should be noted that Paul's discussion of the fate of the Jews in Romans 9–11 quotes from Isaiah no less than 11 times (Isa 1:9 / Rom 9:29; 10:22–23 / 9:27–28; 27:9 /11:26–27; 29:10 / 11:8; 40:13 / 11:34; 52:7 / 10:15; 59:20–21 / 11:26–27; 65:1 / 10:20; 65:2 / 10:21). These references cover the gamut from Israel's propensity to sin to God's determination to deliver them.

All four of the gospels utilize 40:3–5 to show that Christ's coming was foreseen by Isaiah. They do so by identifying John the Baptist as the voice crying in the wilderness (Matt 3:3; Mark 1:3; Luke 3:4–6; John 1:26). Another example of an evangelist's use of Isaiah to identify Jesus as the fulfillment of OT promises is Matthew's well-known quotation of Isa 7:14 in relation to the virgin birth (Matt 1:23). Matthew continues in this way by showing that Jesus' Galilean ministry was in fulfillment of Isaiah's prediction in 9:1–2. Jesus himself set this pattern of identification from Isaiah when he cited Isaiah 61:1–3 to identify himself as the promised Messiah (Luke 4:18–19).

Chapter 53 is quoted or alluded to ten times, with special prominence being given to the servant's substitutionary suffering and death (Matt 8:17; Luke 22:37; Acts 8:32–33; 13:47; Heb 9:28; 1 Pet 2:22, 24–25). One could go so far as to argue that this section of Isaiah may have had a determinative effect upon the early church's understanding of the meaning of the Cross.

One other area where Isaiah was heavily drawn upon was for an understanding of the church's mission to the Gentiles. The mysterious plan of God (29:14—1 Cor 1:19; 40:13—1 Cor 2:16; 66:4—1 Cor 2:9), in which God's people would declare salvation to the entire world (11:10—Rom

15:12; 49:6—Acts 13:47; 52:5—Rom 2:24; 52:15—Rom 15:21), is another Isaianic motif which helped early Christians make sense of their experience.

CONCLUSION

In the book of Isaiah we find the sweep of Biblical theology displayed as in no other single book of the Bible. The great themes that would come to constitute the topics of Systematic Theology are all to be found here. The nature of God, the nature of reality, the nature of humanity, the problem of sin, the effects of sin, the need for redemption, the meaning of life, the hope of eternal life, all are to be found in this book as in no other. Beyond that, these ideas, which could be as dry as dust, are expressed with in comparable literary power and beauty. To be sure, the sobriquet "Prince of the Prophets" is not misplaced when it is applied to Isaiah and his book.

3

Judgment and Hope
The Full-Orbed Gospel[1]

Isaiah is often called "The Prince of the Prophets." Why is this so? It is true that the book is characterized by beautiful language, impressive imagery, and lofty themes. But even the most ardent devotee of the book would be hard-pressed to deny that others of the Hebrew prophetic books possess the same qualities in some measure at least. So what accounts for the special place accorded Isaiah by so many?

I believe it is the comprehensive theology of the book which moves it to the front rank. More than any other biblical book it contains all the great themes of biblical theology. So much is this the case that I would contend that if all the other sixty-five books were destroyed, leaving Isaiah's book alone, we would still have all the essential biblical truth, at least in elemental form. This is certainly a sweeping statement, but consider for a moment. Here are divine transcendence and immanence; original sin and redemption glory; arrogance and humility; implacable divine justice and unmerited favor; the utter untrustworthiness of any created thing and the absolute dependability of God; the majesty of the Divine King and the suffering of the gentle Savior; substitutionary atonement and the destruction of death; salvation by grace alone and the necessity of holy living on the part of the saved; God as the Creator of the Cosmos and the Lord of history; etc. No other prophet comes close to this kind of a binding together of biblical

---

1. The substance of this article was delivered as part of the Kenneth S. Kantzer Lectures in Systematic Theology in February 1996 at Trinity Evangelical Divinity School. It appeared in *Trinity Journal* 17 (1996) 191–202, and is used here by permission.

thought. I would even dare to say that no book of the Bible puts all the elements of biblical theology together as Isaiah does. Of course the NT books present the fulfillment of biblical faith more completely than Isaiah does, but, by and large, they do not do the kind of justice to OT truth that Isaiah does to NT truth. Yes, Isaiah is "The Prince of the Prophets," and in some ways he is the "Prince of Biblical Theology."

For many years the wholeness of the Isaianic theology has been fractured, as higher critical issues and convictions have dominated the study of the book. At least since the appearance of Eichhorn's groundbreaking introduction to the OT in the final years of the eighteenth century, it has not been the unity of the book, but its diversity which has held the attention of those investigating it.[2] As the various theories of multiple authorship gained credence, scholars sought to find the distinctive character of the work of each author or group of authors. Thus, the study of Isaiah came to resemble more and more a group of persons looking at a great painting with magnifying glasses, trying to discern between the brush strokes of the master and those of his disciples.

Thankfully we live in a new day. In recent years, authorship theories about the book of Isaiah have undergone some changes. Now, instead of believing that the present book is the result of combining three somewhat independent books (1–39; 40–55; 56–66) from the same theological tradition, it is argued that the supposedly later parts were written in the full consciousness of the supposedly earlier parts, and with the purpose of developing the themes already there in the earlier parts. Furthermore, it is now believed that someone has woven the parts together with introductions and seems to make the parts into a coherent whole. The difference in the approaches of Christopher Seitz, a contemporary scholar, and William L. Holladay, who wrote in the 1970s, illustrates how much of a change has occurred.[3] To be sure, those contemporary scholars who are re-emphasizing the unity of the book are very careful to distance themselves from those of us who suggest this phenomenon might point to unity of author as well, but we can be grateful for their recognition of what seems to us an unassailable fact: the book is a unit, not because of accidents of redactional history, but because of design.[4]

2. J.G. Eichhorn, *Einleitung in das A.T.* (3 vols.; Leipzig, 1780–1783); cf. also J.C. Döderlein, *Esaias* (1775).

3. C.R. Seitz, ed., *Reading and Preaching the Book of Isaiah* (Philadelphia: Fortress, 1988); W.L. Holladay, *Scroll of a Prophetic Heritage* (Grand Rapids: Eerdmans, 1978).

4. I suspect that it will be impossible to maintain the unity of the book *and* the multiplicity of authorship, but it will be interesting to trace the ways in which both points of view are sought to be maintained in coming days.

When we begin to look at the elements of that design, the first which strikes us is what may be called "bi-polarity." More than most of the biblical books, perhaps more than any other, Isaiah seems to stress polar opposites. So exaltation and degradation, glory and shame, desert and garden, and a host of others, some of which were mentioned above, appear. Perhaps the most prominent of these is judgment and hope, in part made more prominent because they seem to coincide with the two most obvious divisions of the book: chapters 1–39 and 40–66. In 1–39 judgment receives the major focus, while hope receives it in 40–66. This particular bi-polarity has so much impressed some scholars that they have gone so far as to suggest that all appearances of the other theme in the other section are the work of another hand.[5]

But we do not have two dissimilar books, one about judgment and one about hope, inside a single slip-jacket, as it were. There are too many overtones of hope in chapters 1–39, and there are too many overtones of judgment in chapters 40–66, especially chapters 56–66. Eventually, of course, the recognition of the differences between 40–55 and 56–66 led to the proposal of a third main section of the book (56–66) with authorship different from that of 40–55. I believe, and seek to demonstrate in chapter 5 below, that this third section is designed to synthesize the teachings of the first two sections.

But however we understand the question of chapters 56–66, it seems clear that we are not intended to read the parts of the book, nor its two great themes, in isolation from each other. Judgment must never be separated from hope, and hope is always seen as coming through judgment and not in spite of it. That this is the way the book is to be read is made very clear by the introduction (chaps. 1–5). It has often been wondered why the call of the prophet does not appear until chapter 6. Did the prophet start preaching before he was called? Of course, that would not be the first or the last occurrence of that phenomenon, if it were the case, but it seems more likely that the arrangement of the opening chapters is for literary and theological purposes than for chronological ones. What is that purpose? In order to answer that question, we must look at the content of the chapters. One of the first things which strikes the attentive reader is the abrupt and dramatic interchanges which occur. Chapter 1 opens with a powerful word of judgment upon a stupid and rebellious people whose thought processes are so confused that they cannot perform the simplest kind of cause and effect equations. Then without any transition or explanation, the opening five verses of chapter 2 depict the day when all the nations will flow to the

---

5. See, for instance, Holladay's discussion of whether any of the hope sections in chaps. 1–39 actually came from "First Isaiah" (*Scroll*, 91–113).

house of Judah's God to learn his ways so that they may walk in them. Note that this same thought is reiterated at the end of the book, in chapter 66 (vv. 18–21), underlining the importance of the idea for understanding the book.[6]

But then in verse 6 of chapter 2, the scene changes again. Once again there is a pronouncement of judgment upon the house of Jacob, a people who have become enamored with human glory and greatness. The point which is driven home again and again is that preoccupation with that human glory which is only a dim reflection of the true Glory can only reduce the persons so preoccupied to utter degradation: "Men shall enter the caves of the rocks and the holes of the ground from before the terror of the Lord and from the glory of his majesty, when he rises to terrify the earth" (2:19, cf. also 2:10, 21). This theme continues on through chap. 3 until it ends with a picture of Jerusalem as a gorgeously bedecked woman who is suddenly reduced to squalor (3:16–4:1).

But the remaining five verses of chapter 4 return suddenly to hope, with the announcement that the daughters of Zion will be holy and clean, dwelling under the kind of protection and guidance which had been Israel's when she came up from Egypt. When this segment is compared to the previous announcement of hope, it is interesting to note that the former deals with the worldwide promulgation of the law of God, which chapter 1 said Israel did not know, while this one speaks of the exaltation and purification of a Zion which had defiled itself by idolizing human glory. In other words, the announcements of hope are not chosen at random, but are directly related to the prior statements of judgment.

But the happy picture of Israel sheltering under the canopy of God's presence is not the final one in the introduction. For once again, judgment abruptly blots out those pleasant images. Chapter 5 uses the figure of a carefully prepared and tended vineyard which only yields bitter grapes to describe Israel's condition. And like the frustrated owner who turns the cattle into the vineyard, the Lord announces that he has called distant nations who are coming with incredible swiftness to devour the nation.[7]

---

6. It is well-known that Isa 2:2–4 exactly duplicates Micah 4:1–3. If either is the original, it seems likely that it is the Micah passage, since it fits into the context of Micah more smoothly. Some scholars suggest that both are dependent upon a common original. But in either case, it appears that Isaiah has deliberately inserted the piece here, and this underlines the intentionality of the contrast with chap. 1 and the remainder of chap. 2.

7. The rubric, "For all this his anger is not turned away and his hand is stretched out still," which appears at the end of 5:25, is the same one which appears at the end of each of the four stanzas of the pronouncement of judgment in 9:8–10:4. Some suggest that its appearance here is because of some more-or-less mechanical redactional

Before turning to the significance of the abrupt interchanges, we need at least to consider the significance of the author's ending the interchanges on the note of judgment. Obviously, short of asking the author himself, we can only make suggestions. But it may be that Isaiah ended the interchange with judgment because of the reality of the situation he was facing. It is clear that the Israelites expected to hear the note of hope from their prophets, a note which confirmed them in their sinful ways. Isaiah is perhaps wanting to underline that hope is only on the other side of judgment, and that it is the reality of judgment which the people must face and decide how to deal with.

But what of the interchange itself? Why the abrupt oscillations twice repeated? Is not the prophet telling us how to read his book? Is he not prompting us to ask a question and draw a conclusion? Surely the question is, how can *this* Israel become *that* Israel? How can a senseless, rebellious, arrogant, unjust people ever become a holy, submissive bearer of God's revelation to the world? Although the answer to that question is not a central part of this article, let me not leave you in the dark about what I think it is. I believe Isaiah's answer to the question he has prompted us to ask is found in chapter 6. When the nation of unclean lips has undergone the experience of the man of unclean lips, then the nation will be empowered to bear a message to the world as the man was empowered to bear a message to the nation. This is why chapter 6 occupies the place in the book it does, I believe.

But what about the conclusion which the prophet wishes us to draw? Surely it is that for Israel's God hope and judgment are inseparable: judgment, no matter how severe nor how well-deserved, can never cancel out hope. But, by the same token, hope does not cancel out judgment. Israel believed, as we often do, that hope means an escape from judgment, a winking at our sin, or an announcement that we had not in fact sinned at all. They thought, as we do, that it is either hope *or* judgment, that the two are mutually exclusive. Isaiah will have none of it; there is hope, but it is *through* judgment, not in spite of it. Thus he tells us that we are to read the terrible condemnations of Israel and Judah in the improbable light of ultimate hope. But he also tells us that we must never allow the good news of grace to lead us to believe that God's moral law can be ignored. Judgment will always be misunderstood if we forget hope, and equally, hope will always be misunderstood if we forget judgment.

---

decision (cf. Otto Kaiser, *Isaiah 1–12: A Commentary*, OTL [Philadelphia: Westminster, 1983] 65). Fortunately, the present climate tends to put redactional decisions on a more content-based level. If the material was transposed from some other context (a by-no-means-obvious conclusion), it simply points again to the intentionality of the interchange between hope and judgment in this introductory section.

Judgment and Hope

The final chapters of the book confirm this understanding, for we see the same interchange there. There is less concurrence among scholars as to what constitutes the conclusion of the book than there is over the introduction. Many would see chapters 60–66 as filling this function, but others point out how those chapters are integrated with chapters 56–59, and question whether chapters 60–66 can stand alone. Others suggest that 65:17–66:24 are a conclusion, with the announcement of a new heaven and a new earth (65:17) signaling its opening. But 65:17 seems to be closely connected with the earlier part of chap. 65. So there is little agreement on the point.

But be that as it may, the interchanges between hope and judgment are prominent from chapter 56 right through to the end of the book. As most students of Isaiah agree, regardless of their conclusions about authorship, chapters 56–66 are addressed to the post-exilic community. These are the persons who, against all probability, have been set free from Babylon and have come home again. They are the living evidence of God's election love and his undying favor. They are the embodiment of hope. It is not that they did anything to earn God's goodness. They did eventually repent of their sins and believe his promises (as exampled by Daniel's prayer in Daniel 9). But that did not compel God to do anything. God simply did it, as Ezekiel would say, for his holy Name's sake. The obvious conclusion to be drawn then is that as election has nothing to do with obedience, obedience has nothing to do with election; as grace does not depend on righteousness, righteousness need not eventuate from grace.[8]

Isaiah's response to this reasoning is on the same order, and just about as vehement as was St. Paul's seven hundred years later. In 56:1–57:13 and 58:1–59:15, Isaiah speaks of judgment on those who rely on their status as covenant people to exempt them from careful obedience to God's expectations. The prophet, in what could only have been the most shocking of terms, says that a eunuch or a foreigner who keeps the covenant is more pleasing than a pure-bred Israelite who is relying on his birthright, his election, to give him status with God.

---

8. There is a significant difference in the use of *ṣedaqâ* ("righteousness") in chaps. 1–39 from that in chaps. 40–55, which might easily feed this misconception. In chaps. 1–39 the word is regularly used to describe that righteous behavior which persons in the covenant are expected to manifest. But in chaps. 40–55 it is used to describe God's actions in delivering his people from Babylon. Thus, one could easily conclude that the only righteousness which really matters is God's. It is of great significance that 56:1 uses the word in *both* ways: "Keep justice and do righteousness, for soon my salvation will come, and my righteousness (RSV deliverance) will be revealed." God's righteousness (and the hope it brings) is not a release from obedience (and judgment), but ought to be a greater stimulus to such obedience. See chapter 5 below for further discussion of this point.

But interchanged with each of these, that is, in 57:15-21 and 59:16-21, are promises of God to accomplish in his people the righteousness which they are expected to produce, but cannot. Thus, we see the same themes which we have seen before, but from the perspective of a different historical setting. Now, looked at from one perspective, the promised hope will have been realized. Surely the aspect of judgment will be no longer relevant. But the prophet insists that so long as time exists, hope and judgment will be intertwined. As judgment must not be allowed to blot out hope, neither must hope realized be allowed to cancel out the reality of judgment. God's servants, no matter in what state of grace they are, are expected to live in ways that manifest the character of God. These persons who have received the hope are not doing so; is there then only a return to judgment? No, the answer of God is that there is new hope, and that hope is that he will produce in them the righteousness he demands.

This theme is continued in chapters 60-66, where the atmosphere is reversed. In chapters 56-59, the major emphasis is on the failure of God's redeemed to bring about the justice and righteousness that are expected, with a minor emphasis upon the power of God to enable them. Chapter 60 begins with glorious promises of the victory of God in his people and through them in the world, and this atmosphere of glorious triumph pervades the section. But interestingly enough, this is not the only note, as we might expect. Even here our interchange continues. After three and one-half chapters in which God's triumph and the redemption of his people are extolled, there is a shift at 63:15, and there enters the picture again the discordant note of the people's failure to live righteously before God. This element continues through chapter 64 and into chapter 65 until the proclamation of the new heaven and new earth beginning in 65:17. We might reasonably expect that now all would be glory through the final verse of the book. But this is not the case. Even here, against the backdrop of the millennial kingdom, the insistence that disobedience brings judgment is interwoven, with 66:1-4, 15-17 making it clear that mere membership in the community is not what God is calling for. Persons who believe that may as well sacrifice pigs or make a ceremonial meal of mice for all the good their superficial worship will do. And the contrast still prevails to the very end of the book. The last three verses read:

> For as the new heavens and the new earth which I will make shall remain before me, says the Lord, so shall your descendants and your name remain. From new moon to new moon and from sabbath to sabbath, all flesh shall come to worship before me, says the Lord. And they shall go forth and look on the dead

bodies of the men that have rebelled against me; for their worm shall not die; their fire shall not be quenched, and they shall be an abhorrence to all flesh. (66:22–24)

Again, as you might imagine, scholars dispute the originality of the final verse, or even of the entire paragraph. Westermann sees the paragraph as someone's attempt to add what they see as a corrective to the excessively universalistic tone of the previous paragraph (vv. 18–21). There, he says, Judaism is defined in terms of the world. Here the move is back to redefining the world in terms of Judaism.[9] It seems to me that such a point of view fails to take adequate account of the structure of the book. As for verses 22–24 being a corrective to the "real message," verse 23 says precisely what 2:2 said, and in fact what 66:20 says ("They will bring all your brethren . . . to my holy mountain Jerusalem"). No, the point is to close the book as it began, but in reverse order. There judgment for rebellion (Heb. *pešaʿ*) (1:2, 28) is followed by the hope that all the world will learn to know God through these people 2:2–4). Here the promise that all the world will learn to know God through them is followed by the assertion that rebels (Heb. *pošeʿîm*) will not escape the judgment of God. Thus, as the first example insisted that judgment cannot blot out hope, the second example asserts that hope does not nullify judgment. Surely we must at least grant the possibility that the final verses of the book are there as an expression of the central theme of the book and not merely as a result of the narrowly ethnic bias of an unknown redactor.

If the beginning and end of the book speak of the inseparability of judgment and hope, what of the middle sections? A survey of these materials shows that the theme which is laid out in the beginning and is reiterated at the end is equally important there. There are, of course, the two significant sections: chapters 7–39 and chapters 40–55, which generally describe judgment and hope. An important initial observation is that if the point I have been trying to make is correct, then neither of these sections as we now have them was meant to be read in isolation from the other. If judgment and hope are inseparable, then chapters 7–39 and chapters 40–55 are inseparable. The hope which is proclaimed in chapters 40–55 is unintelligible unless we understand that it is proclaimed to the blind, deaf people who were judged in chapters 7–39. In the same way, the judgment which is constantly restated in chapters 7–39 is a judgment upon the people who will, one day, with clear minds and clean lips, show the glory of the holy God to the whole world.

---

9. Claus Westermann, *Isaiah 40–66: A Commentary* (Philadelphia: Westminster, 1969) 427–29.

When we look at chapters 7–39, we immediately observe that the material is bracketed by historical sections, and that both sections have to do with the same subject matter: the response of a Judean king, a son of David, to an external military threat. The kings are of course father and son, Ahaz and Hezekiah. And the son's threat is the result of the father's refusal to trust God in the face of his threat. Moreover, the place where the son's threat is announced is the very place where the father was called upon to believe (by the pool on the highway to the fuller's field, 7:3 and 36:2). For these reasons, I can only say that I consider the tendency of commentators to refer to chapters 36–39 as an historical appendix to be gross misinterpretation.

What we have then are three sub-divisions in chapters 7–39. The first is chapters 7–12, where Ahaz' refusal to trust God and the consequences of that refusal are discussed. Then follows the section where the wisdom of trusting God is developed at length, chapters 13–35. Then, in chapters 36–39, a son of David is given another opportunity to trust God, and God responds with deliverance.

It is not within the scope of this chapter to develop the theme of trust as it appears in chapters 7–39, but I do want to show how judgment and hope continue to be intertwined here, and intertwined around that theme. Judgment is pronounced again and again upon a people who, instead of demonstrating the glory of the holy God to the nations by trusting him, are constantly seduced by the glory of the human nations into distrusting God. This theme is introduced with Ahaz in chapter 7, and it is the final note in chapter 39. Over and over God says to Judah and Israel that whatever they trust in place of him will at the least fail them, and, more likely, will turn on them and destroy them. This is the word which Isaiah announces to Ahaz when he turns to Assyria in the face of the threat of Israel and Syria (7:13–25; 8:5–22). It is the word he declares to Hezekiah's craven counselors when they advise dependence upon Egypt against Assyria (28:1–30:17). And it is what he says to Hezekiah when Hezekiah tries to impress the Babylonians with his wealth instead of telling them how God has healed him (39:3–8). The word is, "Woe to those who try to make themselves independent of the Lord" (cf. 30:15–18).

But squarely in the midst of all these pronouncements of judgment, hope keeps springing forth. And it is not just in one prominent place, as in Jeremiah 30–33, nor at the end, as in Amos 9, or Ezekiel 33–48; it is, as we ought to expect from the introduction and from chapters 56–66, interwoven throughout. The interweaving is intricate, but also done on a larger scale. Thus the section which opens with Ahaz' failure in chapter 7 ends with the announcement of comfort to a redeemed trusting people in chapter 12.[10] Almost too neatly, the section which begins with Hezekiah's great deliverance (chaps. 36–37) ends with the announcement of the coming Babylonian captivity. The overall point seems very clear: in judgment, never forget hope, and in hope, never forget judgment.

On a narrower focus, note the interchange in chapters 7–12. Chapter 8 ends by describing the terrible darkness of a lost people who, cursing king and God, look futilely to the occult for some kind of guidance. But suddenly 9:1 proclaims that God's light will spring forth from the very place where the first incursions of the enemy will begin, Galilee. As the succeeding six verses show, that light is the true Son of David. But the coming of that light should be no source of pride for Jacob, because 9:8–10:34 tell us that unless Israel chooses to live the life of Israel's God, God will lay the ax of Assyria against the root of Jacob. Nevertheless, out of the stump of Jesse will come a shoot, and from that shoot will spread the whole peaceable kingdom of God's grace (11:1–12:6). Back and forth the pendulum swings, between hope on the one hand, and judgment on the other.

The same phenomenon continues throughout chapters 13–35, the lessons on trusting God. Chapters 13–23 contain judgments against the nations, and chapter 24 announces with apocalyptic zeal the destruction of earth's proud city. But chapters 25–27 speak of that city whose walls are salvation where God will remove the shroud of death, not just from his own people, but from all humanity (25:7–8).[11]

Chapters 28–33 begin with a picture of the nation of Judah as the armies of Assyria come inexorably closer, just as Isaiah had predicted. Instead of turning to God, the people turn to self-serving and to blind priests and prophets, and the royal court turns to cynical counselors who declare that an alliance with Egypt is the only hope. What none of them will do is to turn to the Lord in patient trust. So Isaiah pronounces doom upon leaders and people alike. But the section does not end with doom; it ends with a picture of a noble king ruling a restored people in a city without walls (chaps. 32–33).

---

10. Chapter 12 sounds so similar to what is found in chaps. 40–55 that many commentators assign it to the so-called Second Isaiah, refusing to attend to the counterargument that its presence at this point might be taken as evidence that Isaiah wrote chaps. 40–55.

11. Again, the similarity of this material with that of chaps. 56–66, and its supposed affinities with apocalyptic, have caused it to be taken from "First Isaiah" and placed much later. But too much attention has been given to rearranging the book according to hypotheses of origins. The most important question has to do with the meaning of the text as it now stands.

The lessons on trust are brought to an end with a fitting and dramatic contrast. Chapter 34 depicts the fate of the godless world: a barren and desolate desert. But chapter 35 says that for those who will trust him, he can take that desert of judgment and turn it into a garden of hope. Importantly, it is not desert or garden, but garden out of desert, hope out of judgment.

As we have already noted, the section on Hezekiah ends on the note of judgment, thus putting the overall stamp of judgment on chapters 7–39. But, as we have seen, that judgment is shot through with hope, hope for the near term, and hope for the long term. However certain doom may be, it is equally certain, that judgment is never God's intended last word.

When we turn to chapters 40–55, the tone is startlingly different. It is hope from end to end, hope that a captive Israel will take part in a new thing, the absolutely unheard-of thing of the return of an exiled people, as a people, to its homeland. But beyond that is the hope that the sin which precipitated the exile in the first place will be dealt with and Israel will indeed become the servants of the Lord to demonstrate to the world the glory of the holy God.

But even here, in a section which begins with the word of comfort and pardon (40:1–2) and ends with the trees clapping their hands and the mountains singing (55:12), there is the evidence that the same sort of people whom chapters 7–39 addressed are being addressed here. Already in 40:27, there is evidence that the people do not really believe the promises: "Why do you say my way is hidden from the Lord?" This impression is heightened in chapter 41 with the reiteration of "Fear not." In chapters 42 and 43, we see that this is still the blind and deaf people of chapter 6 (42:16–25; 43:8) who do not understand the meaning of what has happened to them. They think they have been doing God a favor with their sacrifices, when all they have really been doing is loading him down with their sins (43:22–28). Furthermore, when God announces that he will do a new thing by means of the pagan Cyrus, their response is unbelief. With increasing stridency God calls them to let go of their pre-conceived notions of how "exoduses" occur and allow him to be God and do a "new thing" (45:9–13; 46:8–13; 48:1–19). Again and again, God calls upon stubborn, rebellious people to open their stopped-up ears and listen to his offers of hope.[12] In other words, both parts of the book are addressed to the same people, people who when faced with threats of destruction refuse to believe them and repent, and people who when offered incredible promises of hope refuse to let go of their apathy and believe. So in the midst of the most incredible announcements of hope,

---

12. Recall the use of "rebel, rebellion" in chaps. 1 and 66, and cf. 46:8 in particular.

there is judgment, judgment upon rebellion, the rebellion of refusing to trust.[13]

Although there is some diminution of this emphasis in chapters 49–55, it is there. In 50:1–3, we find a challenge to believe in the power of God's arm, even against the odds. Then, in 51:17–52:2 Isaiah calls the people to rise from apathetic unbelief and prepare for the deliverance which is at hand. And even the great invitation of chapter 54 is a challenge for those who cannot see beyond judgment to believe that he is really the God of hope. By means of Cyrus he will deliver them from the bondage of Babylon, and by means of the Servant he will deliver them from his righteous anger. Will they persist in their blindness and deafness? Or will they dare to believe?

Now what does all this have to do with Christian theology? I hope that most of the insights have become obvious along the way. But given the possibility that they have not been as obvious as I wish, let me belabor some of what I believe are the most important points. Above everything else, of course, is the wholeness of judgment/hope. These are not two ideas, but one. There is no hope apart from judgment, and there is no judgment apart from hope. This flows from the character of God. Fallen as we are, we constantly hope that we can have God's love without his holiness, his glory without his righteousness. But this is impossible. God will be holy and he will be righteous. He can no more live with sin than a plumb-bob can hang at a forty-five degree angle to the ground. When we finally really believe that, we are in despair. If the God of the universe is really, implacably, faithful and just, we are finished; we might as well abandon all hope. But Isaiah cries out, "No! He is implacably just *and* He is endlessly merciful." He will be just and that means judgment, but he will be merciful, and that means hope, and the hope comes through the judgment. What else is the Cross of Christ than the eternal vindication for the justice of God and the eternal proclamation of the mercy of God? If God can use the Cross to bring us to hope, then no judgment need be final.

A second point has already been touched upon: hope is ever through judgment. Like the Israelites, we want to believe that hope is the magical escape from consequences. If the consequences must be faced, then hope is futile. On the other hand, if there is hope, then I can do what I like and not worry about the consequences. But Isaiah says that we find hope through judgment. How was Israel ever to have any hope of becoming the people of God? If God had allowed them to escape the consequences of their sin, they

---

13. For a helpful discussion of this point, see R. Watts, "Consolation or Confrontation, Isaiah 40–55 and the Delay of the New Exodus," *TynBul* 41 (1990) 31–59.

never would have found him, and the Messiah, if he ever came, would have had to come through some other people. They thought that their election was proof against consequences, but it was only through experiencing the consequences that they were able to live out their election. Precisely because they were the elect, judgment was inescapable. It was the only way for them to gain their hope.

How desperately we need Isaiah's insights as we look at the Christian hope. It is too easy for us to see this present world as an unreal place where our actions are unimportant. After all, we are the people of God, and God is going to relieve us of all of the consequences in the end anyway. All too quickly, we begin to believe that God is going to relieve us of the consequences now, as well. But Isaiah says that we can never realize God's plans for us by avoiding the consequences of our actions. In fact, it is as we learn to appropriate God's grace in and through the consequences of our actions that we are enabled to grow into his likeness. The distinctively American idea that I can do what I want, when I want, and where I want without either responsibility or accountability is neither biblical nor Christian. Christianity is a religion of becoming, a becoming which is the result of the grace of God being revealed in the conflict between the realities of our character and the realities of God's character.

But someone may say, does this not nullify grace? Only if we have a view of grace's primary purpose as being a kind of fire insurance. Isaiah's view, as is Paul's, is very hard on the idea that grace's purpose is to deliver us from the consequences and leave us where it found us. But if grace's purpose is transformation, Isaiah's vision is entirely congruent. Ultimately, it was only through judgment that the Israelites learned the extent of their sins. Then it was that they were able to believe God as they had not before. As he had done with Jacob, so God brought Jacob's descendants to the loss of all things. But God brought Jacob to that point of clarity in order to give him the greatest thing of all, the blessing of God. He brought the nation of Israel to the same point with the same purpose.

Isaiah teaches us that hope is ever new, but that the way of hope is through renunciation and loss into endless abundance.

4

Holiness in the Book of Isaiah[1]

THE CONCEPT OF HOLINESS seems to be especially prominent in the book of Isaiah. Certainly a major cause of this perception is the frequent occurrence of the phrase *the Holy One of Israel*. But that is not the only reason. Terms for holiness occur frequently in the book, and when study of these is coupled with that of *Holy One of Israel* some helpful insights emerge. This study seeks to unveil some of those insights. To do so it will be divided into three parts: in the first part, the occurrences of *the Holy One of Israel* will be studied in a synthetic way to see how the usage of this term contributes to a theology of holiness; the second part will look at other occurrences of terms for holy and holiness in the book for what they might add. In the third part, the concept of holiness will be looked at in the context of the overall structure of the book.

It has long been recognized that the phrase *the Holy One of Israel* as applied to God is one of the distinctive characteristics of the book of Isaiah. It occurs only thirty-one times in the Bible, and of these, twenty-six are in Isaiah.[2] It appears throughout the book—13 times before chapter 40 and 13 times after, a fact which has been appealed to frequently by those who see the book as the product of a single author.

Since the phrase is rare outside of Isaiah,[3] yet relatively common and widespread within the book, it seems likely that this term provides a

---

1. This chapter is a heavily revised version of material that first appeared in *The Herald*, 87/3 (1975) 16–18; 87/5 (1975) 16–18; 88/1 (1975) 19–20; 88/3 (1976) 14–15, 18; 88/5 (1976) 12–13, 24. It is used by permission.

2. Including the one occurrence in the Bible of "The Holy One of Jacob" (Isa 29:23).

3. Pss 78:41; 89:11; Jer 50:29; 51:5; the occ. in 2 K 19:22 is a duplicate of Isa 37:23.

significant key to Isaiah's view of God. What does God's holiness mean for this man? What is the specific content of God's holiness for him? Is Israel's God a holy one in the sense of any other deity—separate, non-human, dangerous? Any discussion of human holiness must surely be built upon the answers to these and similar questions.

Immediately one must face the objection that this phrase has no special meaning for Isaiah, but that it is merely a label for God which the author (or editor) has gotten into the habit of using. Every speaker and writer has favorite language patterns which he or she uses again and again without attaching any conscious significance to them. It must also be noted that *the Holy One of Israel* appears in parallel with more common terms for God, such as *Lord* (eighteen times), *Lord of Hosts* (four times), and *Lord your God* (three times). An example is: ". . .who have forsaken the Lord, and spurned the Holy One of Israel" (1:4). Students of the Old Testament are reminded not to make much of the differences between the synonyms in such parallel constructions. For the poet, the words were synonymous and thus interchangeable. Therefore, it is said by some that it is impossible to assert that *the Holy One of Israel* really meant any more to Isaiah than merely *Lord*, *Lord of Hosts*, etc.

While it may be granted that we often use favorite phrases unconsciously, it is also true that when we first begin to use a phrase or term more commonly than usual, there is a reason for it, even if it is an unconscious one. This is especially true if the phrase is meaningful, as this one is, and not just a space filler, or a routine term, such as a conjunction. We may conclude that whether or not Isaiah was conscious of every use he made of *the Holy One of Israel*, he would have had a reason for adopting it into his working vocabulary. The phrase's rarity in the rest of Scripture suggests that this reason was a conscious one. Perhaps it was that tremendous vision of God in chapter six, whose central emphasis is the holiness of God. One can well understand how the impact of that experience could alter the prophet's expressions about God for all his days.

Furthermore, Isaiah's use of the phrase in synonymous parallelism with *Lord* and other terms, ought not to be taken to mean that *the Holy One of Israel* means nothing more to him than *Yahweh*. What it does mean is that these two terms say something about each other. Who is this Holy One? Is it some new, unknown deity who is replacing the old worn-out one? By no means! He is Yahweh, the God of our fathers, the One who has revealed Himself to us, delivered us, led us, struggled with us, and kept faith with us. And who is Yahweh? Twenty-six times the prophet says that any concept of Yahweh which is not formed by a recognition of His holiness is an inadequate one. But he is not merely the Holy One. He is Israel's Holy

One, One who has given himself to this people and delights to be known by them. That makes all the difference. Thus we can argue that *the Holy One of Israel* is not merely a synonym for *Yahweh,* but is intended to be a powerful qualifier of the divine name.

One other factor ought not to be overlooked. If the Biblical text is divinely inspired as the church has insisted from its earliest days, then that doctrine has a bearing on the present discussion. While we must be wary of using this faith commitment to prove a point which cannot be proven otherwise, if God's Spirit did so superintend each writer's words that they became God's Word, this does give a further reason to believe that Isaiah's use of this phrase is neither accidental nor meaningless.

USAGE OF THE PHRASE

A rapid survey of the use of the phrase *the Holy One of Israel* as well as the eight other places in which Isaiah relates *Holy* to God, reveals seven usages:

1. His exaltation and glory (and yet)
2. His association with the humble
3. His righteousness
4. His capacity to give joy and gladness (because of)
5. His faithfulness
6. His creatorship and
7. His redeemership.

In what follows, each of these concepts will be explored as they contribute to a theology of holiness.

Exaltation and glory

As is well-known, holiness in the ancient Near East was that combination of qualities which marked off a being as a deity. Power, mystery and separateness were chief among these. Yahweh's holiness certainly included these. The vision recorded in chapter six is primarily a vision of God's holiness and it is obvious that power, mystery and separateness are all explicit there. Similarly in 57:15 his holiness is expressed in the fact that he is high and exalted. To exalt oneself against him (37:23) is to play with fire in a most literal sense as Assyria was to discover (10:17).

But there is something more to God's holiness. Verse 6:3 says that the whole earth is full of his glory. This must mean, at the least, that God's might and power are everywhere seen in his world. But does it mean more? What visions did the term *Glory of God* evoke for the Hebrew? It must have evoked the pillar of cloud and fire which rested upon, and filled the tabernacle in the days of the wilderness wandering (Exod 40:34). As such, it was the physical manifestation of a God who wanted to reveal Himself to His people, and wanted to live in their midst.

So what is Isaiah saying? That the glory of God fills the physical temple only? No. The whole earth is his temple. Why? Because this God's holiness is not primarily manifested in that which is life-destructive, but in that which is life-enhancing. He does not wish to be cut off in a sacred place, but yearns to extend his sacredness to all the world. He wants to share his life and this means that his people must be of such a character as to be able to live in his presence.

Association with the humble

What character is it which people must have if they are to know the joy of God's glory in their worlds? Verse 57:15 is perhaps the key verse in the entire book of Isaiah, and it is surely a key to this study:

> For thus says the High and Lifted up who inhabits eternity, Holy is his name, "In a high and holy place I live, but also with the downtrodden and lowly of spirit, to revive the spirit of the lowly and to revive the heart of the downtrodden."

God in his holiness abhors the proud and self-sufficient (10:17; 31:1; 37:23), but is drawn in compassion to the downtrodden and lowly (29:19).

The worst outcomes of human pride are twofold. First, pride may delude itself to think that the Holy One and his character are basically irrelevant to its concerns. So the Israelites told the prophets not to trouble them about the Holy One (30:11). Such a delusion would finally lead Israel to depend upon her enemies rather than upon her God (10:20).

Perhaps even more disastrous than this is the tendency to make God in one's own image, to assume that his character and purposes are equal to one's own. So the Israelites naively looked for God to accomplish his purposes, not realizing that God's holy purposes would destroy a sinful Israel (5:19). How different this is from Isaiah's reaction as he prostrated himself in repentance before God! For one who has really seen the Holy One, human pride is ridiculous

Righteousness

However, it might be said that God's abhorrence of human pride does not necessarily indicate any moral quality to his holiness. Pagan gods also became angry if their clients intruded on the divine prerogatives. But when one studies the phrase further, the point becomes more clear. When Isaiah fell on his face before God, his reaction was not, "You are so great and I am such a worm." Rather, it was, "You are so holy and I and my people are *unclean*."

How were they unclean? Was it ritually, because they had not been keeping the ceremonial laws carefully? Possibly. Surely their involvement with idolatry would have been a factor there. However, a study of chapters one through five leads one to believe that the chief reasons for their uncleanness were moral ones. Why were they not fit to live in God's holy presence? Not because they were finite, not because they were ritually unclean, but because they were morally unclean.

That realization is heightened when the source of God's exaltation is recognized. Was he exalted and holy because of his power, etc.? No. He was, and is, exalted and holy because of his justice and righteousness (5:16). It is these attributes which set him off from humanity and all the powers and principalities. It is because of these that he has the right to direct his world.

God's holiness means that he is high and exalted without rival in either the human or divine realms. As a result, human pride, which revels in its capacity to make a god of itself, is utterly abhorrent to God's holiness. It is through humility that God wishes to exalt us to fellowship with himself. However, it is not only our pride which separates us from God in his holiness, but an "unrighteousness," a moral uncleanness. God's holiness involves a moral character which is a part of his divine essence. Humanity is all that it is—sinful, evil, iniquitous and corrupt–because it has forsaken the character of God (1:4). If one wishes to turn aside into crookedness, corruption and evil, it involves no less than a conscious rejection of God's teaching (5:24; 30:12; 48:17), and a rejection of God himself and his character (1:4). Thus, if humanity is to live in God's sanctuary, something must be done about that moral uncleanness which destroys us and separates us from his true *Glory*.

Source of joy and gladness

So human beings go on their proud, sad way, conscious that something is deeply wrong in them and their society, yet unable to bring themselves to the point of admitting their situation and experiencing the fire of his cleansing (6:5–7). Isaiah makes it clear that that sadness can be replaced by joy. The meek and lowly will see God accomplishing things through them which pride could never achieve (29:16). And the joy will be all the greater because of a humble sense of being used by God to do things never possible in one's own strength (41:15, 16; cf. also Ps 51:12, 13).

For the believer who has known what it is to be born of the Spirit, yet has slipped back into bondage to self, there will come a nagging sense of not being the true child of God (cf. Gal 4:21–31). He or she will be tempted to struggle on, trying to do supernatural work with only natural capacities. The only result will be a certain dull sadness (Isa 31:1–3). What joy replaces that sadness when the chains of bondage are broken and, filled with the Spirit of Holiness, that same person discovers the supernatural character and work of the Holy God being performed through him or her (Gal. 5:22–26). Then they know themselves to be the true child of God, the child of the promise.

Faithfulness

The root of this joy is in the faithfulness of God. The peculiar character of God's divinity, his holiness, is seen not only in his righteousness, but in his faithfulness. Here is a God who is faithful regardless of the circumstances. What he says, he will do. In the ancient world of the gods, as well as in the modern human world, faithfulness was an unusual quality. Since the gods were only a projection of human character, it was not to be expected that they would be true to their word, or to their followers.

What a cause for joy, then, when the Hebrews received the revelations of God's utter faithfulness (12:6)! The world, which had been unpredictable and terrifying, became a place of confidence and hope (10:20). This quiet confidence in a dangerous world is only available to those who have come to the place of surrendering their own right to master themselves (30:15–16). In reality, of course, to insist on self-mastery is to be defeated and enslaved. On the other hand, to be mastered by Christ is to be master over all other things, for the holy God keeps his promises (31:1; 29:23).

As we have said before, God intends to share his holy character with his followers. This means that we humans can be faithful as he is—faithful to him, faithful to our callings, faithful to one another and faithful in the performance of tasks no one else will ever see. How? Because there will be a spirit of Truth about us rather than a spirit of falsehood. It is no accident that the Hebrew word translated "faithful" is also translated "true." God is true in all he is and does. Jesus is the Truth (John 14:6), embodying all of God's faithfulness. And when Jesus promises to send the Spirit of Truth to abide in us, he is not merely saying that we will know true facts (John 16:13), but that we will be true in ways we have longed for but have never been able to achieve (John 14:15–17). This is cause for joy.

Creator and Redeemer

In the second half of the book, *the Holy One of Israel* is used most commonly in context with his roles of Creator and Redeemer. They are not restricted to that part (as his exaltation and glory are not restricted to the first part), but they are most frequent after chapter 39. This is not surprising because the second half of the book is a promise to redeem. The earnest of this promise is the fact of God's creatorship. The Maker is capable of redeeming.

What is perhaps more to the point is to ask why Isaiah chooses to relate God's holiness to his creatorship. In verse 17:7 the two may be coordinate, as he seems to be saying that when Israel comes to her senses she will no longer worship the unholy idols who did not make her. However, the fact that the terms are in synonymous parallelism does suggest an even deeper meaning: that only the Creator of this world has any right to the term Holy. No other being, principality or power has the right to call itself divine, and therefore holy.

Furthermore, as the Creator, he is qualified to indicate what his purposes in Creation were. Isaiah's assertion is that God's holy character is intimately involved. He created humanity to be righteous (45:11–13) and he will not be satisfied until that purpose is achieved. However, to achieve that purpose God is going to have to do a new thing unlike any before. He will not only have to redeem his people from physical captivity, but from an inner captivity. Otherwise his holy purpose will be frustrated. Can he do this? Certainly he can. The One who did a brand new thing in creating his world is also able to do a brand new thing in redeeming it (40:25–28; 41:20; 43:15–2 1; cf. also Ps 51:10). God's purpose in creating us was that we be right. If we are not, is the Creator capable of making us such? Yes!

But not only did he make us to manifest his righteousness, He also made us to bask in his love, to be his bride. Once again Isaiah links this with God's holiness (54:5). While the love element here is only specifically mentioned with respect to holiness, one must recognize in the light of all of Scripture (both the Old and New Testaments), that the motivating cause of God's faithfulness is his love. Thus, this unbelievable love is as much a part of His distinctive character—holiness—as is his righteousness or his glory (43:3, 4).

Given all of the above, if God is to remain true to his holy character, he *must* redeem his people. His glory cannot abide the pride of evil nations (43:14; 47:4). His righteousness and faithfulness cannot endure the thought of his children, his bride, forever missing what they were created to be (54:4–14). His love can only find expression if there are those who can gladly receive it, unhindered by selfishness (44:5). Being who he is, *the Holy One of Israel*, he *must* redeem.

But if *the Holy One of Israel* redeems, what does that mean about the nature of redemption? For too long both Calvinists and Arminians have been obscuring an essential point, namely, that we are saved *for* good works (Eph. 2:10). The Calvinist obscures it by implying that whether or not we are actually righteous is unimportant since Christ's righteousness is imputed to us. (The best Calvinistic teaching abhors such an implication, nevertheless, it is often drawn).

Wesleyan-Arminians obscure the relation between salvation and good works by an often over-neat distinction between "salvation" and "sanctification." We imply that "salvation" takes care of going to heaven, while "sanctification" has to do with righteousness. This is unfortunate, for while two divine infusions of grace are involved, there is only one process: growing up into the likeness of Christ. In this sense redemption is one process and its purpose is that we might cease from being false and become true. *The Holy One* redeems in order that we might be like him.

Before bringing this study of the occurrences of *the Holy One of Israel* to a close we must explore one further aspect of redemption. It was pointed out above that God's glory is an aspect of his holiness. Isaiah tells us (55:5; 60:9, 14) that God intends to share his glory with the redeemed. It is significant then that John's Gospel portrays Jesus as the "glory of God" (John 1:14), and has Jesus saying that He has bestowed that glory on humanity (17:22). *The Holy One* has found a way, despite our sin, to restore us to Himself and to share His nature with us.

PART 2

In Part 1 we discussed the occurrences of the phrase *The Holy One of Israel* in their contexts seeking to gain insight into the character and nature of God as seen in Isaiah's use of the phrase. This part of the study explores the further uses of the words for "holy" in Isaiah as they apply to God, things and people.

When "holy" is applied to God in other ways than in the phrase already noted, three additional insights appear. The first occurrence is in 8:13

where Isaiah is told to dread and fear God, who is to be called holy. Isaiah is not to be fearful over what his contemporaries see as a conspiracy. The historical context of this statement is important. The Judean king Ahaz, fearful of the conspiracy of Israel and Syria against him, has paid Assyria, mortal enemy of both Israel and Judah, a large sum of money to defend him (2 Kgs 16:5–9). When Isaiah had challenged Ahaz to trust God and had offered a sign that God was truly with them (Immanu-el, "God with us," 7:14–17), Ahaz had refused to believe.

If God is truly holy with all that the word implies in the context of Isaiah, he alone is worthy of fear. His moral perfection and his infinity of power ought to produce a reverence and an awe for him which would shape the rest of our lives. About the closest which the Old Testament comes to such a term as "religion" is "the fear of the Lord." A person who operated his or her life on the basis of the fear of the Lord could be expected to treat others humanely because that is what their divine Master expected. A person who predicated their search for wisdom on this correct understanding of God could be expected to find wisdom (Prov 1:7). The fear of the Lord would leave one clean, as opposed to the defiling, debasing fear of all things less than God (Ps 19:9).

At the same time it is important to stress that this "fear of God" is not merely the fear of punishment, or of his anger (1 John 4:17, 18). We ought to obey him because we love him, not because we are afraid of him. This "fear of the Lord" is that reverential ordering of our lives which is the result of a true estimate of his terrifying power, his perfect purity and his unchanging faithfulness—his holiness. That such a being loves us is a wonder beyond words. But that love is valuable precisely because of his transcendent character.

What Isaiah 8:13 suggests, then, is that Ahaz and his compatriots were terrified over the conspiracy against them because they had not really come to grips with the holy God. Someone has said "Either the fear of man will drive the fear of God from your life, or the fear of God will leave no room for the fear of man." (cf. Ps 56:3, 4, 11) Those who have seen that the major question in life is: "What is my relation to a holy God?" and have permitted God to rectify that relation, may step into life confident and kindly, secure and serene.

The second insight concerning God's holiness is found in verses 5:16 and 29:23. "The Holy God is sanctified in righteousness," and "Jacob will sanctify my name, they will sanctify the Holy One of Jacob." These passages suggest that the Holy One can be made holy. On the face of it, that is a strange statement. However, when one begins to explore the possibilities, a profound point emerges. Whether or not God's holiness is seen and appreciated depends in large degree upon human responses. It does little good to mouth "Praise God" and to prattle on about God's deity unless our own lives are marked by conspicuous evidence of his character. God's holiness is displayed in the righteousness of his children's lives. If we live unrighteous lives, his character is profaned (see Amos 2:7).

His holiness is also displayed in his ability to deliver and redeem. An unrepentant, judged Israel was tempted to call God unjust, unfair and impotent—unholy. However, verse 29:23 promises that on a day when Israel's repentance will permit God to show himself mighty on her behalf, Israel will see the offspring God has given, and will declare to all the world that he is holy. The question then is: are we allowing God's redemptive power to be seen in our lives? If so, then we are sanctifying him in all we do.

The third insight is found in verse 52:10 and it is rather similar to the final point above: God's holiness finds its ultimate expression in redemption. God has laid bare his holy arm for the sake of his people. Here his majesty, his power, his righteousness, his purity, his faithfulness (truth) and his love meet. They meet most particularly in chapter 53 in the person of Christ. Any experience or expression of God's holiness which does not issue in a concern for, and efforts toward human redemption is counterfeit.

When holy is applied to other objects than God in Isaiah, it expresses the idea of that which is sacred because it belongs to God, and is set apart for his use. So heaven is called God's holy abode (63:15); the Sabbath is his holy day (58:13); a festival to God is necessarily holy (30:29); and in the millennial age, when Tyre's mercantile wealth is given over to God's use, that wealth will be holy (23:18).

These references provide an opportunity to remark that holiness is both positional and experiential. That which belongs to God and is separated for his use is rightly called holy. The stress is primarily upon the fact of a relationship between possessor and possessed. So anything or anyone which is committed to Christ ("the Holy One of God," Mark 1:24) may correctly be said to be holy (cf. "the saints" at Corinth, and also the warriors whom God has chosen to punish Babylon—13:3). But this holiness is not something inherent which the person or thing then possesses in and of itself. Something can be set apart for God's use only through continued atonement. Thus, the great high altar which was continually used only for sacred service had to be atoned for annually (Lev 16:18, 19).

However, to say that there is a valid relational or positional aspect to holiness is not to deny the experiential reality of holiness. Far from it. All of the prophets, and Isaiah is no exception, look forward to the day when Israel through a genuine commitment to God will live out his holiness. With exquisite sarcasm, Isaiah mocks the whole idea of a holiness which does not bear the mark of God's character, as he points out the ridiculousness of those who are manifestly unclean claiming to be more holy than someone else (65:5; 66:17).

Isaiah's references to Jerusalem further illustrate this point. From one point of view, Jerusalem is holy by virtue of the fact that it is God's temple city. On the other hand, in some fourteen references it is made plain that God's possession of Jerusalem is vain unless the activities which go on there are a credit to his name. Simply because the temple is called by his name does not guarantee its continued existence, nor that of those assigned to it (43:28, 64:10, 11).

In fact, if the activities there are unholy, he is all the more likely to destroy it precisely because it discredits him (48:2; 63:18). But punishment does not mean abandonment. The whole thrust of the promises of return is that he will now make holy in fact what was previously holy in name. The sanctuary (holy place) will now be a place of peace (11:9; 65:25), of righteousness (56:7) and of cleanness (52:1). It will be the place to which a genuinely holy people return.

As just noted, what may be said of Jerusalem is also to be said of the people. Chosen of God, they may be called his holy people (63:18). However, this in no way exempts them from judgment if they are not holy in fact. But the purpose of judgment is to bring them to that place of experiential holiness (6:13). The forest of Israel's pride may be burned to the ground, and the future may look very bleak. But in one of those burned stumps there is life (6:13; 11:1), life which will be poured out in order that the people might be genuinely like God (4:3; 62:12). When this occurs, when holiness in name and holiness in fact unite, then redemption has taken place.

PART 3

In the previous two parts of this study the uses of the word "holy" in the book of Isaiah have been studied. In the first part it was seen in connection with the use of the phrase *The Holy One of Israel* that God's holiness is expressed in his exaltation and glory, coupled with his association with the humble, in his righteousness, and in his capacity to give joy and gladness, because of his faithfulness, his creatorship and his redeemerhood. In short, God's holiness encompasses all that is unique to him, in Isaiah's view. The second part dealt with the other uses of the word "holy" in the book. Here was noted the dread and awe of the holy God, the intimate connection of holiness to righteousness, and the fact that redemption was seen as the ultimate expression of holiness.

However, a study of word usages in a piece of literature may be deceptive. One must ask how that concept appears in the larger context of the whole. It is conceivable that what might have appeared to be so from a study of individual usages could be substantially contradicted when seen against the backdrop of the whole. This being so, we ought not to conclude our study of holiness in Isaiah without surveying the book as a whole to see whether the above findings are supported or altered by the total content. This third part of the article will address itself to that task.

In what light, then, does the book of Isaiah as a whole portray holiness? How central is it to the character of God? What is its relation to Israel and Israel's destiny? Where does this concept fit into the total development of the book? Is it central or peripheral? How is holiness related to human life? Is it primarily positional, experiential, or both?

Isaiah may be divided into sections fairly easily. It is divided by chapters as follows: 1–5, 6, 7–12, 13–23, 24–27, 28–33, 34–35, 36–38, 40–48, 49–55, 56–59, 60–62, 63–66. But when we come to group these into larger sections, the work becomes more difficult and there is less agreement among commentators. However, the following seems likely to me:

    I. 1–5

    II. 6

    III. 7–39

    IV. 40–55

    V. 56–66

Seen in this way, the book portrays a shift from the oppression of untrusting arrogance to the service of trusting humility. The introductory chapters (1–5) depict this contrast starkly. Chapter 1; chapters 2:6–4:1; and chapter 5 depict a nation which is anything but God-like. They have rebelled against him and in consequence are estranged from him (1:4, 5). They have become unrighteous, unfaithful (literally untrue), unjust and in short, unclean (1:16). They admire the haughty, the noble and the rich and seek to emulate them (3:16–23) while oppressing the poor (3:13–15). God had created them for justice and righteousness (5:7), but his "vineyard" has only produced the wild grapes of greed (5:8–10), self-indulgence (5:11, 12), spiritual insensitivity (5:18, 19), and finally, moral bankruptcy where evil is called good and good, evil (5:20). All of this is in direct contrast to a God whose holiness is shown in his righteousness (5:16).

Yet 2:1–4 and 4:2–6, in striking contrast to both what immediately precedes them and immediately follows them, depict a redeemed and restored nation which has been made holy and clean (4:3, 4), a people which can be the tabernacle of God among whom his presence will be manifest (4:5), and to which the world will come to learn Yahweh's *torah* (2:1–4). Surely this is not a positional holiness or a positional cleanness. Surely God does not mean for them to continue in the unclean practices of the past, only having been somehow declared holy by a certain mechanism on his part. If there was any lingering doubt, 2:3 and 4 make it very plain that God intends for his ways, his law and his word to become so much a part of the life of his people that all the world will be drawn to him through them.

In this striking contrast is seen one of the great themes of the book: an unholy people—arrogant, unrighteous, oppressive—is to become a holy people—humble, righteous, serving. The question which the contrast forces on the mind, however, is how? How can this tremendous change be brought about? Although no explicit connection is made, it seems logical by the very position of chapter six after the first five chapters that it is offered as an example of the means by which God would restore his people. If what was experienced by the man "of unclean lips" could be extended to the nation "of unclean lips," restoration could be realized along with the accompanying mission to the nations. Central to that experience of Isaiah's is a sense of divine holiness and human uncleanness. If this people is to be restored there must come a vision of who God is.

The preceding chapters make it plain that human arrogance and rebellion stem from a fundamental failure to recognize God as God. We see him as a small comfortable being, made in our image, with whom we may do as we want. The thought that he is wholly righteous and true, all-powerful, beyond our manipulations, One who will not accept cease-fire, but only unconditional surrender, is an idea we resolutely try to push from our minds. Yet, he alone can deliver us from the awful sickness which rages through humanity: moral filthiness.

Thus, it is no accident that the description of God which flows from the burning lips of the seraphs is, "Holy, holy, holy is the Lord God of Hosts; all the earth is full of his glory." The problem of the Hebrews, and all of us, is that we want a deity who is less than holy, less than God. As has been said above, holy does not refer to one aspect of his being, it refers to all that makes him God, central to which is righteousness, faithfulness, love and power. The people of Israel were in the terrible condition they were because they refused to see God as holy. If they, as we, can ever get a glimpse of who God really is, as Isaiah did, we will be on the road to healing.

It is significant that Isaiah, faced with the overwhelming majesty and greatness of God, does not say, "Woe is me! For I am undone, for I am finite." The recognition which thrusts itself upon him is not that God is so great and he is so small, but that God is so clean and he is so unclean. The crushing difference between God and man is not a matter of immensity or power, it is a matter of character. And until a person realizes that his or her character is as different from God's as a leper's body is from that of a whole person's, they cannot be restored.

This is why people raised in a good moral atmosphere often have difficulty coming to vital faith. Having never really seen God, they cannot believe that their character is so different from his. How hard it is to admit that selfish pride is the most defiling of all sins. Yet, it is Isaiah, whose life we have no reason to think was other than exemplary, lying prostrate before God, convinced in the presence of such blazing purity that he is a hopeless moral leper doomed to destruction like a filthy rag before an open blast furnace.

That, of course, is not how the story turned out. God does not reveal himself to us in order to destroy us. He did not wrestle all night with Jacob simply to bring Jacob to a hideous self-knowledge which would leave him groveling in the dust. He wrestled through the night in order to bring the Israel he had designed out of the Jacob Jacob had made. Only through self-recognition can God bring us to the persons we really are. That is his ultimate purpose.

The nature of God's response to Isaiah's despair is very important. It involves Isaiah directly. God does not make a forensic statement from his throne that in view of a sacrifice made on Isaiah's behalf, Isaiah is now clean in principle. Rather, the consumption of the sacrifice by fire is applied to Isaiah's own person. Truly, Isaiah could not cleanse himself. God had to provide the sacrifice. But, unless Isaiah himself enters into the fiery death of the sacrifice in some real way, the sacrifice would be meaningless. The pain, the surrender, the self-denial which the innocent Lamb underwent for our sakes must become a real part of our own lives if his death and resurrection are to have any effect in our lives.

Beyond this, note that two effects are achieved when the cauterizing fire is applied: atonement for past sins, and a taking away of the iniquity, that perverse twistedness, which produces sin and transgression. In other words, this experience relates to the present and the future, not merely the past. What a mockery it would have been if God had said to Isaiah, "You still cannot be clean in your future life and activity, but I will forgive you what is past!" What a cruel act for God to reveal his purity to Isaiah, if in fact, Isaiah could never really know anything other than a continual recurrence of his present uncleanness. The point of the whole passage is that Isaiah, and Israel, do not have to continue to live defiled, unclean lives. By God's grace and the provision of a sufficient sacrifice in Christ, the past may be atoned for and the present and future may see us sharing God's holy character with clean hearts.

How is such an about face possible? When God is seen as he is, and persons see themselves in that light, and when persons, in despair of their very existence, are willing to receive God's provision for their uncleanness, then they can begin to realize the growth of the character of God in them; then they can know the exaltation of servanthood to God and humans. That is what holiness is all about.

The initial chapters of Isaiah thus seem to set forth the problem and the solution: unholiness vs. holiness. How this solution was worked out in the nation is the focus of the rest of the book. However, these six chapters are enough to make it plain that this holiness of God and man are central issues in Isaiah.

Three major groups of chapters remain in the book. They are: 7–39, 40–55, 56–66. In an interesting way they detail some of the significant steps on the road to realizing God's character in one's life. They take us through trust, the basis of servanthood; redemption, the motive and means of servanthood; and righteousness, the character of servanthood.

Chapters 7–39 deal with the basis for servanthood—trust. Until one has realized what God's holiness means, namely the folly of reposing one's confidence in human pride and self-sufficiency, and the wisdom of casting oneself upon God's infinite trustworthiness, one can never find that harmony with creation, that fulfillment in serving, which we were meant to know.

The section is bracketed by two historical segments which are the antitheses of each other. Chapters 7–12 show us untrust and its results. Chapters 36–39 show us trust and its results. Between these two segments is a group of chapters (13–35) which depict how wrong it is to trust the pomp and the glory of the nations of mankind when God, the Holy One, is in control of all their destinies (see especially chap. 31). As such, they explain what was wrong with the response in chapter 7 and provide the basis for the correct response in chapters 36 and 37.

In chapter 7, the king of Judah, Ahaz, faced with a threatened attack by Israel and Syria, rejects Isaiah's appeal to trust God, the God who would send Emmanuel, in favor of help from his mortal enemy Assyria. Isaiah then relates how Assyria will one day turn upon Judah and enslave her. Yet, in a way reminiscent of chapters 1–5, these dire predictions are interspersed with promises that they as a people will learn to trust God and be restored (chaps. 9 and 11). Chapter 12 is a lovely song of trust in which the prophet anticipates the new attitude of the people in that new day.

In chapter 36, the first part of the above prediction has come true. Assyria is in the process of destroying the last of Judah's strongholds and is preparing to besiege Jerusalem. Hezekiah has apparently learned the lessons of chapters 13–35, however, and refuses to cast away his confidence in God. In his prayer in chapter 37 he calls on God to deliver them, not for their sake, but that the world might know he is the living God. This is an excellent example of that correct understanding upon which trust can rest. As a result of that trust the arrogant Assyrian army was destroyed in a single night.

Yet the section does not end on the high note of trust and deliverance. Instead, chapter 39 brings it to a close with a sad story of Hezekiah's braggadocio and pandering to another foreign nation, Babylon. We may well ask why. Chapters 7–12, which began with untrust on Ahaz's part, ended with a picture of a restored nation living in trust. But this section, beginning with trust, ends with failure and the promise of exile to come. Why? Perhaps it is to remind the reader that however strong and faithful Hezekiah might appear beside some of Judah's other kings, he is not the fulfillment of the predictions in chapters 9 and 11. He is not the promised Messiah. He is not the final fulfillment of God's plans for his people's holiness. Hezekiah cannot redeem and restore. He can only be an example, both of the necessity of trust and of the certainty that, apart from the grace of God, the end of the human story is always failure.

These two truths having been demonstrated, it is possible to move to the next level. If the basis for servanthood is trust, what is the motive for servanthood, what will actually take it from theory to reality? Chapters 40–55 answer this question. It is the recognition of our restored relationship to God, the recognition that we are chosen and forgiven, which motivates us to offer ourselves as servants.

Chapters 40–48 have three great themes: the universal greatness and majesty of God; his unreserved affection and love for Israel; and the proclamation of Israel's redemption as the chosen of God. As such, the three are inter-related. God is shown to be the only One deserving of the title Holy. The other gods are nothing. They did not create; they cannot destroy. They did not plan what has happened; they cannot adjust to what is happening nor relate to what will happen. God alone is holy. Therefore, Israel's sin cannot defeat him. Israel will be redeemed, not in *spite* of God's holiness, but *because* of it. Because he alone is the Holy One he can do that new thing which is called for by Israel's sin. In the meantime, Israel can know her standing: accepted in the beloved. As such, she ought to be bearing joyous witness to the only God through the world. A good summary of these ideas appears in chapter 43:14–21.

However, a problem remains. It is to God's eternal glory that He can and will redeem a people or a person who will see His greatness and trust Him. Yet what about their conduct? They have been rebellious, blind, self-serving. How can a holy God redeem such? Simply by closing his eyes to their state? Surely not! Chapters 49-55 indicate there is a means by which redemption is made possible. In a very subtle, yet evident way there is a shift in these chapters. Instead of the chosen servant Israel who will bring glory to God through witness of undeserved salvation, we are confronted with the righteous servant Israel who will bring Jacob back to God (see chaps. 42 and 49). Does this mean Israel was to save herself, somehow to make herself holy in God's sight? Hardly. Rather, it appears there was to come One who would be the true Israel. What Israel was meant to be (42:1-7), and yet had never been (42:18-25), he would be. And by virtue of that righteous obedience (50:4-9; 51:4-6; 52:13—53:12), God can justly forgive the sins and rebellions of the nation Israel, and indeed, of the world (53: 10-12). Redemption does not negate righteousness. Rather, the importance of righteousness is highlighted when we see the frightful cost in love and self-giving necessary to meet its demands.

The invitation of chapter 55 is a fitting climax to the whole section. We are saved, not because we deserve it, but because God in his love sees us through the suffering and death of Christ. However, this is not to say that God ignores the demands of righteousness in order to save us. Christ met these demands and we must honor them if we are to know the merits of His death (55:6, 7).

This latter fact is underlined in the final division of the book, chapters 56-66. From one point of view, it might appear that the book should end at chapter 55, closing as that chapter does with its lovely benediction. After all, what more can be said than the proclamation of our acceptance in Christ? Yet the book does not close at that point. It continues, and the emphases with which it continues are of crucial importance.

These emphases have to do with the moral and ethical life of the believer. Yes, we are his chosen servants. Yes, our sins are forgiven because of Christ's emptying himself and assuming the role of servant. But what of our character? Is it just as it was? Do we feel we have some special claim on God regardless of how we live (chap. 56)? Is the spirit of pride and possessiveness still reigning (57:14-21)? Do we evaluate the quality of our lives in terms of our religiosity rather than of our attitudes to the unfortunate (chaps. 58 and 59)? If so, we need the Divine Warrior (59:15b-21; 63:1-6), who is the anointed Messiah (61:1-3) to defeat our sins in a climactic way so that the Spirit of the Lord can make us like himself (59:21). If that happens, light (60:1), freedom (61:1ff.) and joy (65:17ff.) will result, and the nations will be drawn to them inexorably. No longer will there be a mockery of holiness (63:3-5; 66:17), but it will be so in fact, and all the nations will join together in worship of the God who makes this possible (66:18-24).

This study has shown that *the Holy One of Israel* is not merely a title in the book of Isaiah, but reflects one of the book's key themes: the holiness of God and its implications for our understanding of the divine purpose in human life. If we understand that Yahweh is the only Holy One, the sole Creator of the Cosmos, and that his transcendent otherness (his holiness) encompasses not merely his essence but also his character, we will be compelled to recognize that this has inescapable implications for human life. Those implications are made especially poignant when it becomes clear that that character is marked by self-denying love, truth (faithfulness), justice, and righteousness (Isa 16:5), whereas the human character is marked by self-serving, deception, manipulation, and rebellion. Can rebellious creatures share the holy character of God for the sake of the world? The answer of Isaiah is a resounding "yes."

5

Righteousness in Isaiah
A Study of The Function of Chapters 55–66 in The Present Structure of The Book[1]

THE THREE PARTS OF ISAIAH

IT IS A TRUISM that chapters 56–66 of the book of Isaiah exhibit many differences from the other two sections of the book, chapters 1–39 and 40–55. The differences are striking enough to have led Bernard Duhm to propose a third Isaianic author, Trito-Isaiah.[2] While few today would accept Duhm's proposal of a separate single author,[3] the idea that 56–66 constitutes a separate section has gained a large measure of support.[4] The reason for this degree of acceptance is clear: the theory succeeds in explaining the manifest differences between this section and the others. Recent study has reached

---

1. This material appeared in substantially the same form in *Writing and Reading the Scroll of Isaiah*, vol. 1, ed. C. Broyles and C. Evans, VTSup 70 (Leiden: Brill, 1997) 1:177–91 and appears here by permission.

2. Bernhard Duhm, *Das Buch Jesaia*, HAT 3/1 (Göttingen: Vandenhoeck & Ruprecht, 1892) 14–15, 19.

3. See particularly, C. C. Torrey, *The Second Isaiah: A New Interpretation* (New York: Scribner, 1928).

4. As witnessed by the number of recent commentary series in which chaps. 56–66 are accorded a separate volume written by a different commentator from those who may have commented upon chaps. 1–39 and 40–48 in the same series (e.g., The International Theological Commentary; and Torch Bible Commentaries). See also Elizabeth Achtemeier, *The Community and Message of Isaiah 56–66* (Augsburg: Minneapolis, 1982).

something of a consensus that these chapters were not the work of an individual (as still tends to be maintained of chapters 40–48, at least), but of a community.[5]

But as useful as these proposals have been in explaining the differences of this section from the rest of the book, they have, by their very success, raised another problem: why are these materials included in the Isaianic corpus at all? The proposal that it is included because the authors were disciples of Deutero-Isaiah,[6] even if it could be proven true, still would not solve the dilemma. What was it about these writings, given their apparent differences in outlook from those of the authors' supposed mentor, which caused the believing community to attach them to the larger collection?[7] A historical connection is clearly not enough to explain the phenomenon. Nor is it enough to say that these chapters have been included with the rest because they form a kind of informed reflection upon Deutero-Isaiah's writings. The reflections on chapters 40–55 are neither so explicit nor so thoroughgoing as to require, or even to suggest, inclusion with chapters40–55 in a single book. As has been shown by M. Fishbane and others, inter-textuality is a feature of the entire Biblical tradition, and does not, in and of itself, call for inclusion of the reflection in the same scroll with the text being reflected upon.[8]

I believe the reason chapters 56–66 of Isaiah have been included with the rest of the book, despite their different focus and context, is not that they are a reflection on chapters 40–55, which are in turn a reflection on chapters 1–39, but that chapters 56–66 are written in the full knowledge of the entire preceding corpus and function to unify that corpus.[9] Without

---

5. So Achtemeier, *Community and Message*, 16. See also Paul D. Hanson, *The Dawn of Apocalyptic* (Fortress: Philadelphia, 1975) 32–41.

6. As per Hanson, *Dawn*, 99, etc. On Hanson's speculative reconstruction of these chapters and his resulting hypothesis concerning the development of apocalyptic, J. Blenkinsopp comments that there are so many gaps in our knowledge of Judaism in the post-exilic period "that trajectories of this kind risk being too speculative to be useful," *A History of Prophecy in Israel* (Philadelphia: Westminster, 1983) 283–84.

7. This problem is as real, or more so, for those who accept the single authorship of Isaiah. What could have motivated Isaiah to write this final section of his prophecy in this way, markedly differently from chaps. 40–55?

8. Michael Fishbane, *Biblical Interpretation in Ancient Israel* (Oxford: Clarendon, 1985). For a convenient summarization, see his "Inner-Biblical Exegesis: Types and Strategies of Interpretation ion in Ancient Israel," in *The Garments of Torah: Essays in Biblical Hermeneutics* (Bloomington: Indiana University Press, 1989) 3–19.

9. On this point, see the helpful contributions of R. E. Clements, "Beyond Tradition-History: Deutero-Isaianic Development of First Isaiah's Themes," *Journal for the Study of the Old Testament* 31 (1985) 95–113; Rolf Rendtorff, "Zur Komposition des Buches Jesaja," *VT* 34 (1984) 295–320; Christopher R. Seitz, *Reading and Preaching the Book of*

these materials, chapters 1-39 and chapters 40-55 could be seen to stand in very serious conflict.

CONFLICTING VIEWS OF SALVATION BETWEEN CHAPTERS 1-39 AND 40-66.

While there are clearly important points of contact between 1-39 and 40-55,[10] their perspectives on several major issues seem to be in marked contrast. The most obvious contrast is in the two sections' understanding of salvation. This is revealed particularly in their differing uses of ṣedaqâ "righteousness." It is common knowledge among students of Isaiah that whereas chapters 1-39[11] commonly use the term to denote living which is in accord with God's character and commands, chapters 40-55 most commonly use it to refer to God's faithful performance of his covenant vows on behalf of His people.[12]

Isaiah (Philadelphia: Fortress, 1988); and Marvin A. Sweeney, *Isaiah 1-4*, BZAW 171 (Berlin: de Gruyter, 1988).

10. So, for instance, there is a sense in which the entire book is about trusting God. In chaps. 1-39, the people are called upon to trust God instead of the nations, whereas in chaps. 40-55 the people are called upon to trust God instead of subsiding into despair. Likewise, it may be said that both sections are about righteousness; the first asking if the people will be righteous, and the second if God will be righteous. There is also a common emphasis upon the incomparability of God; in the first section, as compared to the nations, and in the second, as compared to the gods of the nations. A classic study on this theme as it occurs in Isaiah is C. J. Labuschagne, *The Incomparability of Yahweh in the Old Testament* (Leiden: Brill, 1966).

11. Since many scholars today take chaps. 1-39 to be a literary composite stemming from many different sources and times (a recent expression of this point may be found in H. G. M. Williamson, *The Book Called Isaiah* [Oxford: Clarendon, 1994]), some justification must be offered for taking chaps. 1-39 together as a single unit for study. In fact, without denying the variations in style and perspective which may be found in such segments as 1-5; 6-12; 13-23; 24-27, etc., and without denying the force of some form-critical arguments which point to the possibility of diverse origins of materials within recognized segments, there is still a shared theological perspective in chaps. 1-39 which is readily recognizable and distinguishable from that of chaps. 40-55 and from that of 56-66. These distinctions are by no means absolute, nor do they need to be for the following suggestions to have merit. Neither is it necessary to explain why this common perspective exists. It is enough to recognize it and attempt to understand what its significance is for the present shape of the book.

12. For a useful, though selective, review of the literature on this point, see John J. Scullion, "*SEDEQ-SEDAQAH* in Isaiah cc. 40-66 with Special Reference to the Continuity in Meaning between Second and Third Isaiah," *Ugarit-Forschungen* 3 (1971) 335-38.

What has not been pointed out so frequently is that this differing usage reflects a different perspective. In chapters 1–39 a right relationship with God is only possible in the light of admission of the sin which has broken the relationship, a whole-hearted renunciation of that sin, and an equally wholehearted commitment to living a life of obedience. Unless justice is done and righteousness is lived out there can be no shelter from the storm of God's wrath. Examples of this perspective in these chapters can be multiplied.[13] One example is found in 28:16–17,

> "Therefore thus says the Lord God, 'Behold, I am laying in Zion for a foundation a stone, a tested stone, a precious cornerstone, of a sure foundation: "He who believes will not be in haste." And I will make justice the line, and righteousness the plummet; and hail will sweep away the refuge of lies, and waters will overwhelm the shelter.'"

Unless there is just and right behavior, there is no result but destruction.

On the other hand, chapters 40–55 present a radically different picture. They seem to suggest that obedience to the laws of God plays no part in either securing or maintaining a relationship with Him. The only sin is the sin of giving up hope, and the only failure is failure to remember the infinite power and creativity of the Creator. There is no call for the renunciation of past sins, nor is there any requirement for commitment to righteous living. Rather the repeated call is for the Judeans to entrust themselves into the hand of God, believing that He will deliver them. So 51:12–13:

> I, I am he that comforts you; who are you that you are afraid of man who dies, of the son of man who is made like grass, and have forgotten the LORD, your Maker, who stretched out the heavens and laid the foundations of the earth, and fear continually all the day because of the fury of the oppressor, when he sets himself to destroy? And where is the fury of the oppressor?

In a real sense these chapters teach us that salvation is by grace alone, that the only righteousness with which the elect must concern himself or herself is the saving righteousness of God.

The contrast between the two sections is by no means absolute, as a study of either section will demonstrate. For instance, as Rendtorff has shown, 12:1–6 is one with chapters 40–55 in its emphasis upon the free salvation of God.[14] By the same token, 55:7 makes it plain that the person

---

13. 1:18–19; 11:3–9; 16:4–5; 17:7–8; 26:7–15; 27: 8–9; 28:5–6 14–18; 29:13–14; etc.
14. Rendtorff, "Komposition," 315.

who insists on continuing in an ungodly outlook and life cannot hope to experience the mercy of God:

> Let the wicked forsake his way,
> and the unrighteous man his thoughts;
> let him return to the LORD, that he may have mercy on him,
> and to our God, for he will abundantly pardon.

Nevertheless, the differing emphases of the two sections are clear enough that the discerning reader is left puzzling at the end of chap. 55. Are 40–55 conceived of as a corrective to 1–39? Or is it merely that different historical circumstances (judgment threatened, as opposed to judgment having come) have called forth a different word? But even in this latter case, which certainly seems true enough as far as it goes, we ask ourselves, which is the truer perspective on salvation?[15] This, it seems to me, is exactly what chapters 56–66 are dealing with. This is not to deny that yet another change in historic setting may also be a contributing factor, but the evidence that these materials were written exclusively for the post-exilic community is not as compelling, I think, as is that for 40–55 and the exilic community.[16] In any case, the issue in the writer's mind seems clearly to be: if failure to live according to God's righteous demands brought judgment, and if deliverance from judgment is not to be obtained by living righteous lives, but by continuing to believe in God's election promises, what are the relative places of election and righteousness? Does not the emphasis of chapters 40–55 cancel out that of 1–39? Or, on the other hand, if we maintain the validity of the first part of the book's insistence upon righteous living as per the covenant stipulations,[17] does that not invalidate the second part's insistence upon the unconditional nature of the covenant promises? In short, are election and obedience mutually exclusive, or are they somehow compatible?

---

15. Something of this same unresolved contrast appears in chaps. 1–5, where the stubborn sinfulness of the people (1:1–31; 2:6–4:1; 5:1–30), is contrasted without transitions with the mission which the nation will fulfill in the latter days (2:1–5), and with the clean and holy state they will enjoy (4:2–6).

16. In other words, I think it possible that the writing is as much motivated by logic (as per, say, the book of Romans) as by historic circumstances. On the evidences of a pre-exilic context, see J. B. Payne, "Eighth Century Background of Isaiah 40–66," *Westminster Theological Journal* 29 (1967) 179–90; 30 (1967) 50–58.

17. It should be noted here that the term "covenant" only appears in chaps. 1–39 in 24:5; 28:15; and 28:18, with none of these being an unmistakable reference to the Mosaic covenant. Nevertheless, it seems clear that the Mosaic Covenant, or some form of that covenant, is in the background of the repeated pronouncements of judgment upon failures to behave in ways which that covenant demands. On this point see Walter Eichrodt, "Prophet and Covenant: Observations on the Exegesis of Isaiah, "*Proclamation and Presence: Essays in Honor of G. Henton Davies*, ed. J. I. Durham (London: SCM, 1970) 167–88.

The conviction that they are compatible seems to set the agenda for the last eleven chapters of the book.

ṢDQ IN THE THREE PARTS OF ISAIAH

The place where this fact can be seen most obviously is in the use of the complex of words based on the root *ṣdq*. J. J. Scullion, in his study of these words in chapters 40–66, asserts that they are used in similar ways throughout that section and in distinction from their usage in chapters 1–39.[18] But investigation of the data shows that this assertion is not strictly correct. Chapters 1–39 use the root in one way, chapters 40–55 use it in another way, and chapters 56–66 use it in a combination of the two.[19]

Words having the root *ṣdq* occurs eighty-one times in the book, with one occurrence (49:24) being textually suspect. The denominal verb *ṣadeq* is found six times, the adjective *ṣaddîq* thirteen (fourteen) times, the noun *ṣedeq* twenty-five times and the noun *ṣedaqâ* thirty-six times. This total of eighty (eighty-one) is only exceeded by the Psalms, with 139 occurrences, and the Proverbs, with ninety-four, of which sixty-six are *ṣaddiq*, "the righteous one." After Isaiah, the book having the next highest number of occurrences is Ezekiel, with only forty-three. Obviously, the concept is of considerable importance for the book of Isaiah.

The occurrences are fairly evenly spread throughout the three sections, with twenty-eight in chapters 1–39, twenty-nine (thirty) in 40–55, and twenty-three in 56–66.[20] The connotations of the word in the book are in basic accord with those identified in the various theological dictionaries.[21] The dominant sense is of behavior and/or pronouncements which is, or are, in accord with facts and with accepted (or declared) standards.[22] This is especially apparent

---

18. Scullion, "*SEDEQ-SEDAQAH*," 348.

19. To my knowledge, Rendtorff is the first to point this out, "Komposition," 312–314.

20. It should be pointed out that if chaps. 40–66 are treated as a unit over against chaps. 1–39, then the ratio is twenty-eight to fifty-two (fifty-three). It is apparently on this basis that Johnson, writing in *TWAT* (6:903), can say the root is especially prominent in Deutero-Isaiah. As will be shown below, the usages of chaps. 56–66 should not be grouped together with those of 40–55 against those of 1–39. Nevertheless, it is fair to observe that the root occurs more frequently after chap. 39 than before it.

21. *THAT* 2:507–29; *TWAT* 6:898–923; *TWOT* 2:752–55; *TDNT* 2:174–78; 195–96; 212–14. Other important treatments are Frank Crüsemann, "Jahewes Gerechtigkeit (*sedaqa/sädäq*) im Alten Testament," *Evangelische Theologie* 36 (1976) 427–50; F. V. Reiterer, *Gerechtigheit als Heil: qdš bei Deuterojesaja* (Graz, 1976); and Norman Snaith, *The Distinctive Ideas of the Old Testament* (London: Epworth, 1944) 50–78.

22. Thus, the Septuagint translates throughout with δικαιος or δικαιοσυνή, only

in 5:23 where three different forms of the root (*maṣdîqê* [H ptcp.], *ṣedaqâ*, and *ṣaddîq*) are used to inveigh against the sin of declaring a guilty person right while depriving the person who is right of the right judgment which is due. "Those who justify the wicked for the sake of a bribe, and take away the righteousness of the righteous from him."[23]

This basic usage, that is, to do or say what is the right thing under the circumstances, is found in all three sections of the book.[24] Thus, there are the several statements in chapters 1–39 that the Messianic king will rule in a right manner (11:4, 5; 16:5; 32:1; 33:5). Of these, surely the most graphic is 11:5, which asserts that right behavior will be the Messiah's underclothing.[25] Finally, there is the statement that the destruction which is coming upon Israel is "overflowing with righteousness." In other words, it is an absolutely correct action in view of Israel's behavior.

This same usage, of activity which is right or correct, appears in chapters 40–55, especially in the frequent occurrences of *ṣedeq* (ten times) and various forms of *ṣadeq* (five times). These fall into two groupings: the first has to do with whether a person has or has not made certain statements, and whether these statements are correct. Most of these are in the context of the trial speeches where the question is raised whether it can be shown that any god except Yahweh had predicted the rise of Cyrus (41:26; 43:9, 26; 45:19, 21). An example is 43:9, "Let them bring their witnesses to justify them." A similar usage, but one which does not have to do with the idol controversy, is found in 48:1, where the Lord accuses the people of confessing him "but not in truth or righteousness (rightly)."

The second grouping has to do with Yahweh's call of Cyrus, and the implied question of whether he was right to do so. Yahweh asserts that this call was the right thing to do. This usage occurs four times (41:2, 10; 42:6; 45:13), of which the last, "I have raised him up in righteousness," is typical.[26]

This basic meaning also occurs in chapters 56–66, although not with quite the same frequency (five times) as in the earlier sections. In 58:2, God speaks with some wonder of a nation which, although it behaves wrongly,

---

diverging four times with the use of ελεμοσυνή or ελεος. See J. W. Olley, "*Righteousness*" *in the Septuagint of Isaiah: A Contextual Study*, Septuagint and Cognate Studies 8 (Missoula, MT: Scholars, 1979)

23. Cf. also 29:21.

24. This point deserves to be underscored. Despite differences in connotations between 1–39 and 40–55, both of these sections agree with the third section on the basic usage of the words.

25. That this is the sense, see Jer 13:1–11.

26. For a similar understanding, see C. F. Whitley, "Deutero-Isaiah's Interpretation of *Sedeq*," *VT* 22 (1972) 472–73.

still asks for righteous (right) judgments. Similarly, in 59:4, the prophet protests that no one calls another to court "in righteousness (rightly)."[27] Two other examples of this usage also occur in chapter 59, where it is the rightness of the Victor's cause and behavior which guarantee victory for him (vv. 16, 17).

As we have just shown, the fundamental use of the root, correctness or factuality, is found throughout the book.[28] It is with the other connotations that differences appear and, by means of which, the synthesizing function of chapters 56–66 becomes clear.

In Chapters 1–39

In chapters 1–39 the overwhelming number of occurrences have to do with behavior which is according to moral standards. This tone is established at the outset in 1:21, where it is asserted that whereas justice and righteousness once filled the city, now it is murder which lodges there. By contrast, 5:16 declares that what sets God apart from all creation, which marks him as the one truly holy being, is his justice and righteousness. It is clear from these occurrences, as well as all the rest in this section, that righteousness is understood as morally correct behavior, whether of God or human beings.[29] This conclusion is supported by the fact that, with one exception, the only parallel term used of the root in the first 39 chapters is *mišpaṭ*, "justice." Righteousness is a kind of living which is in accord with the norms of justice. The one exception only confirms this point. It is found in 33:15, which contains the response to the question of 33:14: "Who among us can dwell with the everlasting burnings?" The answer is: "He who walks righteously and speaks uprightly (*mêšarîm*)" Fittingly, this is the last occurrence of *ṣdq* in the first part of the book, and the rest of the verse makes it very plain that righteousness is nothing other than to live according to the moral standards of the covenant:[30]

"who despises the gain of oppressions,

---

27. The similarity with 5:23 is unmistakable.

28. Scullion, restricting himself to the nouns *ṣedeq* and *ṣedaqâ*, insists that "norm" is "a later and western notion" ("*SEDEQ-SEDEQAH*," 336). If he means by this an absolute standard which exists by itself without regard to any situation or relationship, such a position might be supportable, since the only absolute the Bible knows is God. However, if he means, as it seems he does, an accepted standard of "what is so or not so" to which all members of a community would accede, his position is not insupportable.

29. 1:26, 27; 3:10; 5:7; 9:6; 16:5; 24:16; 26:2, 7[2t], 9, 10: 28:17; 32:1, 16, 17[2t.]; 33:5.

30. See note 16 above.

who shakes his hands, lest they hold a bribe,
who stops his ears from hearing of bloodshed
and shuts his eyes from looking at evil."

In Chapters 40–55

As agreed upon by virtually all commentators and authors,[31] righteousness takes on an entirely new twist after chapter 40. But before we explore that new connotation, it is necessary to observe that the one common to chapters 1–39 is not abandoned entirely. There are at least three occurrences where "righteousness" refers to divinely approved moral behavior (48:18; 51:1; 51:7). In these three, the context clearly supports this rendering.[32] In yet four more instances there is some possibility this connotation is intended, but the contexts are ambiguous enough to leave a margin of doubt.[33] Interestingly, however, in none of these cases-in fact, nowhere in chapters 40–55-is ṣdq in any of its forms paralleled with mišpaṭ. Furthermore, the three clear references just mentioned, grouped as they are within three chapters, do not serve to give prominence to the idea of righteousness as divinely approved moral behavior in the section. They strike us, instead, as asides in the middle of a larger argument.

Of much greater interest are the numerous instances where "righteousness" has apparently nothing to do with morally correct behavior, and rather seems to have more to do with salvation, or deliverance.[34] That this is not merely an impression is confirmed by the fact that ṣdq is actually paralleled by forms of yšʿ, "salvation" in five instances.[35]

As von Rad and others have taught us,[36] this equation is not quite as odd as it first sounds. The emphasis in this section is not upon the righ-

31. See note 10 above.

32. "O that you had hearkened to my commandments? Then . . . your righteousness [would have been] like the waves of the sea" (48:18). "Hearken to me, you who pursue righteousness [RSV deliverance], you who seek the Lord" (51:1). "Hearken to me, you who know righteousness, the people in whose heart is my law" (51:7). Some explain the presence of these divergent usages as being secondary additions, and Karl Elliger, *Deuterojesaja in seinem Verhaltnis zu Tritojesaja*, BWANT 63 (Stuttgart: Kohlhammer, 1933) even sees them as stemming from Trito-Isaiah. It does not seem necessary to posit that kind of rigid consistency for an author.

33. 42:21; 45:8[2nd occ.]; 46:12; 54:14.

34. 45:8, 24; 45:25; 46:13; 50:8; 51:5, 6, 8; 53:11; 54:14, 17.

35. 45:8; 46:13; 51:5, 6, 8.

36. Von Rad, *Old Testament Theology*, tr. D. M. G. Stalker, vol. I (New York: Harper & Row, 1962) 370–83.

teousness of the people, which has failed, but upon the righteousness of God. Given the fact that God has acted righteously in punishing his people (10:22), what now remains for him to do? Would he be right to abandon them? Clearly not! For just as the covenant called for certain kinds of behavior from the people, on pain of punishment, so also the covenant contained the promises of restoration (e.g., Deut 30:1-7; Judg 2:1; Ps 89:30-34).[37] For God to act righteously toward his people, he had to deliver them. Here it is not the people's righteousness which somehow earns or requires restoration, but the righteousness of God, who in response to their cries of dereliction, remembers his promise and acts rightly in regard to it (cf. Neh 9:32; Pss 74:18-21; 105:8-11; Ezek 16:60-63).[38] Perhaps the clearest expression of this concept is found in 46:12-13:

> Hearken to me, you stubborn of heart,
>   you who are far from righteousness [RSV: deliverance]:
> I bring near my righteousness [RSV: deliverance], it is not far off,
>   and my salvation will not tarry;
> I will put salvation in Zion,
>   for Israel my glory.

Thus, God's righteousness in Isaiah 40-55 is his adherence to his covenant promises although, from a strictly legal point of view, he is not obligated to do so. This is underlined when chapters 54 and 55 rise to lyrical heights in their proclamation of God's grace in making and keeping an irrevocable covenant with his people (54:10; 55:3-4).[39]

But what is the likely result of such unmerited favor? Ezekiel says that it should result in humiliation and changed patterns of behavior (36:27, 31). When the people of Israel recognize God's faithfulness to them in spite of their prolonged faithlessness to him, surely they will be ashamed of their behavior and seek to live new lives. But there is another possibility, and it is this one which the book of Isaiah seems to address. Election love may

---

37. On this special bonding of judgment and salvation in the present book of Isaiah, see chapter 3 above and chapter 7 below.

38. "Yea, thus says the Lord God: I will deal with you as you have done, who have despised the oath in breaking the covenant, yet I will remember my covenant with you in the days of your youth, and I will establish with you an everlasting covenant. Then you will remember your ways, and be ashamed . . . I will establish my covenant with you, and you shall know that I am the Lord, that you may remember and be confounded, and never open your mouth again because of your shame, when I forgive you all that you have done, says the Lord God."

39. It is very suggestive, especially in light of 5:23 and 59:4, that 53:11 reports that the righteous one, the servant, will declare many to be righteous.

produce pride at having been chosen, and sinful living, since deliverance had not been dependent upon being righteous.

In Chapters 56–66

In my view there are many indications that chapters 56–66 were created precisely so as to address that problem, for when we turn to this section, a different situation obtains immediately, not only in the usage of *ṣdq*, but in the whole tone. That new tone is set with the opening words: "Keep justice, and do righteousness." For the first time since 33:5, *ṣdq* is again paralleled with *mišpaṭ*. But even if that were not the case, the sense would be perfectly clear: we are no longer talking about righteousness as an expression of God's right dealing in regard to covenant or even about a declaration of a righteous condition in the people by God. Rather the command to *do* righteousness makes it very plain that we are once more, as in chapters 1–39, speaking of God's expectation of certain kinds of behavior from his people. If there were any question about this, the content of chapters 56–59 (and of 63–66) lays the question to rest; the people are called to hold fast to the covenant by keeping the Sabbath (56:4, 6), by dispensing with their idols (57:12–13),[40] and by "fasting" from oppression (58:6–8). The similarity with the point of view of chapters 1–39 is unmistakable (cf. 5:8–23; 9:7[8]–10:4; 29:20–21; 31:6–7).

But we do not have here simply a return to the viewpoint of 1–39. The change from that viewpoint appears in 56:1, the first verse in the new segment, through the use of *ṣdq*, for the term occurs twice in the verse, the first in parallel with *mišpaṭ*, as already noted, and the second in parallel with *yešûʿâ*, "salvation."

> "Keep justice,
> and do righteousness;
> For my salvation is about to come,
> and my righteousness is about to be revealed."

In short, there is a whole new motivation for doing righteousness. It is not now so much the fear of impending doom which compels righteousness, as it is the recognition that God is going to mercifully and righteously keep his covenant promises. We should be righteous, the writer says, because of the righteousness of God. This point is followed out throughout the

---

40. As Payne, "Background," and others have observed, the statements about idolatry would seem to be more at home in an eighth-century milieu than in a fifth- or sixth-century one.

section: human obedience should be the natural result of divine faithfulness. This linkage is dramatically underlined again at the end of the first subdivision in 59:14–18. If justice, righteousness, truth and uprightness (vv. 14–15) are ever to prevail, it will be solely because of the righteousness of Yahweh (16–18).

Nor is this human righteousness merely an ephemeral goal. If it does not result, destruction is just as inevitable for the elect as it is for the non-elect. An example of this appears in chapter 66 in two different ways. First of all, there is the picture of Jerusalem as the nursing mother nourishing her many children (vv. 7–14), while God destroys his (and her) enemies all around (vv. 15–16). But then the surprising conclusion is that among his enemies are those who are merely depending upon their ritual purity to secure them a place with God (v. 17). To be among Jerusalem's children does not, in and of itself, guarantee a place among God's children. To have experienced the righteousness of God, his election love, which comes to his people irrespective of their righteousness, does not thereby remove from them the obligation of being righteous.

The second way in which chapter 66 reinforces the expected nature of this connection between divine faithfulness and human obedience follows immediately after the one just mentioned. Verses 18–23 tell how the Israelites will declare God's glory to all the earth, and how the nations will assist in bringing the remnant home so that all flesh may worship the Lord. Here is an expression of the faithfulness of God. But the chilling final verse in the book makes it very plain that unless the response to that faithfulness is obedience, only endless destruction results.[41]

When we look specifically at the uses of *ṣdq* in chapters 56–66, we can see how they bear out the above observations. Twelve of the twenty-three occurrences have to do with the character of the lives of the people of God. Furthermore, unlike the three occasions where this is the case in chapters 40–55, these occurrences are in the midst of substantive discussions about the behavior of the people. In chapters 40–55 the references are in passing, subordinate to the main thrust of the promise of salvation. Here there can be no question that the central question is whether the people will act as God requires or not. God is righteous and he works on behalf of those who act righteously (64:4[5]). But much of the behavior which God's people are calling righteous is actually filthy and polluted (57:12; 58:2; 64:5[6]); their attempts to be righteous have failed (59:9, 14)[42]; and those who really do live

---

41. Note the precisely similar conclusion of chap. 1, even to the use of "rebels" (*pôšeʿîm* in both cases) in 1:28 and 66:24.

42. Both these occurrences are paralleled by *mišpaṭ*.

righteous lives are destroyed (57:1). Nevertheless, God promises that the nation will be truly righteous (58:8; 60:17, 21; 61:3, 11).

It is in this last regard that the synthesizing element appears again. Several references speak of the nation's righteousness being seen by the world (61:10; 62:1, 2). On these occasions, the terms are paralleled with terms for deliverance (61:10; 62:1), or in one case (62:2), glory. On this basis, RSV goes so far as to translate the last two occurrences of *ṣedeq* with "vindication." But I am confident the demarcation between righteousness and salvation is not nearly so clear as that. The righteous living whose absence produced the exile, whose necessity seems abrogated by the gracious restoration, and which the returnees will not be able to produce anyway, that righteous living is still required, but now it is to be the gift of God's grace. Just as chapter 1 (vv. 26–31) promised that in the end Jerusalem would be a city of righteousness in which justice would reign and from which rebels would be destroyed, so chapters 56–66 hold up the same standard. But whereas chapters 1–39 could be misinterpreted to say that such righteousness is the result of supreme human effort, this final section of the book is careful to rule out that possibility. These final chapters make it plain that just as deliverance is a gift of God, so is the righteous behavior which is the logical result of having received such deliverance. This is seen in several ways. First of all, it appears in chapters 56–59 when, after the reports of the people's failure to produce justice and righteousness, God himself does it, putting His Spirit in them (59:14–21). This is reiterated in chapters 63–66 where the people confess their helplessness to do righteousness and God commits himself to create a new Jerusalem in which righteousness will reign.

We are now in a position to see the inaccuracy of Scullion's conclusion that chapters 56–66 use *ṣdq* just as 40–55 do. To be sure, 56–66 show examples of the terms being used in parallel with "salvation" or "deliverance," just as 40–55 do, and as 1–39 do not. But it is also true that 55–66 uses the term to denote righteous behavior (in parallel with "justice") as 1–39 do, and as 40–55 do not. But even more importantly, chapters 56–66 bring both concepts together in ways which neither of the preceding sections of the book do. Those who have experienced the results of God's righteousness in their lives, who know themselves to be part of the elect, cannot do either of two things. On the one hand they cannot consider themselves to be right with God merely because of their birthright. The eunuch or the foreigner who keeps God's covenant has a better right to be in the house of God than the pure-bred Israelite who takes a cavalier attitude toward the provisions of that covenant (56:2–8). On the other hand, they cannot confine righteousness to certain ritual behaviors, all of which have the taint of paganism (65:1–7), while neglecting to treat the helpless with justice (58:6–12), and denying the necessity of the Holy Spirit's guidance in their lives (63:7–19). If they do so, they are doomed to act out the wilderness wanderings all over again and to die in the desert as the ancestors did.

The cure for either of these destructive attitudes, says this final section of the book, is to combine the insights of the two preceding sections: yes, righteous living is always required of the people of God; but human beings are incapable of living that life on their own. We, the writer says, are as helpless to live that life as the Judeans were helpless to deliver themselves from captivity. So just as God alone had to deliver his people from their captivity, he alone must empower them to fulfill his own commands (59:12–16; 64:4–7). This is, of course, similar to the assessment of Ezekiel and the other prophets. Covenant-keeping will not occur simply because people intend it. There is a fundamental flaw in the human spirit. Righteousness is only possible in the long term with an infusion of God's Spirit (Ezek. 36:26–27; but see also Isa 32:14–16).

CONCLUSION

I have sought to show that in their present form chapters 56–66 are a result of a dialogue with both of the preceding sections of the book. As such, this part of the book is not an extension beyond 40–55 as 40–55 is considered an extension beyond 1–39. Rather, it represents a circling back in an effort to tie the two sections together. If its message is entirely appropriate to the returned exiles, its truest context is not historical, but literary and theological.[43]

---

43. The fact that Hanson, *Dawn*, must completely dismember the text in order for it to correctly reflect his reconstruction of the historic setting is a strong testimony in support of this assertion that the first context of 56–66 is not historical.

6

Isaiah Chapters 40–66
Addressed to People during and after the Exile[1]

AT LEAST SINCE THE work of J. G. Eichhorn in the latter part of the eighteenth century, it has been customary to argue that chapters 40–66 of the book of Isaiah must have been written during the Babylonian exile or later.[2] The reason for this argument is that the apparent audience of those chapters is persons of that time. But the book itself seems to be at pains to assert that Isaiah ben Amoz (1:1) was solely responsible for the book. For many, accepting that assertion as a fact has meant that they have felt compelled to maintain that the primary audience of chapters 40–66 was persons alive during the prophet's ministry.[3] This article will argue for neither of the above positions. Instead, it will argue that Isaiah of Jerusalem did indeed address

---

1. This article is a revised form of a paper presented at the 2010 annual meeting of the Evangelical Theological Society in Atlanta, Georgia. It was published with this title in *Bibliotheca Sacra* 169 (Jan–Mar 2012) 33–47.

2. For a discussion of critical issues in the book of Isaiah, see the introductions in Oswalt, *The Book of Isaiah, Chapters 1–39*, NICOT (Grand Rapids: Eerdmans, 1986); and Oswalt, *The Book of Isaiah, Chapters 40–66*, NICOT (Grand Rapids: Eerdmans, 1998).

3. Most recently, see Gary V. Smith, *Isaiah 40–66*, NAC 15 (Nashville: Broadman & Holman, 2009). See also his contrasting view which was presented in the above-named conference and published as "Isaiah 40–55: Which Audience Was Addressed," *JETS* 54 (2011) 701–14. In my view, the evidence he cites is consistent with the materials having been written in the late eighth century, but they do not indicate that they were primarily addressed to persons of that time

persons some 150 years in the future from himself. This is a risky position in that it opens the author to the charge, in the words of Brevard Childs, of believing in clairvoyance,[4] since to him and many others it is incredible that anyone could address persons 150 years in the future.

ISAIAH WRITES TO PERSONS IN THE FUTURE

The charge is a serious one. Other biblical prophets talk *about* the future, but no other talks *to* people in the future, especially as far distant as 150 years from their own day. But consider the alternatives. If we deny that point of address, we are forced to gloss over some very strong evidence, cited below, which points in that direction. On the other hand, if we assume that such strong evidence must point to the materials having been written during the exile and afterwards, we are forced to admit that the later writers and editors did their best to make it appear that their work was actually that of Isaiah, and that he really did foretell the circumstances of the exilic and post-exilic people to the point of being able to speak to them in advance. Childs is forthright in this, stating that the exilic and post-exilic writers would have originally included more specific historical details, in the tradition of biblical writing, and that those details have been expunged to make it appear to be the work of the earlier prophet.[5] But does it not make better sense to recognize that those details were not included because the earlier prophet did not know them, as the book seems to be at pains to assert? A further point which should be very telling is that much of the argument for the superiority of Yahweh over the gods of Babylon found in chapters 40–55 is made to hang on Yahweh's ability to tell the future, namely that Israel would go into captivity and that they would be delivered from captivity by a man named Cyrus. If these "predictions" were the work of the so-called Deutero-Isaiah, writing in about 545 B.C.,[6] after Cyrus had already begun to make serious inroads into Babylonian territory, and if that anonymous prophet had to put them in the mouth of someone speaking 150 years earlier to give them validity, what happens to the argument, let alone the integrity of this unknown person who is called the greatest theologian of Israel?

---

4. Brevard S. Childs, *Isaiah*, OTL (Louisville: Westminster John Knox, 2001) 3.

5. Childs, *Introduction to the Old Testament as Scripture* (Philadelphia: Fortress, 1979) 325–30.

6. So for instance Christopher North, "The 'Former' Things and the 'New' Things in Deutero-Isaiah," in *Studies in Old Testament Prophecy: Presented to Professor Theodore H. Robinson by the Society for Old Testament Study on His Sixty-fifth Birthday, August 9th, 1946*, ed. H. H. Rowley (Edinburgh: T. & T. Clark, 1950) 111–26.

But if we are thus driven back to say that the present book is the work of one person speaking under the inspiration of the Holy Spirit, as the text seems to maintain, what explanation can we give for why this address to future persons would have happened, especially when it seems to have happened nowhere else in the biblical corpus? Since the Bible itself does not give us the explanation, anything we suggest must necessarily be provisional. But here is a suggestion: at the time when the hammer of defeat and exile was falling on North Israel, Isaiah was given a message which would encompass the entire experience of exile and return that would affect God's people from 721 B.C. until 516 B.C. Too often we dismiss the significance of Samaria's destruction for the overall history of the people of God. We seem to think that that event was only an isolated incident with little bearing on the whole nation's self-understanding, and that it was the fall of Jerusalem in 586 B.C. which produced the real crisis in Israel's history and experience. But there was more of a sense of solidarity among the peoples of Israel and Judah than we might sometimes realize. That being so, the fall of Samaria would have had something of a cataclysmic impact on the thought and theology of the Judeans. Thus Isaiah was inspired to see that the events of 721 and following were merely the left bookend, as it were, of a total experience that would include the right bookend of the events of 586 and following. In the context of the events of 721 and following, Isaiah was given a vision of the absolute god-hood of Yahweh in the world, his utter holiness and absolute sovereignty, and the certainty of his redemption of his people. But that understanding could not be permitted to rest solely on Yahweh's ability to deliver Jerusalem from the Assyrians. What about that godhood when Jerusalem was in ruins, just like Samaria, as it would be? Could God's supremacy be so flexible as to deal with the entirely new situation which exile, both Samaria's and Jerusalem's, would portend? Of course the answer is a resounding "Yes!" In short, the theological vision given to Isaiah in his own lifetime would have been called into serious question if it had not been extended out to that point which Samaria's fall inevitably led to 150 years in the future.

It appears that at least some of the proponents of multiple authorship agree with this understanding of the *raison d'être* for the present book. While some, like Otto Kaiser, seem to have believed that the present book is the result of a host of more or less accidental conjunctions of similar key words or phrases,[7] there are others who believe that reflection on the work of the great prophet[8] in a new set of historical circumstances caused students of Isaiah's theology to feel the need to extend it to cover those new circumstances. Once again, it seems that the intense effort to make it appear that this was not the case, but that the prophet himself had had such an all-encompassing vision, would call into question the integrity of these supposed students.[9]

All of this previous discussion of course presumes that chapters 40–66 of Isaiah are indeed largely addressed to persons in the exile and after. If we could agree that that is not the case, much of the previous discussion would be moot. However, I do not believe we can agree on the basis of the evidence discussed below. But before we look at that evidence, it should be said that if the primary audience was during the exile and later that does not mean that these words had no relevance to the people of Isaiah's own day or that they were meaningless for them. In fact, it seems plain that several individual passages assume an eighth century background. In this regard, the work of J. Barton Payne from a generation ago is still very much on target. As he pointed out then, such passages raise serious difficulties for the position that these chapters were only written in the sixth century.[10] However, such observations do not mean that the *primary* address of the materials was to

---

7. Otto Kaiser, *Isaiah 1–12, A Commentary*, 2nd ed., tr J. Bowden, OTL (Philadelphia: Westminster, 1983).

8. Although there is no consensus about exactly how much of "the great prophet's" work we actually have. Many see it as a matter of only a few chapters. To think that such a small beginning point issued in the several hundred years of intense theological meditation and reflection supposed to produce the present book seems even more incredible than that God could inspire a man to speak to people far in the future from his own day.

9. Note that Hugh Williamson has proposed that it is actually "Deutero-Isaiah" and his disciples who are responsible for the present shape of the book and most of its content (*The Book Called Isaiah: Deutero-Isaiah's Role in Composition and Redaction* [Oxford: Clarendon, 1994]). In my mind, that makes it all the more surprising that these later persons would feel so impelled to deny their own work and put it in the mouth of this obscure Judean prophet, of whose work we now have only isolated fragments.

10. One of these factors is the accusations in chapters 56–66 that the people were engaged in idolatrous practices. Yet it is often maintained that the Babylonian exile was what broke the Judeans of persistent idolatry. While it seems probable that that assertion is generally true, there is no concrete evidence demonstrating that *all* idolatrous practices had been left behind in the exile. It seems likely that a syncretistic idol worship, albeit on a limited basis(?), may have been practiced in Judah until the time of Ezra and Nehemiah. But even if there was no idol-worship in post-exilic Judah, we can still see Isaiah saying, out of his own background in the eighth century, that the arrogant self-righteousness of some of the returnees would be nothing other than the worship of idols.

people in the eighth century, or even that those passages which reflect the background of that century had their primary address there. The differing vocabulary and style beginning in chapter 40:1 argue that the prophet has moved into a different world and is speaking to a people who are much less concrete to him than his own people are.

EVIDENCE FOR A SIXTH-CENTURY AUDIENCE

Addressing Different Questions

With this lengthy introduction, let us move to the evidence which points to the sixth century address. While some specific passages will be discussed, it is the change in overall tone and in the issues being addressed that is more impressive. Clearly, chapters 40–55, in particular, are dealing with a very different set of questions than those being spoken to in the earlier part of the book. Chapters 7–39 are focused almost exclusively on the trustworthiness of God. From Ahaz onwards, that is, from the fall of Samaria onwards, the issue was whether one should trust in Yahweh or in the gods of the nations in order for Jerusalem to escape a similar fate to Samaria's. In fact, the Judean people were not inclined to an exclusive trust in Yahweh, but rather tended to try to make use of Yahweh as one of the gods. And if Yahweh did not seem to be producing in a timely fashion, they were quick to turn to the nations and their gods. Thus these chapters frequently ring with the tones of judgment. The human pride and arrogance which is at the base of all idol-making, in Isaiah's view, comes in for sharp condemnation. If there should be no deep and lasting change in these conditions, then in spite of that deliverance from Sennacherib which so demonstrated Yahweh's trustworthiness, Jerusalem was as doomed to fall as Samaria ever was, regardless of how long it might take. This seems to be the point to which chapters 38 and 39 bring us.

But chapters 40ff. are not addressed to a people looking to avoid destruction. These chapters are addressed to a people in despair, a people who believe their condition is hopeless. The affirmations which Isaiah makes are answering questions that would arise from the destruction of Jerusalem and the onset of the exile, not from conditions existing during 739–701 B.C. We can see what the content of those questions would be from chapter 40: does God want to deliver us (vv. 1–11); can God deliver us (12–26); will God deliver us (27–31)? These questions are answered in detail and from several angles in chapters 41–55. They are not questions of a people living with a measure of security in their own land, still reasonably confident that with a little luck and little help from their friends, they can stave off disaster.

In chapters 41–45, as is well known, there are several places where Yahweh calls the idol gods into court to see who is really god. While these scenes could have relevance to other contexts than just an exilic one, the particular literary setting in which they appear confirms that it is the exilic context that is in primary focus. In chapter 41, the stage is set with a proclamation that Yahweh has "raised up one from the east." Who is this but Cyrus, as is later confirmed in 44:28—45:7? It is surely not one of the Assyrian tyrants. Although those tyrants were said to be tools in Yahweh's hands, they were tools for destruction, not deliverance.

The nations are terrified at the onslaught of Cyrus and scurry to make idols (41:5–7), but Israel is told not to fear because she is God's chosen servant. Thus the tone is one of encouragement to the despairing. It is not an admonition to wait on Yahweh addressed to people rushing off to save themselves with political machinations. Not only is Israel not to fear because of their election, but also because the Holy One of Israel is their Redeemer. This is a significant shift in the horizon of this, Isaiah's favorite epithet for God. Counting the one occurrence of "The Holy One of Jacob," this appellation occurs twenty-six times in the book (as against only four unique occurrences elsewhere in the Bible). Thirteen of these twenty-six occurrences are found in chapters 1–39 and thirteen in chapters 40–55. In chapters 1–39 almost all the occurrences are in the domains of sovereignty and trustworthiness, whereas almost all the occurrences in 40–66 are in the domain of redemption. In the face of threatening destruction dealt with in chapters 1–39, the Holy One is depicted as the infinitely trustworthy Sovereign. What would account for the shift to seeing the Holy One as the compassionate Redeemer except a shift of context to the exilic and post-exilic periods, when it is redemption that is needed and hoped for?

Court Cases Challenging the Idols

The first of the court cases against the idols appears in 41:21. Here as elsewhere, Yahweh challenges the idols to two things: explain the past and tell the future, and to do some new thing. This is a very sophisticated attack, because it is aimed precisely at the identity of the gods with the forces of this world. Those forces have neither purpose nor goal; they simply continue on in the endless round of existence. Just as the Sun cannot tell us where it came from, or where it is going, neither can Shamash, the sun-god, tell us where the world came from or what it exists for. In the same way, the gods cannot do anything really new, and they certainly cannot tell us about it in advance. But since Yahweh is the transcendent Creator of the world, he can do all that, and indeed he has. Particularly, as becomes clear in later iterations of this case, Yahweh has foretold the exile, and has foretold something hitherto unheard of–return from exile, even going so far as to name the deliverer, and the Israelites in exile will be God's witnesses that he has done these things.

It seems to me that these attacks on the idol-gods draw their particular poignancy from the exilic context. In that setting it will appear that Babylon's gods have defeated Yahweh in a most complete way. But Isaiah was inspired in advance to lay out the case that, far from disproving Yahweh's universal power, the exile will provide the most stunning proof of that fact. Why is it that the Judeans (alone, as far as we know) were almost instantly ready to respond to Cyrus' decree of restoration? Is it because some unknown prophet of the exile came up with arguments previously unheard of in 545 and somehow captured the imagination of a people who were 40 years into Babylonian assimilation? That is highly unlikely. It is much more likely that a core group never succumbed to the pressure for assimilation because they had not merely the more general assertions of Jeremiah and Ezekiel, but the particular statements of the book of Isaiah which spoke of all these things in advance. In the exilic context what it had said all along now made sense in ways it had done only dimly before.

The Promise of the Servant

Likewise, it is in the context of the exile that the promise of the Servant makes most sense. An Israel that felt it had finally sinned away all of God's covenant promises, had failed to promote God's divine order, his *mišpaṭ*, in the world, and had failed to convey his instructions for living, his *torah*, to the world, yet heard that it was God's chosen servant. How could this be? In chapter 42, we are given a first glimpse of how Israel's servanthood was going to become possible. A Servant whose responses to God and to suffering would be very different from that of Israel would do for Israel and the nations what Israel had failed to do.[11] These wonderful promises would have

---

11. The refusal to allow that this Servant could be Jesus of Nazareth has produced chaos in scholarship concerning the identity of the Servant. While it is not surprising that Jewish scholars have insisted that all references to servant must be to Israel, it is fascinating to see the range of opinions expressed by others with no consensus whatsoever. They range from Deutero-Isaiah himself to Jeremiah to an unnamed leper in the exilic community; and these are only the beginning. For a recent survey, see Joseph Blenkinsopp, "The Servant and the Servants in Isaiah and the Formation of the Book,"

no lodging in the Judah of 700 B.C. It is likely that that Judah is described in chapter 22, where the people are wildly partying (after the deliverance from Sennacherib?) and Shebna, the Prime Minister, is supervising the building of his tomb. People like those have no need of this quiet, unassuming servant who will not break a bent reed or extinguish a guttering candle. These promises are for people who believe themselves to be spiritually hopeless, in short, the people of the exile.

Recurring References to Babylon

Further confirmation of this exilic address is found in the recurring references to Babylon as the oppressor and the one from whom deliverance will be obtained. These are not the more generalized oracles against the nations such as are found in chapters 13–14, and 21, but specific promises of deliverance (43:14–15) and indeed a command to go out of Babylon in 48:20. In chapter 46, it is the Babylonian idols (and no others) who are said to be themselves carried off into exile. But most telling of all is the way in which the unit containing chapters 41–48 is closed. The last of the court cases is completed in chapter 46 with a ringing pronouncement that Yahweh is God, and there is no other (46:9), the chief evidence of which is his ability to bring "a bird of prey from the east" to perform his purpose of salvation (vv. 11–13). Immediately following in chapter 47 is a powerful statement of Babylon's humiliation and judgment. She who said, "I am and there is no other" (vv. 8, 10) will be brought down into the dust by the true "I AM" (45:18; 46:9). She will be herself judged because, although she was Yahweh's tool to punish his people, she did so mercilessly. It is hard to see any of this having been primarily addressed to the people of Isaiah's own day. What did they know of Babylon, but that she was a rich and cosmopolitan city that had been a thorn in the side of Assyria for years and years, and might be a potential ally (39:1ff.)? They did not know her as an oppressor from whom deliverance seemed impossible and as the arrogant center of a world empire unlike any yet seen at that time.

Call for Action

Neither is the call for action in chapter 48 like those found in chapters 1–39. Judah is not called to repent for sins of injustice and arrogance and to turn

in *Writing and Reading the Scroll of Isaiah*, 2 vols., ed. Craig C. Broyles and Craig A. Evans (Leiden: Brill, 1997) 1:155–75.

to Yahweh in humble trust. To be sure, she is to abandon any belief that some special status will save her. But more importantly, she is called to pay attention[12] to God's promises of deliverance and not to become assimilated to Babylon because of lost hope. All Yahweh's claims to absolute uniqueness are summed up, and the effect of that truth is to say that he can do whatever he wants with Babylon (v. 14). None of all this that has happened (namely the exile) would need to have happened, but it has. But that does not mean Yahweh has been defeated either by the Babylonians or by Israel's sins. He will deliver them and in the hour of deliverance, they need to be ready to go.

There is one part of chapter 48 which may have been addressed to people in Isaiah's own day. This is the stanza now delineated as verses 6–8. It reads as follows:

> You have heard; now see all this;
>   and will you not declare it?
> From this time forth I cause you to hear new things,
>   hidden things that you have not known.
> They are created now, not long ago;
>   before today you have never heard of them,
>   lest you should say, "Behold, I knew them."
> You have never heard, you have never known,
>   from of old your ear has not been opened.
> For I knew that you would surely deal treacherously,
>   and that from before birth you were called a rebel.

Surely the most natural way to take this English text is to understand that the announcement of what Yahweh was about to do was not given to anybody other than those being immediately addressed. In other words, there cannot have been two audiences: an earlier secondary one, and a later primary one. For those who believe that the primary address is to the Babylonian exiles, this text is taken as one of the primary evidences that chapters 40–66 could not have been written earlier than the exilic period.[13] But that need not be the case. Two possible explanations could be given. The first is that in this case the words did indeed have primary application to hearers in the eighth century BC. Isaiah would have been establishing to them that he was a true prophet whose message was not merely a repackaging of what

---

12. Note that words for hearing occur ten times in the first eighteen verses of chapter 48. Also, note that in Hebrew thought "to hear" is synonymous with obedience. To disobey is not to "hear."

13. For further discussion, see Oswalt, *Isaiah 40–66*, 270–72.

had happened in the past. Thus, although those persons in Isaiah's own time would not necessarily have understood much of the import of what Isaiah was saying, they could still recognize that Isaiah was a true spokesman for the infinitely creative Yahweh. At the same time, the new things being prophesied were not to occur in Isaiah's lifetime, but many years later. Thus, although in this passage the primary and secondary audiences would have traded places, there would still be two audiences.

The second explanation does not require this shifting of primary and secondary audiences. Here the primary address is still to the exiles, and has to do with their comprehension of what had been actually said many years earlier. As is well-known to students of the Hebrew language, the connotations of the Hebrew verbs *šāmaᶜ* and *yādaᶜ* are much more comprehensive than those of the English words commonly used to translate them. Both of these verbs have a great deal to do with reception and application. Thus, one could "hear" something in the restricted English sense, and yet not "hear" it in the full Hebrew sense of taking appropriate action. In the same way, one could "know" something in the restricted English sense of being intellectually aware of it, and yet not "know" it in the full Hebrew sense of apprehending its significance for ones own life. Thus it could well be that the exiles had indeed not really "heard" or "known" these things until in the context of the exile Yahweh had opened their hearts to perceive the true significance of what had been actually said many years earlier.[14]

Israel/Judah's Sin

When we come to chapters 49–55, it seems to me even more clear that the context is the exile. The three questions introduced in chapter 40: "Does God want to deliver us?"; Can God deliver us?"; and "Will God deliver us?" were fully addressed in regards to Babylon in chapters 41–48. Those chapters showed that the Babylonian gods were helpless to retain their hold on the exiles, and that Yahweh could deliver his people from Babylon whenever he chose. Israel was God's chosen servant whose deliverance would be an inescapable witness to God's supreme power. But the exile raised another issue besides the power of Yahweh in relation to the Babylonian idol-gods. That issue was the one of sin, the sin of Israel/Judah that precipitated Yahweh's handing over of his people into the hands of their enemies. How can sinful Israel ever become holy, servant Israel? Yes, God can deliver his people from Babylon, but what about their sin? How will he deal with that? He can restore the people to their land, but how will he restore them to himself? So

---

14. For a fuller discussion see ibid., 266–72.

chapter 40's three questions come back into focus again in chapters 49–55, but on a whole new issue.

Interestingly, while the language of chapters 49–55 continues to revolve around deliverance from captivity, there is no mention of Babylon, nor is there the kind of explicit reference to deliverance from a political entity that one finds in chapter 41–48. Rather, here the issue is whether, and how, God will deliver them from their alienation from him. Surely, he has rejected ("forgotten") them. In response, God insists that this is not the case, and that he has bared his mighty arm to set them free. On the surface, the appearance in this unit of three of the four of what were formerly designated the "Suffering Servant" passages seems strange, even intrusive.[15] But I contend that when we look more closely at the structure of the unit, we find that these sections are integral to what is being said. A close reading will show that the final passage, Isa 52:13—53:12 is pivotal. From 49:1 to 52:12, there is a growing anticipation: Yahweh is going to restore his Bride to himself; the siege which holds his Zion in bondage is going to be broken. Then, in chapters 54 and 55, we find invitation, in which people are urged to avail themselves of the reconciliation to God that is now available. What happens to change anticipation into invitation? It is the final baring of God's mighty arm, as detailed in 52:13—53:12. But who ever thought the mighty arm would look like that?! Deliverance from alienation from God, the ultimate consequence of sin is in fact made possible through the humble, substitutionary suffering and death of the Servant. This is not the people of Israel dying because of the sins of the Gentiles. As I said above, the first discussion of this individual Servant appears as an introduction to the concept in chapter 42. We are informed in prospect how it will be that God can restore to himself sinful Israel and make them servant Israel. But the full treatment of the topic is reserved for chapters 49–53, where the second and third discussions (in chapters 49 and 50) are preparatory to the climactic one in chapters 52 and 53.

Now we say all of this about chapters 49–55 to say that a despairing sense of alienation from God was simply not in the purview of any but a bare minority of Isaiah's eighth century hearers. As a whole, the people of Judah between 740 and 700 B.C. seem not to have been very conscious of their sin at all. They were shocked and frightened by what happened to Israel, and they were very apprehensive about Yahweh's ability to be of very much

---

15. On the appropriate designation, see T. N. D. Mettinger, *A Farewell to the Servant Songs: A Critical Examination of an Exegetical Maxim*, Scriptura Minora 13 (Lund: Gleerup, 1983). I believe it would be more appropriate to label them "The Individual Servant Passages" (as opposed to those references to the "collective servant" that appear elsewhere in this part of the book).

assistance to them in the looming crisis of the Assyrian threat. But to think that Yahweh had somehow abandoned them because of their sins, and that their most desperate need was for reconciliation with him? Where is any evidence of that at all, except perhaps among the faithful remnant? Chapter 8 describes the situation in Isaiah's own day with frightening accuracy, so that Isaiah saw nothing for it but to seal up the testimony and entrust it to his disciples for another day. Another day when there would be a generation for whom his words would have a saving effect and not a hardening one.

Righteous Living, Mark of a Redeemed People

Finally, we come to chapters 56–66. Here it seems that more of Isaiah's words would have had relevance to his own day. It has been argued elsewhere that the use of *ṣedāqâ*, "righteousness" in chapters 56–66 shows that the author intended to strike a synthesis of the dominant themes of chapters 1–39 and 40–55.[16] The first division (1–39) speaks regularly of righteousness as that which Yahweh requires of his people. But the second division (40–55) hardly ever speaks of righteousness in this way. Instead the term is regularly used of Yahweh's undeserved grace in saving his people. When we come to chapters 56–66 we find once again that righteous behavior among humans is a divine expectation. Yet the humans confess that they are unable to be righteous. This provides the setting for the proclamation that righteous behavior will be made possible by that divine grace revealed in the previous division.

To make the point just mentioned, chapters 56–66 are structured as a very artfully contrived chiasmus beginning (and ending) with a vision of righteous foreigners and eunuchs with whom God is pleased (56:1–8; 66:18–24), then moving to the failure of God's people to be righteous at all (56:9—59:15a; 63:7—66:17), and then to a revelation of the Divine Warrior who will defeat the people's enemies (59:15b–21; 63:1–6), and then to a picture of God's righteous people as a lantern through whom the rising Sun shines out on all the world (60:1–31; 61:4—62:11) and climaxing with the Messiah's self-affirmation of his role as deliverer (61:1–3).[17] In other words, both chapters 49–55 and 56–66 are dealing with the subject of sin. 49–55 are dealing with it from the point of view of its forensic and judicial aspects. The issue is one of cause and effect. "The soul that sins shall die." Is there any way to avoid that effect of sin without nullifying the whole cause/effect structure of the universe? 52:13—53:12 demonstrated that there was. But

---

16. For a fuller discussion of this topic, see chapter 5 above.
17. For a fuller discussion of this structure, see Oswalt, *Isaiah, 40–66*, 461–65.

chapters 56–66 are dealing with sin from the perspective of behavior. Does forgiveness of sin simply leave sinful behavior to proceed as if nothing had happened? To quote a famous Pharisee, "Well then, should we keep on sinning so that God can show us more and more of his wonderful grace? Of course not!" (Rom 6:1–2a NLT).

While it is certainly possible to say that the diatribes against sin and unrighteousness which are found in chapters 57–59 and 63–66 would have been entirely appropriate for an eighth century audience, it is not likely that the confessions of sin which the prophet also includes in those chapters would have found much resonance in that audience. As was said above, in eighth century Judah there was little of the kind of deep soul-searching that we find here. Rather there was more of that kind of complacency that we see in Amos and again in Jeremiah. We can imagine them saying something like this, "It is true that we need to placate our God now and then if he gets upset about this or that, but by and large he needs us at least as much as we need him."

In the aftermath of the exile, the situation was dramatically different. Now there was despair, not only over their situation, but also over their inability to live the life of God. The concern to encourage the people that we find especially in the books of Haggai and Zechariah underlines this point. At the same time, in the light of the content of Isaiah 56–66, we may recognize a parallel attitude signaling a new kind of complacency. It might be expressed like this, "Why did God deliver us from Babylon? It was certainly not because of our righteousness, but because he was keeping his promises to our ancestors. So, what matters here is birthright, not behavior." This attitude would play straight into the issue of ethnic purity that animated so much of the concern of the post-exilic period. Isaiah says that the issue is not ethnicity, but righteousness. This is no argument for syncretism against an Ezra or a Nehemiah, but it is a plea to put the discussion on the right footing. A foreigner who has been fully assimilated into the covenant faith of Israel is more pleasing to Yahweh than a sinful, arrogant, pure-bred Judean.

All this being said, the most natural historical context for what we find in chapters 56–66 is the post-exilic period. The fact that it is difficult to pinpoint exactly where in the post-exilic period these chapters best fit is, to this author's mind, another argument that the material was not written during that period, but rather, was written to address the underlying issue of the whole period from 539 onwards. What was that issue? It may be expressed in three questions: "What is the basis of an ongoing relationship with Yahweh?"; "What is the means of doing that?"; "What is our function as a people in the world?" Those were not questions that most eighth century

Judeans were asking. This is not to argue that they were utterly irrelevant for such persons. If that had been the case, the messages would not have been preserved for later generations. But they were not burning questions for many, whereas they would have been burning questions for those returned from exile.

Two Opposing Groups

Many commentators correctly point out that there seem to be two groups of people to whom the prophet is speaking in chapters 56–66: one whom he is attacking and one whom he is approving.[18] Exactly who those groups might have been is not so easy to define, however. One suggestion that has become popular in the last thirty years is that the group the prophet was attacking were the followers of Ezekiel who were determined to rebuild the temple and to impose priestly restrictions on the people, whereas the group he was affirming were the followers of the hypothetical "Deutero-Isaiah" who supposedly opposed rebuilding the temple and wished for a freer society in which ethics were more internalized. The fact that both of these groups are hypothetical reconstructions which have a marked similarity to groups within North American society raises some serious doubts about the proposal.[19] It seems to me that we can say this: there were people who were proud of their birth-right as Israelites and who believed that ritual precision was what was called for. On the other hand there seems to have been a group of people who, although they were oppressed by those in power, nevertheless were determined to fulfill the spirit of the Covenant in their behavior, while at the same time being very conscious of their failure to do that in the depth that they wished.

I would grant that there is no *prima facie* evidence to prove that such opposing groups did not exist in Isaiah's own day. However, I would insist that particularly as we apply the questions the section is asking to those groups, it is much more likely that they existed in conflict during the post-exilic period. It seems apparent that there were those who came out of the exile as "people of the Book," people who concluded that the reason for the

---

18. Recent scholarship would tend to deny that there is a single prophetic voice in these chapters. Rather, they are presumed to be the work of "the post-exilic community." See, for instance, Elizabeth Achtemeier, *The Community and Message of Isaiah 56–66* (Minneapolis: Augsburg, 1982). However, the failure to arrive at any consensus about which portions relate to which speakers seems to call that conclusion into question. On the other hand, the carefully developed chiastic structure argues that a single mind is responsible for the present form of the text.

19. See e.g., Paul D. Hanson, *The Dawn of Apocalyptic* (Philadelphia: Fortress, 1975).

exile was that Israel had not been exclusive enough and had not kept the letter of the Covenant stipulations carefully enough. This was their answer to the question of what kinds of behavior were necessary to an on-going relationship with Yahweh. Sometimes Ezra is taken to be representative of this group (unfairly, I think). Without becoming a thoroughgoing Hegelian, it is not too difficult to posit another contrasting group, who argue that it is the ethical aspects of the covenant that are important to obey and that while it is indeed important to protect themselves from the influence of the nations, it is even more important to reach out to the nations and draw them in. It is difficult to find evidence that that dialogue was taking place in the eighth century.

CONCLUSION

In sum, then, Isaiah 40–66 is not primarily addressed to the people and the concerns of the eighth century. Rather, these chapters, further developing the implications of what was said to eighth-century people, are addressed to their descendants. Having chastised his contemporaries for their tendency to trust the nations rather than Yahweh, Isaiah lifts the eyes of shattered, despairing persons in the future to see that far from discrediting Yahweh, the exile and its aftermath will give them an opportunity to so live out his life that they can become a light to those very nations their ancestors had been tempted to trust.

7

The Mission of Israel to the Nations

Micah and Isaiah[1]

WHEN WE LOOK AT the prophets as a group, we see two apparently conflicting attitudes concerning the surrounding nations. On the one hand, there is the promise that eventually Israel will be delivered from the destructive hand of the nations, and will in turn destroy them (e.g., Ezek 38:16, 23; Zech 14:12–15). But on the other, there is an underlying sense of responsibility to declare God's glory to the nations (e.g., Hos 14:6–7; Jer 3:17; 16:19). This apparent dichotomy between Israel's privilege and its responsibility seems to be best bridged in Micah and then to a greater extent in Isaiah.

MICAH

On the one hand, as in Amos and Hosea, there is great attention given to the present disastrous condition of the nation and the destruction of the Holy City (by the nations) which those conditions will engender. It is because of corrupt political and religious leaders (3:11) that this disaster will occur (4:11, 12). Yet, in direct juxtaposition to this diatribe against those who have failed in their mission of revealing God in Israel comes the famous

---

1. This material is excerpted from a chapter of the same title that appeared in *Through No Fault of Their Own: The Fate of Those Who Have Never Heard*, eds. W. V. Crockett and J. G. Sigountos (Grand Rapids: Baker, 1991) 85–96, and is used here by permission.

The Mission of Israel to the Nations

statement in 4:1–5 which contains the clear statement of Israel's mission to the nations. Ruined Zion will become the highest mountain of all and all the nations will come to it to learn the law of God. The statement seems to serve two purposes in its present setting. On the one hand, in the light of this future universal role of revelation, the present failures of the leaders in the national context are the more despicable. On the other hand this passage makes it plain that despite the failures of Israel and Judah, God's intentions for them were such that they could not, and would not, be abandoned.[2]

Isaiah's use of this passage is also instructive. Arguments over which prophet originated it have so far been inconclusive.[3] But however the question is answered, Isaiah uses the material to good effect. At the head of chapter 2, it stands in stark contrast to both chapter 1 and to 2:5—4:1, the next section. The contrast is so stark one is brought up sharply by it. How can the harlot city of 1:21 be the fountainhead of law and word which appears in 2:3? To a significant extent this question and its answer set the agenda for the rest of the book: how can rebel Israel become servant Israel for the purpose of revealing God's glory to the world?

But we must return to Micah for a moment. Some might say that any concept of mission in 4:1–5 is negated by the conclusion of Micah 4 (and all of chapter 5) where the daughter of Zion is invited to thresh the nations and give whatever is left as an offering to God (4:11–13). Surely this expression, corresponding to that found in Joel (e.g., 3:18–19), conveyed Israel's normative attitude toward the nations—not obligation, but domination—and 4:1–5 must be read in that light. Thus the flowing of the nations to Jerusalem would be as slaves.[4]

There is no need, however, to force either of these ideas into subordination. They are coordinate. Israel can be both blessing and curse, as indeed can God. To those who come in submission and acceptance he offers blessed sonship. But to those who insist on taking his gifts by force, he shows nothing but implacable hostility. Thus, it is not at all inconsistent that Zion should be at the same time a source of life and a source of death to the

---

2 Micah 4:5 should not be seen as a sign of indifference on Micah's part. There is every reason to take it as a statement of current fact. In spite of the present adherence of the surrounding nations to idols, if Israel would be faithful to her God, the day would come when all nations would recognize Israel's God alone.

3 If one of the two prophets originated the statement it seems likely to have been Micah. The image in Micah 4 follows naturally from 3:12, but seems to break in abruptly after Isa 1:31. See Oswalt, *The Book of Isaiah, Chapters 1–39*, NICOT (Grand Rapids: Eerdmans, 1986) 112–19.

4 For this point of view, see Delbert R. Hillers, *Micah*, Hermeneia (Philadelphia: Fortress, 1984) 49–53.

nations.[5] This same collocation of ideas appears even more starkly in Isaiah 14. Verse 1 tells us that foreigners will unite with the House of Jacob while verse 2 says Israel will enslave the oppressors. These ideas are not polar opposites, but complementary. It is as God destroys the nations which persist in oppressing his people that the nations are moved to seek his mercy and grace.

ISAIAH

None of the other prophets matches Isaiah for his full-orbed treatment of the subject of the nations. From chapter 2 just mentioned until chapter 66 in which we are told that all flesh will worship God (v. 23), the nations are never far from Isaiah's view. In fact, a good case can be made that chapter 6 is in its present position in the book in order to show that just as the man of unclean lips was made able to declare the glory of God to his nation, so the people of unclean lips (as described in chs. 1–5) could be made able to declare that glory to the nations (66:18–20).[6]

When the book is seen in this way chapters 7–39 are a discussion of Israel's need to recognize the glory of God. The great irony of these chapters is that instead of trusting God and thus representing him to the nations, Israel becomes enamored with the glory of the nations and turns her back on God. The burden of the section then, is to show the folly of such a move. Against this backdrop four allusions to mission are noteworthy. The first of these occurs at the end of the description of the Messianic kingdom in chapter 11: the earth will be so full of the knowledge of the Lord that violence and destruction will cease (11:9). While it may be argued with some force that the passage is descriptive and not prescriptive, it is still a witness to what the prophet expected to be the outcome of Israel's experience.

The second allusion appears in chapter 19 at the end of the oracle against Egypt. There in verse 24 it is stated that a day will come when, as a result of God's healing, Egypt and Assyria will join with Israel to become a blessing "in the midst of the earth" (v. 24). Whether this is an allusion to Genesis 12:3 is unclear, but the same concept is certainly at work: God's blessing must be shared.

---

5 See Gen 12:3 for this thought. D. W. Van Winkle reaches this same conclusion (that it is not either-or, but both-and) in his "Relationship of the Nations to Yahweh and Israel in Isaiah 40–55," *VT* 35 (1985) 446–58. Nor is this a new position. It was already espoused by Gustav F. Oehler in his *Theologie des Alten Testaments* (Stuttgart: Steinkopf, 1882) 804–11.

6 See Oswalt, *Isaiah 1–39*, 55ff.

The Mission of Israel to the Nations

The third allusion to a mission of Israel among the nations in Isaiah 7–39 is found in chapter 25. Chapter 24 summarizes the oracles against the nations (chs. 13–23), and speaks of their total destruction. Chapter 25 then says that because this destruction will be a manifestation of God's absolute faithfulness to his own, all peoples will come to "this mountain" (Zion) to worship God. There he will prepare a feast for "all peoples" (v. 6), in the context of which he will destroy death for all the nations (v. 7).[7]

The common thread in all three of the passages just discussed is the idea that it is by means of Israel that God will show himself to the nations. There is a sense in which Israel is passive in all this: it is as the nations observe how God treats his people, and as his qualities are manifested by his people, that the nations are drawn to him. Thus the question must be raised whether Israel has a responsibility to the nations or merely to God. Probably the prophet was not thinking in either/or categories, as 12:4 would indicate. There Israel is commanded to active witness: "Make known his deeds among the nations, proclaim that his name is exalted."

The final allusion to Israel's mission to the nations in chapters 7–39 appears in chapter 39. There Hezekiah's failure to give glory to God before the visiting Babylonians is directly linked to the coming exile in Babylon. More than is superficially apparent, this linkage leads directly into chapters 40–66. It is not merely the mention of Babylon, nor even the allusion to the coming exile that makes this chapter such a bridge. Rather, it is this whole aspect of witness. Hezekiah, and by extension, the whole nation, had failed to be a vehicle for demonstrating God's glory to the nations. Thus, the exile results, but not merely as a punishment; it also becomes the vehicle whereby Israel's mission can be fulfilled.

This idea of representing God before the nations is the key one in 40–48 and again in 56–66. In 40–48 God expresses his unmerited favor to the exiles by telling them that not only has he not forsaken them, he will use them to demonstrate his Godhead against the Babylonian idols. (For this same idea in slightly different words, see Ezek. 36:22–36). Israel's deliverance, a brand-new thing, will demonstrate that their God is indeed God of the whole world. In a whole series of ringing affirmations God insists that Israel will be the means of the nations recognizing their folly and turning to him (41:20; 42:10–13; 44:23; 45:1–6, 14, 22–25).

---

7. Chaps. 24–27 have sometimes been referred to as the "Little Apocapalypse" since they speak in rather universalistic terms about God's triumph over the nations. Whether this is a correct identification of the material is open to question because many of the characteristic features of apocalyptic are not found. See Oswalt, *Isaiah 1–39*, 440–41, and Oswalt, "Recent Studies in Old Testament Apocalyptic," in *The Face of Old Testament Studies*, eds. D. Baker and B. T. Arnold (Grand Rapids: Baker, 1999) 369–90.

Again, as mentioned above, Israel's role here is primarily passive. It is as God delivers them, demonstrating both his own incomparable power and the impotence of the idols that the nations will come to recognize that God alone is God, the "Holy One." This is not to say there is no active role for Israel to play. One need only to think of chapter 39 to see the counterpoise. But it is to remind ourselves that any witness to the nations is predicated solely on the salvific activity of God on his people's behalf.

The identity of the Servant of the Lord in chapters 42–53 is of course a matter of continuing controversy.[8] But it must suffice here to point out that not only is the Servant a covenant for the people (ʿ*am*—surely Israel), he is also a light to the nations (42:6), and filled with the Spirit of God to bring justice to the nations (42:1; see also 49:6 and 51:4, 5). These descriptions are so like those used in unquestionably Messianic passages elsewhere in the book (especially 11:1–6) that one can only believe the Servant referred to here is the Messiah. Thus Israel's Anointed One has an expected worldwide ministry and through him Israel does as well.[9]

The ministry of Israel to the world takes on a more active focus in chapters 56–66. Here the parochial narrowness which seems to have characterized Israel through much of its history is challenged. Genealogical and cultic correctness are shown to be of no value unless they are accompanied by heartfelt obedience. In this respect an obedient foreigner is much more pleasing to God than a disobedient pure-bred Jew (56:6). Nor is this merely an abstract example. God says he will bring the foreigners into his very temple so that it may be "a house of prayer for all nations" (56:7). God will not allow the Jews to turn in on themselves, congratulating themselves upon their good fortune in election or in escaping from Babylon. No, they have a mission to perform, and God will endow them with his Spirit for its performance (59:21).

This mission is made explicit in chapter 60 with its promise that the nations and their kings will come to the light which will dawn upon Israel (60:1–3). To be sure, one aspect of this promised coming is servitude (60:10–14), but this is not the total picture, for there is also the sense that the nations will come to Zion out of recognition of what wondrous things Israel's God has done for her (61:9; 62:2). Again the key concept is witness. Israel is not necessarily commissioned to convert the nations, but she is to make the Lord known everywhere (64:2). This idea is stated in no uncertain

---

8. See the discussion in Oswalt, *The Book of Isaiah, Chapters 40–66*, NICOT (Grand Rapids: Eerdmans, 1998). See also chapter 12 below.

9. For the purposes of this discussion it is important to note that even if we were to agree with medieval Jewish exegesis and conclude that the Servant is always Israel, the import for our topic would be unchanged: Israel has a mission to the wider world.

The Mission of Israel to the Nations

terms in the final chapter of the book, where we are told that God will send survivors from the Jews to the nations to declare his glory so that all flesh shall come to worship before him (66:19–23).

Thus, the book of Isaiah ends on the note first introduced in chapter 2: God's ultimate purpose is that the nations should know and worship him, and Israel is the instrument by which that purpose will be accomplished. Nor is this a late concept, as the reechoing of chapter 2 makes plain. Since that passage is duplicated in Micah, which is securely dated to the last half of the eighth century B.C., we can confidently argue that the concept is endemic to the classical prophets from the earliest days of the movement.

8

The Nations In Isaiah
Friend Or Foe; Servant Or Partner[1]

LIKE MANY OF THE so-called "writing prophets," the book of Isaiah views the momentous political and military events of the ninth through the fifth centuries B.C. through the lens of the sole lordship of Yahweh in the world.[2] In this respect it is no different than Jeremiah or Ezekiel, or for that matter, Habakkuk. Each of these books represents all the nations as existing under the direction of Israel's God and acting according to his purposes.

Yet, it can be argued that Isaiah's view of the nations is much more comprehensive and nuanced than that of the other prophetic books. The book in its present form is not content merely to insist that the nations move at Yahweh's behest, or that the activities of the nations are directed to achieve Yahweh's purposes on behalf of his people. Rather it also argues that Israel has a mission to the nations and that the nations will eventually join Israel in Jerusalem where they will not only serve Israel, but also share with Israel in the worship of God. This complex understanding has sometimes been seen as a result of the book's recensional complexity.[3] Thus, differing editorial viewpoints contributed to different views concerning the nations.

---

1. This material appeared in substantially the same form under this title in the *Bulletin for Biblical Research* 16/1 (2006) 41–51, and appears here by permission.

2. G. Ernest Wright, "The Nations in Hebrew Prophecy," *Encounter* 26 (1965) 225–37.

3. So, for instance, William L. Holladay, *Isaiah: Scroll of a Prophetic Heritage* (Grand Rapids: Eerdmans, 1978) 20. See also Marvin A. Sweeney, *Isaiah 1–39 with an Introduction to Prophetic Literature*, FOTL 16 (Grand Rapids: Eerdmans, 1996) 46–47.

In this study, I will seek to examine how the present shaping of the book seeks to condition our reading of the relationship of the nations to Israel.

The total picture presented may be stated in the following way:

1. Israel should not be seduced by the glory of the nations into trusting them.
2. If Israel trusts the nations instead of Yahweh, those very nations will turn on Israel and destroy her.
3. When Israel has been destroyed, God will call the destroying nations to account.
4. God will deliver Israel from the nations.
5. This deliverance will be an expression of the glory of God.
6. Israel will declare the glory of God to the nations.
7. Israel will be the means whereby God's rule of justice will come to the nations.
8. The nations will come to Jerusalem bringing gifts to offer to God and by extension to God's people.
9. The nations will either serve Zion or be destroyed.
10. The nations will join Zion in worshipping Yahweh.[4]

When these concepts are studied in the light of the present ordering of the materials in the book, it may be asserted that the relationship of Jerusalem/Zion to the nations forms the central core of what the book is saying.[5]

The two extreme poles of this relationship appear in chapters 1 and 2. In the first chapter the point is made that because of Israel's disobedience "strangers" are devouring the land (1:7). Then the option is put to them: obey and eat the best of the land, or rebel and be eaten by the sword (1:9). In neither of these cases does one of the words for "nations" appear, yet the

---

4. The Hebrew words which may be translated "nations," chiefly *goy, goyim, ʿam, ʿammim, leʾum,* and *leʾumim,* occur more than eighty-five times in the book.

5. Roy F. Melugin, "The Book of Isaiah and the Construction of Meaning," in *Writing and Reading the Scroll of Isaiah,* eds. C. C. Broyles and C. A. Evans (Leiden: Brill, 1997) 1:39–56, argues that the variety of structures which have been proposed for the book argue that meaning is the province of the reader. I continue to believe that it is possible to discover what the originator(s) of a piece of communication intended. On Isaiah's comprehensive view of the nations, see Hans Wildberger, *Isaiah 1–12: A Commentary,* tr. T. W. Trapp, Continental Commentaries (Minneapolis: Fortress, 1991) 94–96. On the unity of message in the book, and the relationship of the nations to that message, see R. E. Clements, "A Light to the Nations," in *Forming Prophetic Literature: Essays on Isaiah and the Twelve in Honor of John D. W. Watts,* ed. J. Watts and P. House, JSOTSup 235 (Sheffield: Sheffield Academic, 1996) 60.

nations are clearly in view. If Israel is disobedient to God, the nations will be his tool of punishment. But the first five verses of chapter 2, the segment shared with Micah (4:1–6), present a radically different picture. Instead of the nations being a tool of God's judgment, they are supplicants coming to Jerusalem to learn the Torah of Jerusalem's God. Here, in the very opening words of the book, we are presented with two apparently contradictory pictures. Will the nations come to Israel to destroy or will they come to worship? Thus, the reader is invited to ask how this opposition can be worked out, and the rest of book as it now stands is organized in such a way as to answer that question.

The question begins to be addressed at once in 2:6ff. If Zion is to be the means of declaring God's glory to the earth in his Torah, then clearly it is God's glory which must fill Israel. But instead, it is the glory of the nations that fills Israel. They have made alliances with "foreigners" (2:6b) and are filled with their wisdom (6a), with their wealth (7a), with their weaponry (7b), and their idolatry (8). They are enamored with all the great things of the earth (12–17), especially those which promote human pride, and the result is that all pride in human achievement, especially that represented by making divinity in human form, will be humiliated. It will be humiliated by a revelation of the "terror of the Lord, and . . . the glory of his majesty" (10, 19, 21). This idea emerges again in chapter 6, where the declaration of God's unique holiness is accompanied by the statement that it is his glory which fills the earth. It is not the glory of humanity, as epitomized by the nations, that fills the earth, but God's, and Zion must somehow learn that.

In whose glory then will Judah/Jerusalem trust? This becomes the central issue around which chapters 7–39 are organized. Will they trust God and become the means of declaring his glory to the nations? Or will they trust the nations, having been seduced by their glory, and be destroyed by them? Chapters 7–12 lay out the whole sequence of events which refusal to trust God will set in motion. Then chapters 7–35 demonstrate the folly of trusting the nations, and chapters 36–39 show another Judean king, Ahaz' son Hezekiah, being given the test of trust again.

The sequence of events in chapters 7–12 is initiated by Ahaz' refusal to trust God for deliverance from Syria and Israel. He does so because he has already made a defensive alliance with his greater enemy Assyria. In response, Isaiah informs him that Assyria will shortly overflow the land (8:7–8).[6] Because Ahaz has trusted the nations and their glory instead of God and his glory, he will soon find himself being destroyed by the very repository of his trust.

---

6. Interestingly, the land is not described as Ahaz's land, but Immanuel's.

But, somewhat surprisingly, the story does not end there. God does not intend to allow the nations to decimate his people. So in a dramatic contrast to the oppressive might of Assyria, God offers the kingdom of the child (9:1-6; [E. 2-7]). Through the repeated use of children in this segment the writer is asserting that God's weakness is stronger than the might of the nations.[7] Thus, in spite of their strength, the nations must ultimately confront the One whose purpose they are fulfilling (10:5-19; 27-34), with the result that their illusion of being self-directing and self-perpetuating will be shattered. But as with Israel, God does not intend that the nations will be exterminated. They are drawn to this king, who will be like a signal flag for all to see (11:10).[8] They will come to worship him, returning the captive Israelites to their Lord (11:12). As a result the Israelites will no longer rely on their oppressors, but on their Lord (10:20). Chapter 12 represents the final outcome of this sequence of events. Because of God's deliverance Zion will trust the Lord and not be afraid of the nations (12:2). The inhabitants of Zion will declare to the nations the glorious work God has done in delivering them (12:3-6).

There is a sense in which chapters 7-12 provide us with a summary of the rest of the book. Chapters 13-39 explore in greater detail the question of whether God is greater than the nations. Is he their ruler, and is their destiny in his hands? Can he really be trusted in view of Judah's smallness and the nations' greatness? Then chapters 40-55 consider the question whether Judah, having experienced the predicted result of trusting the nations, really can be delivered from them. The answer is, as it was in chapters 10-11, a resounding "yes." Not only that, but Judah will be the means both of demonstrating to the nations the unique deity of Yahweh and of establishing His rule of justice among them. Thus, chapters 56-66, presupposing an at least partial restoration, ask how this rule of justice will be established and how the mission to the nations will be carried out.

Chapters 13-39 address the question of trusting the nations through the juxtaposition of five blocks of material: 13-23, 24-27; 28-33; 34-35; 36-39.[9] Without arguing that the structure is entirely intentional, it still may

---

7. Shearjashub 7:3; Immanuel 7:14; 8:8, 10; Maher-shalal-hash-baz 8:1, 3; Isaiah's children 8:18; the Prince of Peace 9:1-6; the child who counts the trees 10:19; children playing with deadly animals and reptiles 11:6-8.

8. 10 of the 20 occs. of *nes* are found in Isaiah (5:26; 11:10; 11:12; 13:2; 18:3; 30:17; 31:9; 33:23; 49:22; 62:10). Of these, 8 have to do with calling the nations to serve God's purposes. The two which do not are 30:17 and 33:23.

9. Some writers have proposed including 34-35 and 36-39 in a subsequent division of the book. For a recent example of this approach, see Sweeney, *Isaiah 1-39*. I believe the continued prominence of the question of trust in 36-39 argues conclusively for their inclusion with the earlier chapters.

be noted that there is an interesting interchange of focus in these five blocks: they move back and forth from specific to general. Chapters 13–23 address specific nations; chapters 24–27 speak of the world in general; chapters 28–33 return to a specific focus upon Judah and the temptation to trust Egypt during the last two decades of the eighth century; chapters 34 and 35 then sum up the alternatives in general terms: trust the nations and join them in a barren desert (34), or trust God and find the desert turned into a garden (35). Finally, chapters 36–39 offer two specific test cases in trust.

The oracles against the nations in chapters 13–23 detail God's charges against each of the nations, including Judah herself (chap. 22).[10] There is a sense of world-wide coverage beginning with Babylon on the east and concluding with Tyre on the west. Between these two, almost every nation which had any bearing upon Judah is included.[11] The function of Babylon at the beginning of the list is significant, because it is plain from the sweeping language used in both chapters 13 and 14 that Babylon is being treated as a representative of the glory of all nations and their rulers. At the other end of the collection of oracles Tyre also seems somewhat representative. This is confirmed by the way in which the book of Revelation uses Isaiah's language for Tyre to describe Babylon (Rev. 18:9–17). By placing this very wide-ranging collection of oracles at this point, the author or the editors seem clearly to be saying that it is foolish to put ones trust in the glorious nations of earth when they will all be brought down to destruction by Judah's God.

The generalizations found in chapters 24–27 both confirm and expand on this conclusion. Chapter 24 sums up the particular judgments announced in 13–23 in general statements relating to the whole world. The chapter concludes with a vision of God reigning in glory on Mt. Zion, not merely over the nations, but over the entire cosmos.[12] As in chapter 12, the consequences of Yahweh's destruction of his people's enemies are songs of praise to him (25:1–5) and expressions of trust in him (26:3–4). These are intimately related to the divine promises of restoration from among the nations. So 27:12–13 which promise that God is going to thresh the fields of Assyria and Egypt and bring the good grain home has a very similar tone

---

10. For a study of the genre of national judgment oracles, see Duane Christenson, *Prophecy and War in Ancient Israel: Studies in the Oracles Against the Nations in Old Testament Prophecy* (Berkeley, CA.: Bibal, 1989).

11. Only Ammon and Edom are missing, and Edom comes in for special attention in chapter 34.

12. Interestingly, the picture of world destruction is interrupted by the sound of nations from all over the world singing praise to God (24:14–16a), but the prophet seems unwilling to hear these songs from Israel's former enemies yet. He cannot forget the treacheries which will still occur (16b).

to 11:15–16 where the author speaks of drying up the waters of Egypt and Assyria in order to make a highway to bring his people home.[13]

But there is one feature in this section for which the reader is perhaps not so prepared. This is the assertion that one of the key events of the feast in chapter 25 is the removal of the shroud of death that is cast over all nations (vv. 7–8). The rejoicing in God's glory is not only for Zion, but also for the whole world. This was intimated in 11:9–10, but is made entirely explicit here. As with Israel, so with the nations; God's purpose in judgment is not extermination, but restoration.

The particular point at issue in chapters 28–33 is whether Judah will put its faith in Egypt, following the advice of the national leaders, who are described as blind and drunken. There are six repetitions of "Oi," or "Woe" found in the unit (28:1; 29:1; 29:15; 30:1; 31:1; 33:1). The first five of these serve to focus the issue of trust ever more sharply. They move from general statements about the foolishness and cravenness of the leaders (28:1; 29:1) to an explicit statement of woe on those who trust Egypt instead of God (31:1).

Rather like what appeared in chapter 7, the real folly of trusting in one nation for deliverance from the threat of another nation is that God has already settled the fate of the threatening nation. So it is said several times throughout the unit that God will fight against the Assyrians and that their end is certain (29:5–8, 17–24; 30:19–33; 31:8–9). This is made clear in the final woe (33:1) which, true to form, is addressed to the oppressing nation. The true king has appeared (32:1) and the oppressor cannot stand against that kingdom. Again, as above, the result of Yahweh's deliverance is an expression of trust (33:2). The people who would not wait for God, but rushed off to make alliances with Egypt now express their willingness to wait on (trust in) him.

Chapters 34 and 35, as stated above, serve as a general conclusion to what has been said in 13–33. They sum up the consequences of trusting the nations or of trusting God. Interestingly, the two chapters presuppose the recurrent situation described above. The people will not trust God from the outset and thus avoid the desert of human pride.[14] Rather, they will trust the

---

13. H. G. M. Williamson notes this similarity but does not believe it indicates the same hand at work (in his case, that of DtIs), *The Book Called Isaiah: Deutero-Isaiah's Role in Composition and Redaction* (Oxford: Clarendon, 1994) 178–79.

14. The fact that Edom is mentioned in chapter 34 has caused some commentators to overlook the generalization which characterizes the chapter. However, this use of graphic examples to underscore a general point is a characteristic feature of the present book. Two occurrences of this feature are found in 3:16–4:1 and 25:10–12. In the former a beautiful, finely-dressed, elegantly-coiffed woman is used to illustrate Jerusalem's pride which will be humiliated. In the latter, Moab is used to illustrate the proud city of

nations first and will end up in the desert. But God's true trustworthiness will be shown by his willingness and ability to make a garden bloom in that desert (35:1–2) and to make the place where the jackals lay (34:13) become a meadow (35:7).

In the light of this understanding of the materials from 7 to 35, it can be seen that chapters 36–39, far from being a historical appendix, as some older commentaries called them,[15] are an integral part of the argument of the book.[16] Isaiah had confronted Ahaz on the highway to the fuller's field, and challenged the king to trust God in the face of the threat from Syria and Israel. Ahaz refused to do so and Isaiah told him that Assyria would soon threaten the very life of the nation. Now that prediction has come true: the Rabshakeh stands on the highway to the fuller's field and dares Hezekiah (whom he does not deign to call king) to trust in God. No less than six times the Assyrian officer lays out the issue: in whom do you trust? He quickly dismisses the thought of trusting in Egypt and puts the point very simply: there is no point in trusting God; he is just one more of a string of national deities which the Assyrian king (not the Assyrian gods!) has destroyed. On the other hand, he says to the people, if you will put your trust in the Assyrian king, he will treat you very favorably. Clearly, the reason for the inclusion of these materials at this point in the book is to present them as a test case of all that has been said in chapters 13–35. If God will be trusted instead of the nations, he can and will deliver from the nations.

On the other hand, if God is not trusted he will not deliver. This is the point of the second test case, chapters 38–39. Here, in an incident which almost certainly occurred 10 years or more before Sennacherib's attack, Hezekiah had an opportunity to declare the glory of God to Babylon and failed to do so, choosing rather to attempt to impress the Babylonian envoys with his wealth. The result is predicted destruction by Babylon. We do not

---

earth which refuses God's grace.

15. J. A. Alexander, *Commentary on the Prophecies of Isaiah* (New York: Scribner, 1846); C. von Orelli, *The Prophecies of Isaiah*, tr, J. S. Banks (Edinburgh: Clark, 1889); J. Skinner, *Isaiah, Chapters I–XXIX*, The Cambridge Bible (Cambridge: Cambridge, 1930). See also Otto Kaiser, *Isaiah 13–39*, tr. J. Bowden, OTL (Philadelphia: Westminster, 1974).

16. For one expression of such an understanding, see Christopher R. Seitz, *Zion's Final Destiny: The Development of the Book of Isaiah: A Reassessment of Isaiah 36–39* (Minneapolis: Augsburg, 1991). For a counter argument, see Williamson, *The Book Called Isaiah*, 189–211, who concludes that the material was first composed by those familiar with Isaiah's writings, then incorporated into the Deuteronomic History, and then incorporated into the book of Isaiah. I do not believe he solves the problem created by the fact that chaps. 38 and 39 refer to events chronologically preceding the events of chaps. 36 and 37, a reversal that serves Isaiah's purposes, but not those of Kings.

have time here to discuss all the hermeneutical issues which this structuring of the materials raises. But with regard to the theme of the nations, the basic point seems clear. In fact, Judah would not follow the later example of Hezekiah, but the earlier one. They would not trust God in the face of the Babylonian threat, and as a result would not experience the kind of deliverance Hezekiah experienced from Assyria. The unit serves then to conclude the lessons on the trustworthiness of God with two graphic illustrations. But it also serves to introduce another phase in the discussion of Zion and the nations. What happens if God does not deliver from the nations? Does that not mean God has been defeated by them? Chapters 36–39 prepare us to hear that the answer is "no."

Since the folly of trusting the nations and the complete trustworthiness of God was vindicated in chapters 7–39, it is not surprising that it is not a major point in what follows. Here, particularly in chapters 40–55, the issue is: can Yahweh do what he promised in chapters 10, 11, 14, 19, 27, 29, 30, 33, and 35? That is, can he restore a remnant of his people from among the nations, and can he do it in such a way that it will make his glory manifest to the nations? The answer is a resounding yes, both from the point of view of God's willingness to do so and of his ability to do so. The lawsuit against the idols in chapters 40–48 is really a lawsuit against the nations. Sennacherib had said that God could not compare to him, the representative of all human glory. Now God says the nations cannot compare to him; they are a drop in a bucket, dust on a scales, grasshoppers on the earth, in fact, less than nothing (40:15–17, 22–23). Given the exilic audience of these statements, they are truly stunning ones. Is the mighty Babylon who holds Judah in her hand really nothing? The answer is "yes," and thus it is not surprising that Babylon becomes the graphic example of this point in chapter 47.[17] Babylon has said of herself what only God can say: "I am, and there is none beside me." (47:8, 10; cf. 43:11; 44:6–8; 45:14, 18, 21–22; 46:5; 9). As a result God will use another of the nations to bring Babylon down into the dust. Cyrus exists to carry out the prior plans of God. Just as God could use an Assyria or a Babylon to carry out his plans for Israel, so he can use the Medes and the Persians to carry out his plans for Babylon.

But as it emerged earlier in the book, in chapters 11 and 25, God's purposes for the nations are not merely to punish them for their pride and their unwarranted cruelty. He wishes to establish his *mišpaṭ*, his rule of justice, among them. He is not the God of Israel alone, but the God of the whole earth.[18] While this thought is first introduced in chapter 42, it is

---

17. For this feature of graphic summarization in the book, see n. 14 above.
18. D. Hollenburg, "Nationalism and the Nations in Isaiah XL-LV," *VT* 19 (1969)

more prominent in 49–55. Again, how astonishing this sounds against the backdrop of the exile. Of all times when one would think that it would be unlikely for an oppressed nation to believe that God could rule benevolently over all nations, this would be it. But the fact remains that this is the context where these pronouncements are to be heard. God intends to bring justice to all the nations. Specifically, he intends to do this through his servant (42:1, 6–7; 49:6). Obviously, this is not the place to go into the vexed question of the identity of the servant.[19] Nor is it necessary for the purposes of this study to make that identification. The point is that God is not content merely to restore his Israelite servants from captivity. That is only the beginning of his purposes for the nations. He expects that his salvation will reach to the ends of the earth (49:6; 52:10). Is this just that the ends of the earth might see the salvation God is giving to Judah? While 52:10 might be construed that way, 49:6 can hardly be done so. Furthermore, 2:1–5 at the beginning of the book and 66:23 at the end tell us that the nations are to be participants, not merely spectators, in the worship of God. As argued above, the strategic placement of those statements supplies the context in which the final redactors intend for us to read the book.[20]

My point here is that even in chapters 49–55, where the focus is specifically upon God's desire and ability to solve the alienation which has arisen between him and his bride, the nations are not forgotten. God's restoration of his people to fellowship with himself will be the paradigm for the restoration of the nations to himself. The servant, whoever we may conclude this person to be, has a work which is not only for Zion, but for the entire world (49:6). Zion's task is to be a witness to the antiquity of God's good promises for them and to his incomparable ability to carry out those purposes against all the odds (55:5). Not only does fallen Zion look to the mighty arm of the Lord for deliverance, so do all the ends of the earth (51:4). The apparent weakness of that arm when it appears will be shocking to all, including the nations and their kings (52:14), but this is consistent with what was said in chapters 7–12: God demonstrates his power through weakness.[21]

23–26, argued that the universalism here is only an extension of nationalism. Duane L. Christensen, "A New Israel: The Righteousness from among the Nations," in *Israel's Apostasy and Restoration: Essays in Honor of Roland K. Harrison*, ed. A. Gileadi (Grand Rapids: Baker, 1988) 251–59, has presented evidence showing that this need not be the case.

19. For a discussion of the options, see Oswalt, *The Book of Isaiah, Chapters 1–39*, NICOT (Grand Rapids: Eerdmans, 1986) 49–52, 58–59. A select bibliography appears in the companion volume, *The Book of Isaiah, Chapters 40–66*, NICOT (Grand Rapids: Eerdmans, 1998) 113–15.

20. R. E. Clements, "A Light to the Nations," 68–69.

21. Roy F. Melugin, "Israel and the Nations in Isaiah 40–55," in *Problems in Biblical*

Chapters 56–66 explore how it will be possible for Zion to play its part in the achievement of God's plans for the nations. The change in atmosphere from 40–55 is apparent. There offers of God's unfailing, undeserved love are repeated in lyrical tones. Here we see something more like chapters 7–39 with their demands for obedience. I have proposed elsewhere that the function of this section as it now stands in the book is to synthesize the two views of righteousness which appear in 1–39 and 40–55.[22]

But what of the nations in all of this? They appear prominently in three places: at the beginning (56:1-7), in the middle (60-62), and at the end (66:18-24). These observations seem to support the proposal of Charpentier that the contents of these chapters are arranged chiastically.[23] While it is possible to push proposed details of this structure too far, it does seem that the facts support the general hypothesis. The Messiah stands at the apex in 61:1-4 (part E); on either side are descriptions of the glory of redeemed Israel in the sight of the nations (part D and D,' 60:1-22; 61:5–62:12); on either side of those is the Divine Warrior who does for Zion what it cannot do for itself (parts C and C,' 59:15b-21; 63:1-6); on either side of those are blocks of material describing restored Zion's inability to do righteousness (parts B and B,' 56:9–59:15a; 63:7–66:17); and on either side of those, at the beginning and end of the division are paragraphs describing the worship of foreigners (parts A and A,' 56:1-8; 66:18-24).

I propose that by placing the worshipping nations at the beginning and end of the section, the author or editor is signaling to us the readers the significance of this idea for understanding the section. When the nations are again given prominence in the center segments, we are prepared to recognize that prominence and to read it appropriately. The opening and closing sections confirm to us that God's salvation described in 40–55 is indeed not for Israel alone. To be sure, that salvation is always in conjunction with Israel's, as 66:18-24 makes clear. Nevertheless, it is in full partnership with Israel, as 56:1-8 shows. In fact, that opening segment also introduces the key theme of the second levels (56:9–59:15a and 63:7–66:17): the apparent inability of Zion to live out the kind of obedience the foreigners and eunuchs are

---

Theology: Essays in Honor of Rolf Knierim, eds. H. T. C. Sun and K. Eades (Grand Rapids: Eerdmans, 1997) 249-64, comments that chaps. 40–55 do not adequately address the issues of justice (261). He points especially to the statements about the nations submitting to Zion in 45:14-17 and 49:22-26. Two comments should be made: may this not be a defect of reading 40–55 independently of the rest of the book, and should we not consider the surprising degree to which justice *is* promised to those outside of Israel, given the historical backdrop of the exile?

22. See chapter 5 in this volume.

23. E. Charpentier, *How to Read the Bible*, tr. J. Bowden (New York: Gramercy, 1991) 77; G. Polan, "Salvation in the Midst of Struggle," *The Bible Today* 23 (1985) 90-97.

offering. The point seems to be that the evidence of being a member of the covenant people is not birth, but behavior. God's salvation is for the ends of the earth, and any, whether they be foreigners or eunuchs, may participate in it if they will live God's life. The temple is to be a house of prayer for all nations (56:7–8). The reminiscences of chapter 2 are unmistakable.

Zion, expected to be the means by which God's rule of justice comes into the earth (see above on 49–55), is unable to produce such justice. Therefore, the divine warrior must do this by himself (59:15b–21 and 63:1–6).[24] As a result, God's light will shine out of Zion to all the nations (60:1–22 and 61:5–62:12). In response to the dawning of that light the nations will stream to Zion. Specifically, it is said they will do three things. They will bring Israel's children back to her (60:4, 9; see also 49:22). Along with the children, they will bring their wealth as a gift to proclaim God's praise and to honor the name of the Holy One of Israel (60:6, 9; 61:11; 62:7). And finally they will serve the people of Zion. Kings are led in triumphal procession and the nations that will not serve Israel will be destroyed (60:11a–12, see also 49:23). Foreigners will take the menial tasks so that the inhabitants of Jerusalem can perform the role of priests (61:5–6).

How are we to read these last passages? Should we see them as an alternative view which has not been synthesized adequately? Whatever we may think about the recensional history of the components of 56–66, it is clear from the way in which the material is presently structured that we are not intended to see these statements as ultimately contradictory. By making 56:1–7 and 66:18–24 the base upon which the triangle rests, it is clear that we are to understand the statements about submission of the nations to Zion (not only in 60–62, but also in 45:14–17 and 49:22–26) as partial and not final. God wants the nations to come into his house (56:7) to worship him (66:23) and while the antecedent is not entirely clear in 66:21, there is a strong likelihood that the "them" from whom priests and Levites are drawn in 66:21 are the nations who are bringing the Israelites' brethren back from captivity.

Then why are these statements about servitude here? I suggest the solution is to be found in the very last verses of the book where it is said that all flesh will come to Zion to worship God, and that they will go out to view the destruction of the rebels. This book does not espouse a universalistic salvation. It does envision salvation being made available to all. But all are not said to accept it. The point is that while all nations will recognize God's Lordship, not all will do so willingly.

---

24. If we ask the identity of this Warrior, it is surely the Spirit-anointed one described in the apex section (61:1–3).

In its present form the book of Isaiah presents a strikingly fully developed theology of the nations. And Zion, from being devoured by the nations to being a light to them, is at the heart of the presentation. The way in which this theme is developed through the present arrangement of the materials in the book bears witness to the intentionality of that arrangement.

9

God's Determination to Redeem His People
Isaiah 9:1–7; 11:1–11; 26:1–9; 35:1–10[1]

THE PRESENT FORM OF the book of Isaiah conveys a remarkably wholistic conception of salvation. It is one which comprehends both the seriousness of sin and the power of God in the face of sin. It offers neither easy solutions, nor helpless despair. In this way it presents a more complete picture than any of the other prophets. That is, its view of judgment is more pervasive than any of the post-exilic prophets,[2] while its view of salvation is more thoroughgoing than any of the pre-exilic prophets.[3],[4] Deliverance is to be

---

1 This is a slightly revised version of an article that first appeared in *Review and Expositor* 88 (1991) 153–65, and is used here by permission.

2. The post-exilic prophets have the task of convincing the returnees that there really is hope for their continuance as the people of God. For those prophets, judgment is past and they must lift their people's faith so that they may believe for what is to come; cf. Zech 8:9–13. For Isaiah, salvation only comes through judgment and cannot be separated from it.

3. For the pre-exilic prophets, the horrifying sins of the people and the unthinkable, but inevitable exile filled their vision. They all, to a greater or lesser degree, could see the restoration beyond the exile, but the harsh reality of the immediate future filled their vision so completely that even for someone like Jeremiah the distant hope is confined largely to chapters 30–33, and the promise is a kind of a gauzy hope-against-hope. Not so in Isaiah, where the hope of redemption is treated with the same air of certainty as is the threat of judgment.

4. This comprehensive theology is usually explained today as being the result of a continuous process of editing and addition which extended from the time of the

found *through* judgment, not in spite of it, and the election-love of God is not called into question by judgment, but rather, *demonstrated* by it.

But as important as the book's concept of judgment is, it is apparent that judgment is never an end in itself. This is made plain in the introductory and concluding chapters and especially in chapter 6. God has no satisfaction in reducing Isaiah to a gibbering mound of flesh on the floor. Bringing him to the point of realizing that he cannot even exist in the presence of God is not the purpose of the vision. Rather, that horrible realization is designed to prepare Isaiah to receive the purifying fire on his lips, which is in turn designed to prepare him for his mission. So it is with Israel, the nation of unclean lips; they undergo the fire not merely so that God's just wrath may be propitiated, but so that they may declare to the world that the glory which fills all Creation is nothing other than the glory of the Holy One of Israel.

This latter point is of great importance. For just as judgment is not an end in itself in Isaiah, neither is salvation. God's purpose is that the world might know Him, and while the saved might legitimately glory in their salvation, they may not use that salvation as a justification for drawing into themselves in "holy" pride (56:3-8). It is when the world sees the glory of God in and through Israel that their salvation will have reached its intended fruition (60:1-3).

The four passages discussed in this study all occur in the first large segment of the book (chapters 1-39, sometimes referred to as "First Isaiah"), but they can all be paralleled with passages which appear in 40-66.[5] What this means is that the ideas found in these segments are not merely those of a few isolated spots in the book, but are representative of the thought of the book as a whole. Neither are they typical of just the first part of the book; they represent the distilled positions and convictions of the whole. Furthermore, by their positioning in the early part of the book, which is normally associated with judgment, they help to show that a facile categorization of the message of the parts of the book (1-39: judgment; 40-66: hope) does a disservice to the more subtle structuring of the book's thought. In this Biblical book, more than most, it is the whole which provides the necessary context for the understanding of any part.[6]

---

prophet whose name the book now bears until sometime in the fourth century B.C. For an argument that the character of the book is better explained by authorial unity, see Oswalt, *The Book of Isaiah, Chapters 1-39* (Grand Rapids: Eerdmans, 1986) 17-28.

5. Compare 11:4-11 with 65:17-25; 11:1-5 with 61:1-4; 9:1-7 with 63:1-6; 26:1-9 with 62:6-12; 35:1-10 with 42:14-17, etc.

6. Some recent works which underscore this important thought are: P. R. Ackroyd, "Isaiah 36-39; Structure and Function," in *Von Kanaan bis Kerala*, ed. W. C. Delsman, et. al., AOAT 211 (Neukirchen-Vluyn: Neukirchener, 1982) 3-21; Walter Brueggemann,

What the previous statements mean for this particular study is that the present structure of the book argues that the restoration was not some sort of "plan B" after the unexpected disaster of the exile. As the book represents it, particularly in chs. 7–12, the promise of salvation was coupled directly with the threat of devastation right from the outset. This is seen in capsule form in the name of the son whom Isaiah is commanded to take with him to his first encounter with Ahaz: "A Remnant will Return" (*shear-yashub* 7:3). Scholars have argued over the import of the name, with some saying it is wholly threat,[7] while others have argued that it is primarily promise.[8] But surely it is not a case of "either-or." The name contains equal proportions of threat and promise. Everything of the present vital nation will be lost except for the tiniest fragment, *but* by means of that fragment the people will continue to exist and fulfill the ancient promises.[9] Israel will not disappear, as would so many of the surrounding peoples.

Thus we are brought face to face with the divine resolution of the seemingly-insoluble problem of human sin: how can God be both just and faithful? How can he punish the sins of the nation without annihilating the nation? How can he keep his promises to the patriarchs without simply ignoring the sins of the descendants of the patriarchs? The solution is in the inseparable joining of the exile and the restoration, and in the extension of those truths far beyond mere political realities to metaphysical reality itself. By itself the exile suggests that God is defeated, if not by Babylon, then by sin, and cannot keep His sweeping, unqualified promises (Gen 15:5, etc.). But, on the other hand, promises of Israel's perpetual existence under the good hand of God (Num 24:15–19), seem to smack of favoritism, if not outright injustice, in the face of Israel's persistent rebellion. In Isaiah, these are resolved.[10] The accumulated disobedience of many individual Israelites

---

"Unity and Dynamic in the Isaiah Tradition," *JSOT* 29 (1984) 89–107; R. E. Clements, "The Unity of the Book of Isaiah," *Interpretation* 36 (1982) 117–29; Clements, "Beyond Tradition-History: Deutero-Isaianic Development of First Isaiah's Themes," *JSOT* 31 (1985) 95–113; Rolf Rendtorff, "Zur Komposition des Buches Jesaja," *VT* 34 (1984) 295–320; *The Old Testament: an Introduction* (Philadelphia: Fortress, 1986) 190–93, 198–200; J. J. M. Roberts, "Isaiah in Old Testament Theology," *Int* 36 (1982) 130–43; Christopher R. Seitz, "Isaiah 1–66: Making Sense of the Whole," in *Reading and Preaching the Book of Isaiah*, ed. Christopher R. Seitz (Philadelphia: Fortress, 1988) 105–26.

7. Sheldon H. Blank, "The Current Misinterpretation of Isaiah's She'ar Yashub," *JBL* 67 (1948) 211–15.

8. Gerhard Hasel, "Linguistic Considerations Regarding the Translation of Isaiah's Shear-Jashub," *AUSS* 9 (1971) 36–46.

9. In contrast, see Amos 3:12, where the reference to fragments does seem to be wholly threatening.

10. They are also resolved to a significant extent in Ezekiel, but more as a by-product

will ultimately bring the nation to destruction. But God will not give up the nation, and will ultimately find persons who will repent of the *nation's* sins and thus become the basis for restoration.[11] Thus in Isaiah the concepts of judgment and salvation, which seem to involve an irreconcilable contradiction, are welded together in such a way as to make sense of each other.

As Isaiah presents it, God's determination to save his people is global in nature. By this I mean that he is not merely speaking about saving persons from the effects of their sins—the exile—but also from sin itself. This is the significance of the Messianic promises. If political restoration were all that was in the writer's mind, then the "messiah" Cyrus (Isa 45:1) would be the only one necessary. But it is plain that the book envisions something much more comprehensive than mere political restoration. Unless something is to be done about the sin which caused the exile, then the restoration is no solution to the problem. Thus, the Davidic Messiah is envisioned; one who will reign in truth and righteousness, and one whose reign will result in the earth being full of the knowledge of the Lord (11:9). How the Messiah will achieve this work is not specified in the four passages under consideration here, but if I am correct in asserting that the entire present book is intended to provide the context for any part, then it must be insisted that the so-called "Suffering Servant" passages of chs. 42, 49, 51, and 53 provide the key.[12] Detailed discussion of those passages is outside the province of this article, but some reference will be made to them below.

9:1–7 (HEB. 8:23—9:6)

In my understanding of the structure of the present book, chs. 7–39 form a single larger unit focusing upon the issue of trusting God or the nations (see further below on 26:1–9). These chapters reflect a time when Israel and her neighbors were in profound crisis. Almost as soon as Tiglath-Pilezer III had ascended to the throne of Assyria in 745 B.C., it had become plain that the small nations on the eastern coast of the Mediterranean Sea were not going to

---

of other arguments than directly.

11. For examples of such repentance, see the prayers of Daniel (9:4–19) and Ezra (9:6–15).

12. It is argued by many modern scholars that these passages have no connection with the Messiah, e.g., R. N. Whybray, *Isaiah 40–66*, NCBC (London: Marshall, Scott & Morgan, 1975); Roy F. Melugin, *The Formation of Isaiah 40–55*, BZAW 141 (Berlin: deGruyter, 1976). Surely the repeated reference to saving the people of Israel (42:6–7; 49:6, 8; 53:8) from their sins can only point to a Messianic figure in the overall context of the book. For a concise recent statement of this point of view, see H. Blocher, *Songs of the Servant, Isaiah's Good News* (London: InterVarsity Press, 1975).

be able to avoid direct confrontation with Assyrian imperial power. Those nations stood in the way of a renewed Assyrian drive toward Egypt, and it now appeared the Mesopotamians had both the will and the power to complete that drive. As might be expected, Egypt used every means at her disposal to persuade her northern neighbors to resist the Assyrians. For some 60 years this drama played itself out, and against that backdrop of conflict and diplomacy, of braggadocio and terror, of courage and deceit, Isaiah kept calling Israel and Judah, and then Judah alone, to a radical trust in God.

The larger unit is divided into three parts: chapters 7–12, which discuss Ahaz' refusal to trust and the implications of that decision; chapters 13–35, which depict the reasons for trusting God (see below on 26:1–9 and 35:1–10); and chapters 36–39, which are a mirror image of chapters 7–12, with the Davidic monarch, Ahaz' son, Hezekiah, having learned some of the lessons of the intervening chapters, now displaying a willingness to trust God in the face of a much more serious threat than his father had faced earlier.

The material of chapters 7–12 divides into 4 segments. The first, 7:1–9:7 (Heb. 9:6), revolves around three children who, along with Isaiah, are seen as signs of the promise. The second segment (9:8[Heb. 9:7]–10:4) details the moral reasons why any kingdom comes under divine judgment. The third (10:5–11:16) shows that although God may use Assyria to punish Judah, Assyria is not ultimate, and her oppressive rule must give way to the blessed rule of the Messiah. The fourth segment is a lyrical conclusion to this evidence of God's determination to save, 12:1–6.

The poetic stanza 9:1–7 comes at the end of the first segment. Here Isaiah had challenged Ahaz, king of Judah, to radical trust in God in the face of threats by Israel and Syria to invade and depose Ahaz if he would not join them in a coalition against Assyria. In response to Ahaz' falsely pious refusal to accept this challenge, Isaiah had assured Ahaz of two things: one, within twelve years, Israel and Syria, of whom Ahaz was now so deathly afraid, would be destroyed (7:13–16), and two, the Assyria to whom Ahaz had fled for help instead of to God (2 Kgs 16:7–9), would strip Judah of almost everything it possessed (Isa 7:17–25). Ahaz was to learn by hard experience that on the one hand God can be trusted and on the other whatever we trust in place of God will one day turn and destroy us.

These assurances are directly tied to a prediction of the birth of a child to be called Immanuel, "God With Us." This twofold context of promise and threat makes it very likely that, like Shear-yashub (see above), the name has both a positive and a negative connotation. On the positive side, since God is with us, Israel and Syria need not be feared. But on the negative side, since God is with us, our attempts to manipulate our lives and insure our success without reference to Him are doomed to failure.

This far is clear enough, but from this point the waters become more murky. To whom does Immanuel refer? We must come to some answer to this question because it has a direct bearing upon the identification of the child in 9:1–7. We have neither the space nor the warrant to discuss the Immanuel question in any detail here.[13] It must suffice to observe that a good case can be made for the single sign's having two references, a near one, perhaps Maher-shalal-hash-baz,[14] and a distant one, the Messiah.[15] That something more than the birth of a normal baby is ultimately intended is indicated by the stupendous language used to describe the sign ("higher than heaven, deeper than Sheol," 7:11), the mysterious language surrounding the description of the conception, and that the land is said to be the possession of Immanuel (8:8). Note also that the phrase "God with us" is used in the introductory oracle to 8:11–9:7. All this suggests that while it is plain the sign has an immediate reference for Ahaz and his own time, it also has a more distant all-encompassing reference. This is nowhere clearer than in the two uses of the word *immanu-el* in 8:8 and 8:10. In 8:8 the land is referred to as Immanuel's land, a land which will be filled with the outspread wings of Assyria—threat. But suddenly, and without any transition, 8:9 begins to speak of the nations being broken and dismayed because *immanu*-el, "God is with us" (8:10)—promise. Here the more distant implications of the Immanuel sign begin to be unfolded, culminating in the promise of the Davidic Messiah in 9:1–7.

But if that promise is to be experienced, the Israelites will have to get their eyes off the supposed conspiracies which they like to think control their destiny—because it absolves them of responsibility for that destiny—(8:12), and get them onto the Holy One who really does rule their destiny (8:13–14a). If they will not turn to God, and instead turn to this world for guidance, then God Himself will become a stumbling block (8:14b–15), and they will find only darkness (8:19–22). In that case, the truth which is embodied in the message of Isaiah and in his name ("The Lord Saves") and the names of his children will simply have to wait until history has created a more fertile soil for its germination (8:16–18, and cf. 6:11–13).

Nevertheless, this segment (8:8–9:7) is not just a reiteration of the threat of 7:17–8:9, for 9:1 cries out that God will not allow judgment to be the final word, nor darkness the final experience. Beyond judgment there is

---

13. For further discussion see Oswalt, *Isaiah 1–39*, 209–14.

14. For evidence for this point of view, see Herbert M. Wolf, "A Solution to the Immanuel Prophecy in Isaiah 7:14–8:22," *JBL* 91 (1972) 449–56.

15. Note that this would conform very well to the suggestion that the name has a double connotation, with Maher-shalal-hash-baz embodying the threat and the Messiah the promise.

redemption, and beyond darkness there is light. Furthermore, that light is to rise first in that very part of Israel which first felt the lash of the Assyrian conquest—Galilee (9:1). Threat may be immediate and promise may be long deferred, but they are inseparable in the mind of God. So, to limit "God with us" to the time of Ahaz is impossible if Isaiah's total vision is to stand.

But it must be asked exactly what Isaiah has in mind in this lyrical announcement. Is it not possible that he is merely speaking in hyperbolic language about the birth of a Judean prince (v.7), perhaps even Hezekiah?[16] This is certainly not inherently impossible. Isaiah could have viewed the birth of this child who would be more faithful than his father had been as an evidence of the presence of God with his people. But if this is so, then Isaiah had to admit before the end of his ministry that he had been sorely mistaken. Chapters 38 and 39 show us in unmistakable terms that Hezekiah is *not* the promised Messiah. Not only is he distinctly mortal (38), he is also distinctly fallible (39). No, the present shape of the book tells us that the child here should not be read as Hezekiah, and if not he, then which other Judean prince of that day?

But even if the larger book did not call this interpretation into question, the poem itself does. From the opening reference to Galilee to the description of the person as "Mighty God," '*el gibbor*, there is no way in which any Davidic monarch contemporary with Isaiah could have been being referred to. Neither Ahaz nor Hezekiah, and certainly not Manasseh, had any hope of restoring Galilee, or even Ephraim, to the Judean Monarchy. And to call any of those persons God could be nothing other than blasphemy.[17] Furthermore, verses 3 and 4 are clearly addressed to God, who is the deliverer. By itself, this would not rule out a strictly human reference in verses 6 and 7, but when coupled with the title of verse 6, it seems conclusive. In sum, the prophet's primary reference is clearly to an eschatological redeemer who will bring light to those groping in darkness (vv. 1–2), relief to those who are oppressed by tyrannical military power (vv. 3–5), and a just and reliable political order to those weary of corruption and cowardice (vv. 6–7).

The means by which God will accomplish these things is hinted at by the emphasis upon the Messiah's coming as a child who is born (v. 6). This emphasis is very significant in this context for two reasons. In the first place, it serves to make explicit the connection with Immanuel which has already been alluded to above. Immanuel as he was born in Ahaz' time (especially if he is to be identified with Maher-shalal-hash-baz), was a sign of threat

---

16. So, for instance, Sigmund Mowinckel, *He That Cometh*, tr. G. W. Anderson (New York: Abingdon, 1954) 102–10.

17. Cf. L. Rignell, "A Study of Isaiah 9:2–7," *LQ* 7 (1955) 31–35.

God's Determination to Redeem His People

because of refusal to trust in God. But the Immanuel who was to be born in the future was to be a sign of the utter trustworthiness of God. After the nation had reaped the entirely predictable results of its failure to trust God, He would demonstrate the real depths of His trustworthiness by restoring and redeeming them through the new Immanuel, now not merely a sign, but the very fulfillment of the promise of hope.

The second significance of the reference to the child is to be found in the contrast between the oppressor and the deliverer. What is God's answer to the monstrous oppressions of the aggressors of the world? How will he break the oppressor's rod (v. 4)? Is it simply a larger dose of oppression and aggression, but now directed at the former aggressors instead of by them? This is the typical human answer, but it is not really an answer. It simply compounds the problem. God's answer is of another order entirely. It is not spelled out in full here-that development only comes in 42:1–53:12, but the reference to the child hints at it. God's answer to the world's cruelty and arrogance will not be more cruelty and arrogance, but less! His answer is a child. The innocence and vulnerability of the child will swallow up the darkness and oppression and corruption of the world and give back light and freedom and justice. *That* is strength.

It should be noted that the picture of salvation here is almost wholly political, whereas the ministry of Jesus Christ, whom the New Testament and the Church have taken to be the primary referent,[18] is anything but political. Two extremes should be avoided in interpreting the passage. On the one hand, we should avoid using it to justify the more extreme positions espoused by liberation theologians. These persons, seeking to address corrupt political regimes and recognizing the Church's general quiescence, if not acquiescence, in the face of such evils, have tended to say that there is no Biblical picture of salvation except political salvation. We cannot do this because of the New Testament's insistence that the chief human problem is not political, but spiritual. Our greatest problem is not of political injustice, but separation from God because of sin. We have no warrant as Christians to dismiss the New Testament because the Old Testament is prior in time.

On the other hand we dare not attempt to explain away such language by making it all metaphorical of the personal spiritual life. If nothing else, the results of this approach during the last 2000 years should alert us to its fallacy. Over and over the Church has winked at injustice and oppression because it has said that salvation has nothing to do with politics. And over and over again the Church has ended up becoming enslaved to the very power it should have stood against in the beginning.

---

18. Cf. Luke 1:32–33; John 1:4–5; 12:34; Eph 2:14.

So how are we to hold these two understandings together? We need to let each inform the other. It should not surprise us if the Old Testament talks of deliverance and redemption in very concrete terms. This is the way it discusses everything of an abstract or spiritual nature. So sin is a thing, a burden which must be rolled off ones back; blessing is resolutely material in nature[19]; memory is primarily a way of acting, etc. Spiritual truth is taught by means of object lessons. In some cases, as for instance sacrifice and dietetic laws, the object lesson has no direct connection with the truth being taught and can be discarded after a sufficient time. But in other cases the object lesson is actually an initial phase of the truth. In cases like these, while the object lesson is not complete in itself and must continually point beyond itself, neither can it ever be discarded; it is essential to the whole. That is the case here: political darkness, oppression, and corruption are manifestations of a deeper spiritual darkness, oppression, and corruption which if left uncorrected will forever poison society. In this initial phase we are told that the Messiah will deliver from these external manifestations. Eventually, it is revealed that this will be made possible by an inner deliverance. Nevertheless, it is plain that any deliverance on the inner plane which does not then affect the social and political world is a deliverance in name only.

11:1–11

The second reference to salvation through the Messiah in chapters 7–12 comes after two segments which seem to answer the implied question, "If Judah is spared from the attacks of Israel and Syria because they in turn are attacked by Assyria, does this not prove that Ahaz' alliance with Assyria, far from being a damnable thing, was the right thing?" 9:8–10:4 assert that the reasons for Israel's fall have nothing to do with Ahaz' political maneuverings or Assyria's might, but with Israel's moral condition. It is God with whom she has to do, and it is God's hand, not Assyria's which is stretched out against her (9:12, 17, 21; 10:4).

The second segment (10:5–34) underlines this point by insisting that Assyria has no power of independent action, but is simply a tool in God's hand (v. 15). As such, Assyria is as much accountable to God as Israel and Judah are. Such a thought would be incredibly distasteful to the proud Assyrians who believed themselves to be masters of their own fate (vv. 13–14).

---

19. It is interesting that those liberationists who say that the Old Testament's picture of salvation is normative hardly ever say that its picture of blessing is normative. By the same token, some in the modern Charismatic movement want to make the Old Testament understanding of blessing normative, but not its picture of salvation.

They expect to defeat and capture the god of Jerusalem (v. 11); they hardly care to see themselves as nothing more than His agents (v. 12). But God will punish Assyria for its arrogant boasting, cutting it down before Jerusalem (vv. 27–34) and delivering a triumphant remnant of His people from the jaws of the Assyrian lion (vv. 20–27).[20]

Over against the fallen forest giant that is Assyria, the spindly shoot which emerges from the burned-out stump of Jesse (cf. 6:13) is unimpressive in the extreme. Nevertheless, this is God's work, both to cut down the arrogant empire and to prosper the fragile and the helpless Redeemer. The picture of the Messiah and his kingdom in 11:1–11 is chiefly marked by its quiet peaceability, particularly in contrast with the boasts of Assyria in ch. 10. Here the implications of the child ruler discussed above on 9:6 are developed more fully. This kingdom is not secured by the mailed fist of a conqueror, but by a kind of wisdom, counsel, and knowledge which could only have their origin in the Spirit of God (v. 2). Because this ruler's only concern is the approval of God, he will not be impressed by human pomp and power. In his eyes the poor and the helpless will be as worthy of royal succor as anyone else (vv. 3–4a). His only weapon will be the word of truth, and with this he will destroy the wicked (v. 4b). Righteousness and faithfulness will not be showy outer garments put on occasionally by the Davides to impress people. Rather they will be as personal, as regular, as intimate, as much a part of his daily life, as underclothes (v. 5).

All this is pictured in the world of nature, as the normally rapacious animals are depicted as co-habiting peaceably with their previous prey (vv. 6–8). Whether this was ever intended literally is almost impossible to say. But clearly if it is, it could only be in another world than the one we know now, since the lion would have to have a very different set of teeth than it presently has to survive as a herbivore. It seems more likely that Isaiah is simply utilizing a favorite device of his—the extended figure—to make a point about the nature of the Messiah's rule among humans.[21] We do not need changed teeth or digestive systems to participate in a kingdom where there is neither hurt nor destruction, but we do need changed hearts where the experiential knowledge of God reigns supreme (v. 9; cf. Hos. 4:1–3).

The message just outlined is, in some ways, an amplification of one aspect of 9:1–7. That statement chiefly emphasized the results of the child-king's rule. However, in verse 7 reference was made to the qualities of the king, namely justice and righteousness. Here in 11:1–9, the qualities which

---

20. Note the recurrence of *shear jashub*, "a remnant will return" in v. 21 (cf. 7:3). This reinforces the ideological unity of chs. 7–12.

21. See, e.g., 3:18–23; 5:1–7; 10:27–34, etc.

the Messiah and his kingdom will manifest receive the major emphasis. This has the effect of insuring that the Messiah cannot be misconstrued as merely one who "could make it happen" for the elect in the political realm. Instead, He is characterized by qualities which can only spring from an intimate association with God, qualities which, in fact, have their sole source in God. This does not diminish the importance of external outcomes, but it does underline that those outcomes are wholly dependent upon the presence of qualities which are profoundly spiritual.

Verses 10 and 11 introduce the second part of chapter 11, a section which extends to the end of the chapter. The Messiah will be the signal flag by which the remnant will be called home from around the world.[22] In the day when God's kingdom prevails the powers which had held the people captive will be able to do so no longer. It is not clear to what historic events this promise refers. The return in 539 B.C. was not led by the Messiah, although some believe Haggai thought of Zerubbabel in those terms.[23] The formation of the church at Pentecost with persons from all over the world being drawn into the New Israel might satisfy the terms of this statement, but that event would certainly not be anticipated in advance merely from reading these verses. At this point then the only satisfying literal reading of the passage is to anticipate a time still to come when a mass return of dispersed Jews to Israel is also accompanied by a general acceptance of Christ. Although there is a persistent resistance to reading prophecy with such long-term reference (due in part, no doubt, to the excesses of those who read all of the prophets in these ways), if we grant any divine prediction to the prophets, this kind of reading cannot be ruled out of court.

In any case, Isaiah was just as convinced of the restoration as he was of the exile. If judgment was coming with awful inevitability, salvation would follow it with joyous certainty. All of this followed from the prophet's view of the transcendence of God. The coming struggle was not a battle for supremacy between the Lord and the gods of the Mesopotamian powers. It was solely an act of judgment on Gods part. And since Assyria came only at the hand of God, she could not go one step farther, nor keep her captives one day longer, than God decreed. Let the world babble on about the fact that once a nation went into captivity it never returned. The Lord was not bound by the cycles of the past. He was the Narrator and the story would reflect

---

22. There are several key words and themes which recur throughout the book. One of these is *nes*, "ensign, signal flag" (5:26; 11:10, 12; 13:2; 18:3; 30:17; 31:9; 33:23; 49:22; 62:10). Its most common use is to refer to calling people, whether enemies or the remnant, from afar.

23. R. Mason, *The Books of Haggai, Zechariah, and Malachi*, CB (Cambridge: Cambridge, 1977) 25.

His faithfulness and His righteousness, and if that meant doing something unheard of, a brand new thing,[24] the restoration of his people, that hardly constituted a problem for Him.

26:1–9

Chapter 11, ending as it does with promises of the restoration of Israel from among all the nations, raises an immediate question: can God really carry through on such sweeping promises? Does He really have the power to make good? Can He really be trusted? Chapters 13–23 serve to answer this question in very particular ways. From East to West, from the glory of Babylon to the wealth of Tyre, the nations are brought to the bar of God one by one and their fates are declared. God rules their destiny and calls them to account (cf. esp. 14:24–27).

The focus then turns from particular to general. Looked at from one point of view, God is a secondary figure in chapters 13–23. The nations are at center stage and God could be conceived as a somewhat reactionary figure: the nations act and God reacts. He reacts in a very final way, to be sure, but still reacts. If that understanding should have arisen from a reading of those chapters, it is quickly laid to rest by chapters 24–27. Here there is no question but that God is the sovereign actor on the stage of history. By no means is He portrayed as puppetmaster, pulling the strings of robot-like peoples, but He is the central figure in the action. It is His character, nature, and will which determine the direction of affairs and their ultimate outcome. Since this point of view is especially characteristic of apocalyptic literature, these chapters are often referred to as "The Little Apocalypse." However the chapters manifest few of the other characteristics of apocalypse, so if they are a part of that genre, they are a very early example.[25]

Chapter 24 speaks of the destruction of the nations in general, while chapter 25 contrasts the fate of the faithful with that of the arrogant, as symbolized by Moab. 26:1–9 sums up the central point and many of the key themes of the section. God can be trusted to keep his promises of salvation (vv. 3–4), and those who do put their trust in him will be singing songs of joy (v. 1), because He will break down the proud city of rebellious humanity (vv. 5–6) and set up the city of salvation (vv. 1–2). Key to all of this is righteousness (vv. 2, 7). God will certainly not act on behalf of the unrighteous,

---

24. Cf. 43:19, etc.
25. See Oswalt, "Recent Studies in Old Testament Apocalyptic," in *The Face of Old Testament Studies*, eds. D. Baker and B. T. Arnold (Grand Rapids: Baker, 1999) 369–90.

but those who have a passion for the same character as God's (righteousness and faithfulness, cf. 11:5)[26] may depend upon him in patient hope.

This patient waiting for God the judge on the part of the righteous is also a theme in several of the Psalms, especially those known as Royal psalms (cf. 96; 97; 98). It is rooted in a fundamental confidence both that God can be depended upon to want to do right on behalf of all people, and that he has the power to carry out what his nature predisposes him to do. It is also born out of a recognition that human attempts to deliver ourselves are always flawed by our short-sightedness and our tendencies to self-serving. When I act on my own behalf the results will be equivocal at best. But when God acts in deliverance, the world discovers what true righteousness looks like (v. 9).

There is a wonderful peace (26:3) in this kind of "ceasing from one's own works" (Heb 4:10). But this is not merely passivity nor is it yet stoicism. Those attitudes merely reflect resignation, an acceptance of the inevitable since nothing can be done to change it. This is the farthest thing from what Isaiah has in mind. This peace is a result of the confidence that the almighty God is at work on my behalf. It sings with anticipation, remembering what good things he has done for me in the past, knowing the best is yet to be. It is a peace which is rooted in the goodness, the righteousness, and the power of God. That being the case it delights to burrow itself deeper and deeper into the consciousness of him (v. 9).

The section (chs. 24–27) ends with a reiteration of the promise of restoration from captivity (27:12–13). God is indeed the Master of the nations and is able to keep all of his promises to his people if they will only fix their minds on him. They need not worry about the power of the nations and they should not be blinded by the glory of the nations. God is the source of their strength and hope.

35:1–10

Chapters 28–33 return from the focus on God's lordship over the nations to the situation in Judah in Isaiah's own day. The chapters are united by a series of woes (28:1; 29:1, 15; 30:1; 31:1; 33:1) pronounced upon those who will not trust God. The historical settings seem to range from shortly before the fall of Samaria in 721 B.C. until as late as 701 B.C. Assyria was continuing her southward push during these years and even before Samaria's fall was

---

26. RSV "your memorial name" is odd; NEB "your name and memory" is better. God's "name" is his character and reputation as established by his acts in Israel's history, acts of fragrant memory.

active as far south as Philistia. After Samaria fell, nothing stood in the way of Assyria, and wisdom seemed to dictate some sort of alliance between Judah and Egypt. To this Isaiah reacted with utter scorn. What could fickle Egypt offer that God could not duplicate a hundred times over (e.g., 31:1–3)? So the prophet foresees nothing but a funeral ahead for Judah and he re-echoes the funeral cry, "Woe, woe!"[27]

Chapters 34 and 35 provide a graphic conclusion, not only to chapters 28–33, but indeed to the entire section on trusting God or the nations (chs. 13–33). The choices and their results are laid out with unmistakable clarity and simplicity. Chapter 34 shows that to trust the nations of humanity with all of their pomp and power is to reduce the world to a desert. As in chapter 26, where Moab is used as an example, here Edom provides the specific illustration. But the opening four verses make it plain that it is the world which is being addressed and not Edom alone.

By contrast, chapter 35 precisely reverses the situation. For those who will trust God, though they be blind, deaf, lame and dumb (vv. 5–6), the desert will become a garden, and the road home a highway upon which even the most helpless cannot get lost. In place of a wilderness inhabited only by owls and vultures forever (34:15–17), this garden will be dwelt in by the redeemed of the Lord, who will fill it with singing.

Thus these two chapters together sum up the choices which Isaiah has set before his people. The nations of earth are under the judgment of God (13–23); God is telling the story of history and will bring it to its appropriate end (24–27); those who put their trust in God will triumph, but those who trust in horses will be disgraced (28–33). So trust God!

The theme of streams in the desert which is central to chapter 35 is preparatory to the thought of chapters 40–55 (cf. 43:19–21; 44:3–4; 48:21; 49:9–10; 51:3; 55:12–13).[28] In those chapters the primary focus is upon God's promises to restore his people from the exile into which their refusal to trust Him will have brought them. While there is a certain sense in which the promises of water in these passages have a literal application to the return of the Babylonian exiles around the northern rim of the Arabian Desert, it is apparent that their primary reference is figurative. There is no indication

---

27. But, as is typical for the book of Isaiah, not even this section, largely filled with foreboding, can be allowed to close on that note. Beginning with 31:6 the prophet speaks of the hope which lies in the future for those who will turn to God: a righteous king will reign (32:1); the Spirit will be poured out from on high (32:15); the destroyer will himself be destroyed (33:1); the Lord will act on behalf of His people (33:10).

28. Note that this imagery is not exclusive. It is also said that God can dry up rivers so that the redeemed can cross (42:15–16; 44:27; 50:2). This is undoubtedly reflective of the other aspect of the Exodus imagery.

that these phenomena actually accompanied either the return in 538 or the later one in 458. Rather they speak of the fruitful lives of those who, admitting their own helplessness to achieve God's goals, accept his provisions for their lives. To be sure, this will have some external ramifications, as it did for the returning exiles. But unless springs of water also break out from within, producing spiritual vision in place of blindness, and spiritual sensitivity in place of deafness (cf. 32:15–17), there will simply be a recurrence of the same sins which brought on the exile in the first place.

"Glory," *kabod* (35:2) is used in three closely related ways in the book. In all three cases it stands for that which is judged to be significant and impressive. When it is applied to the nations of the earth, it is used to show that all which they have achieved is, in fact, insignificant (e.g., 16:14; 21:14). When it is used of Israel, it is in the setting of promise (4:2; 35:2; 62:2). But that promise is not of something which Israel will achieve through her own efforts; it is always the result of God's glorious work on her behalf. It is as the unfading reality of God and His love, that is, His glory (6:3; 24:23; 66:18), is revealed in the salvation of Israel that Israel herself will be seen as glorious (esp. 60:1–3). That is precisely the point being made in 35:2: it is as God reveals his glory in the salvation of Israel that Israel takes on her true significance, not a field of briars but a mighty forest. This is the paradox of human worth. When we attempt to make ourselves persons of worth through our own achievements, our own hollowness is only made more manifest. But when we discover that we are worthy of the supreme sacrifice of the only truly Glorious One in the universe, we become persons of inestimable worth. No wonder such persons—redeemed and ransomed—sing an unending song (vv. 9–10).

The four passages studied in this article reveal what the book holds to be an irrefutable truth: the God who created the world and who delivered Israel from Egypt will neither wink at Israel's sin, nor will he allow any of his promises to fall to the ground. He is powerful enough, creative enough, and loving enough to save his people. Nor will he save them in spite of judgment. Rather, through judgment he will bring them to the place where they will trust him and his provisions for a restoration not only to the promised land but in their own spirits. The Messiah will establish the kingdom of God not only on earth but in their hearts.

10

The Significance of the ʿalmah Prophecy in the Context of Isaiah 7–12[1]

ONE OF THE CENTRAL areas of controversy in the topic of Biblical authority is that of Biblical prophecy. Clearly, if it can be demonstrated that the many future events which were predicted in the pages of the Bible subsequently occurred, the argument for the more-than-merely-human origins of the Bible are greatly strengthened.[2]

But some may argue that this mode of reasoning[3] is a later rationality forced upon the Hebrews, who supposedly reasoned in a much less syllogistic way.[4] Those who say such a thing have not looked carefully at Isaiah's lawsuit against the gods found in Isaiah chapters 40–48. Over and over God through the prophet challenges the gods to bring forward evidence to show that *just once* they have done what is characteristic of Him: specifically predicted some event which has subsequently occurred as predicted.[5] Bernard

---

1. This is a slightly revised version of an article which appeared in *The Criswell Theological Review* 6 (1993) 223–35. It appears here by permission.

2. See, for instance, the arguments of James Orr, *The Problem of the Old Testament* (London: Nisbet, 1907) 455–560.

3. Accurate, specific prediction is the province of the transcendent Creator alone; the Bible contains accurate, specific prediction; therefore, the origins of the Bible are to be sought for in divine inspiration.

4. See, for instance, John Barton, *The Oracles of God* (Oxford: Oxford University Press, 1986) 132.

5. Cf. Isa 41:21–24; 43:8–10; 44:6–8; 45:21; 46:8–10; 48:5, 14–16.

Duhm, in his well-known commentary, says that only one who was quite unfamiliar with pagan religion could make such an overblown statement. Anyone with even an elementary knowledge of Babylonian religion would surely know that the gods regularly predicted the future.[6] But the fact is, Isaiah's statements are neither naïve nor overblown. As Claus Westermann points out, we look in vain in the non-Biblical literatures for anything approximating the duration and specificity of the prophecies of the exile, for instance.[7] In fact, the pagan oracles were noteworthy for their ambiguity. Thus, whatever happened, it could be argued that the oracle was correct.[8]

But even recognizing this characteristic ambiguity, if Isaiah were merely saying that the gods had never predicted the outcome of some event correctly, his argument would be open to question. Anyone familiar in any way with the ancient world could have surely pointed to some case of that happening. What Isaiah is clearly talking about has to do with what Westermann saw. Isaiah is talking about the prediction of a pattern of specific events shaping the course of history out into the far-distant future. It is this which the gods could not even begin to duplicate, as the inspired prophet well knew.[9]

---

6. Bernhard Duhm, *Das Buch Jesaia*, HAT 3/1 (Göttingen: Vandenhoeck & Ruprecht, 1892) 307–8.

7. Claus Westermann, *Isaiah 40–66: A Commentary*, tr. D. M. G. Stalker, OTL (Philadelphia: Westminster, 1969) 91. Cf. also G. E. Wright, *The Book of Isaiah*, Layman's Bible Commentary (Richmond, VA: John Knox, 1964) 103.

8. Two well-known examples are the oracle to Croesus and the one regarding the Persian threat to the city of Athens. Croesus took the oracle about a mighty empire's being lost to refer to the Persians, and therefore inferred that he would triumph. After he lost the battle, it was declared that the empire being referred to was Croesus.' Similarly, when the oracle declared that the Athenians would be saved by "the wooden wall," it was assumed that the reference was to the walls around the city. Later, when the Greek fleet had removed the threat of attack by destroying the Persian fleet, it was declared that "the wooden wall" must have referred to the fleet. See Botsford and Robinson, *Hellenistic History*, 5th ed., rev. by D. Kagan (New York: Macmillan, 1969) 102, 147.

9. Thus, Isaiah's use of the terms "former things" (41:22; 43:9; 44:7, etc.) is significant. Brevard S. Childs believes this is "II Isaiah" speaking of "I Isaiah's" predictions, as in 38:6 and 39:5–7 (*Introduction to the Old Testament as Scripture* [Philadelphia: Fortress, 1979] 329–30). More plausibly, R. E. Clements, "The Unity of the Book of Isaiah," *Int* 36 (1982) 117–29; and C. Stuhlmacher, "'First and Last' and 'Yahweh–Creator' in Dt.-Is," *CBQ* 29 (1967) 495–511, believe it refers to the Exodus events (the importance of the Exodus events as a paradigm for understanding the return from Exile in Isaiah 40–55 is widely recognized).But I believe even this is too limited. I am confident that all of God's promises from Abraham through Moses and David to Hosea are in the prophet's mind. How can Israel even think that the God who has called the nation into existence by such promises and preserved it against all the odds by wondrously fulfilling those promises while giving even greater ones could either forget them or could be just one more of the gods (40:27; 43:11–12)?!

This insight has bearing upon the significance of the Cyrus prophecy for our

It is within this context that I wish to discuss the prediction in Isaiah 7:14. Is that prediction part of this larger pattern of promise which characterizes God's work in Israel, or is it merely an isolated example of God's ability and purpose.[10] I am convinced this is not merely a matter of academic interest. The reason why it is not a matter of mere academic interest is because of what the New Testament does with that prediction. Without question there are genuine predictions from God in the Old Testament which are significant for their own time alone. They are genuinely supernatural in origin, and they have a part to play in God's overall plan for Israel, but, in and of themselves, they do not constitute a revelation of that plan. Such, for instance, would be the prediction of the division of Solomon's kingdom (1 Kgs 11:29–40). By contrast, there is the promise to David that he will have a descendant upon the throne of Israel forever (2 Sam 7:8–17). Both of these are specific predictions from God; both of them have been dramatically fulfilled. But the one is primarily of punctiliar significance, while the other is of enduring significance. To which of these types does Isaiah 7:14 conform?

Part of the significance of that question lies in a larger understanding of the connection between prophecy and fulfillment. At least since the writing of the Gospel of Matthew (and, in fact, before that, as I will show below), this prediction has been taken to have had enduring significance. It was revelatory of the deeper purpose and plan of God. This understanding was guaranteed, it was thought, by the New Testament's explanation of the passage. For virtually its entire history the Church has accepted that if the New Testament describes some event as being the fulfillment of an Old Testament statement, then the Old Testament statement was intended from the outset to have a New Testament fulfillment. With the rise of the

---

understanding of the authorship of the book of Isaiah. Surely the centerpiece for Isaiah's claims for the uniqueness of the Lord is the Cyrus prophecy. "Have the gods ever made this kind of prediction? Of course not!" If indeed the prediction was penned 125 years before Cyrus was born, then the claim was absolutely correct. On the other hand, if, as those who support multiple authorship claim, the "prediction" of Cyrus' victory was only made after Cyrus had begun his conquests, there is, in fact, nothing unique about Isaiah's predictions, and his arguments are indeed dependent upon misuse of logic. For the claim that Isaiah's predictions were only made after the emergence of Cyrus, see C. R. North, *The Second Isaiah* (Oxford: Oxford University Press, 1964) 105.

10. Two examples of Old Testament theologies which see the promise element as the organizing principle in Old Testament thought are Gerhard von Rad's *Old Testament Theology*, 2 vols. tr. D. M. G. Stalker (New York: Harper & Row, 1962); and Walter Kaiser's *Toward an Old Testament Theology* (Grand Rapids: Zondervan, 1978). The former sees promise/fulfillment as the general scheme which shapes the emerging theology. The latter more correctly, in my view, sees the specific promises of the Old Testament, and their outworking, as expressing the predetermined plan of God for the saving of the race.

Enlightenment and its skepticism of anything but natural causes, this linkage came to be sharply contested. In fact, it was argued, genuine prediction was not possible, and particularly not over the long span of time between the Old and New Testaments. Thus, what the New Testament writers did, it was supposed, was to comb the Old Testament in a flush of enthusiasm for their new-found faith, looking for correspondences which would suggest that this man, whom they increasingly took to be God Incarnate, was indeed part of the eternal plan of God.

Historically, those who have espoused positions like these have been divided into two camps: believers and unbelievers. The unbelievers (like August Comte and, more recently, John Hick),[11] have simply seen the attempt as an exercise in mass delusion. The believers (like G. Adam Smith)[12] have argued that while the original intent was purely punctiliar, the New Testament writers were providentially guided in their discovery of links between the Old and New Testaments. The early Fundamentalists were surely right in their insistence that neither of these positions did justice to the Biblical claims.[13]

This is not the place to enter into a defense of the orthodox position on prophecy and fulfillment. But it is the place to register a note of concern. Recently the "believers" position which I have described above seems to have begun to gain currency among the descendants of the Fundamentalists, the Evangelicals. In various ways it is being said that imaginative reflection upon the inspired texts in which connections to one's own time are found, although those connections were not originally intended, is consistent with a high view of inspiration.[14] Thus, it has been argued that both propositions are true: Isaiah 7:14 bears no reference to the heaven-sent Messiah; Matthew 1:22–23 is inerrantly inspired when it says that the virgin birth of Christ was "to fulfill what the Lord had spoken by the prophet."[15] The only way such a logical contradiction can be maintained is to say that the New Testament writers did not mean by "fulfill" what the English word normally means. Frankly, this looks like sleight-of-hand and does not give confidence

---

11. John Hick, *The Myth of God Incarnate* (Philadelphia: Westminster, 1977).

12. *The Book of Isaiah*, 2 vols., The Expositor's Bible (London: Hodder & Stoughton, n.d.).

13. All the discussions of J. Gresham Machen, *The Virgin Birth of Christ* (New York: Harper, 1930) 287–294, a classic treatment of the passage.

14. This understanding has gained impetus through the study of the kind of exegesis done at Qumran and elsewhere by early Jewish exegetes. That this kind of exegesis, known in one form as Pesher, and in another as Midrash, was engaged in is clear. What is not clear is whether it was the only kind of exegesis used, and more to the point, why the literary links between it and the New Testament writings are so few.

15. John Walton, "What's in a Name?" *JETS* 30 (1987) 289–306.

The Significance of the ʿalmah Prophecy

in the argument. One must ask why a more correct translation of *pleiromai* has never come into use if that is the case. No, the New Testament writer believes himself, and wishes his readers to believe, that Isaiah predicted the virgin birth of the Messiah and that that prediction was completed, fulfilled, in the virgin birth of Jesus Christ. The choice before us is either to accept or reject that claim. The Fundamentalists were correct in insisting that there is no middle way.[16]

But is it possible to accept Matthew's claim? Even if we grant that such long-distance prediction is possible under divine inspiration, is there genuine reason to believe that it took place? Does not a careful historical-critical investigation of the text in the light of normal Biblical usages suggest that the passage was only intended to be used in a punctiliar way, that it was only intended for Ahaz' time? Certainly some weighty arguments can be mounted in defense of such a position. Especially strong is the evidence from within the text itself that the prediction was to be fulfilled, in one sense at least, within Ahaz' own lifetime. But does that realization demand that a later, fuller reference be given up? I think not. When the arguments for limiting the reference are examined, significant weaknesses can be found.[17]

---

16. Walton's attempt to solve the problem with reference to the OT use of names falls far short. He argues that children are given names in the expectation that those names will somehow become significant, but without any assurance of what that significance will be. He sees this as analogous to OT prophecy. First of all, this does not apply to Isa 7:14 as he sees it, since he has deprived it of any larger predictive significance. But beyond that, this model of open-ended and amorphous possibilities does not correspond to what the prophets claimed for themselves. See the arguments above.

17. The article by Walton cited above lists a number of these arguments. In the interest of completeness they will be responded to in brief from here. 1) The author asserts that *ḥarâ*, in 7:14 is an adjective which cannot have a future connotation. He cites the comparable phrases in Gen 16:10 and Judg 13:3, asserting that there also the word is an adjective and that only the converted perfects in those contexts give the future meaning. The forms are not adjectives in any of the three contexts, but fem. participles. Thus, the future rendering is entirely appropriate. 2) He misrepresents the argument that the LXX in translating ʿalmah with *parthenos* was correct and must not be overlooked. He suggests that since "virgin" is not the meaning of the term ʿalmah, but only a connotation, it is never correct to translate it with that meaning. No recent commentator has suggested that ʿalmah should always be translated "virgin." But when it has been, that is not to be dismissed. 3) He asserts that 'ot, "sign," does not connote anything miraculous. He makes this assertion on the basis of three passages, 1 Sam 2:34; Jer 44:29–30; 2 Kgs 19:29. But this overlooks two important aspects: the general usage of the word and its specific context in Isaiah 7. In general, the word is connected with "wonders" in the recitals of the Exodus. The Exodus signs were surely miraculous in nature. This is brought closer home by the miraculous sign of the shadow in Isa 38:7–8. But most important of all is the passage in which Ahaz is directly encouraged to ask for a miraculous sign "as high as heaven or as deep as Sheol." Thus there is every reason to believe that the sign which God eventually gave was miraculous. 4) He argues

But of greatest significance, in my opinion, is the evidence of the literary context, and it is to that which we now turn.

Although most recent commentators do not regard chapters 7–12 to be a literary unity, there are good reasons to consider the chapters as a unity of thought. First of all, they show a very clear demarcation from what follows (chap. 13ff.), and a reasonably clear demarcation for what precedes (chap. 6).[18] Furthermore, when the ideas are considered, there seems to be a clear progression of thought extending from Isaiah's opening challenge to Ahaz to trust God (7:9) to the closing hymn of the redeemed extolling God's trustworthiness (12:1–6). That progression moves through several stages: terror at the Syro-Ephramite threat (7:1–6); refusal to accept God's word of promise (7:7–16); the forecast of destruction by Assyria (7:17—8:8); reflection on the blindness of the people of God (8:9—9:1); the promise of the child deliverer (9:2–7); explanation of the reasons for Assyria's coming (not geopolitical power, but Israel's moral failure, 9:8—10:4; thus Assyria is merely a tool, and, as such, accountable to Him who wields it, 10:5–34 [since Israel's destruction is not the result of Assyria's will but of the will of the morally responsible, trustworthy God, Israel's destruction will neither be complete nor final]); the glory of Israel's return to the Messianic kingdom (11:1–16); the hymn of redemption (12:1–6; cf. Exod 15:1–18). Thus, there is a clear thread of continuity which proceeds from the opening announcement of

---

that the only possible meaning of the statement is that a young woman of the harem already pregnant at that time will have reason to name her child "God-with-us" by the time it is born. This is based on the three errors already noted and compounded by a too-easy dismissal of the high likelihood that the initial occurrence of the sign was in Maher-shalal-hash-baz, the son of Isaiah himself (8:1ff.). The "fulfillment" which Walton suggests breathes none of the air of mystery and wonder which is found in the passage itself. 5) He does not pay adequate attention to the use of "Immanuel" in chapter 8 and the way it extends the significance of the sign beyond the immediate present.

18. The lack of agreement among commentators as to whether ch. 6 should be included with chaps. 1–5 or 7–12 is an indication of the chapter's transitional function, in my view. Looked at from the perspective of chaps. 1–5, chap. 6 provides a clear solution to the problem posed in those chapters: how can proud, perverse, rebellious Israel (1:1–31; 2:6–4:1; 5:1–30) become clean and holy (4:2–6), the one to whom the nations come to learn the law of God (2:1–5)? The answer is that the nation of unclean lips can have an experience of God analogous to that of the man of unclean lips. But when chapter 6 is looked at from the perspective of chs. 7–12, there are many ways in which it functions as an introduction to those chapters. Like them, it has a firm historical rootage; it provides a clear explanation for the blind and stubborn refusal of the promises of God which characterize the response in those chapters; it predicts the destruction which will result from that refusal; it sets the stage, with its final glimmer of hope, for the Messianic promises which conclude the unit. Thus, any simplistic inclusion or exclusion with/from either 1–5 or 7–12 is to be avoided. Rather, both segments must be interpreted in the light of that pivotal chapter.

terror (7:2) to the final pronouncement of fearlessness (12:2), with each successive topic growing out of the preceding one. This sense of continuity is enhanced by the recurring treatment of certain themes. Some of these are: the house of David (7:2, 13; 9:7; 11:1, 10); children as signs of threat and promise (7:3, 14; 8:3, 18; 9:6; 11:6, 8); Assyria (7:17, 18, 20; 8:7; 10:5, 12, 24; 11:11, 16); the remnant (7:3; 10:20, 21, 22; 11:11,16); God's sole trustworthiness as seen especially in his will to deliver (7:7-9; 8:9-10; 9:1-7; 10:20-27; 11:11-12, 15-16; 12:1-6). All of these reasons argue strongly that, despite a diversity of literary forms (poetry, prose, threats, oracles of salvation, etc.).[19] these materials have been put in this particular sequence because they are intended to be understood in context with one another.[20]

This understanding of the contextual unity of chapters 7-12 is significant for the interpretation of 7:14. The author, or compiler, has signaled to us that he understands this passage, as well as all the rest of the materials in the unit, as a part of that larger picture. Thus, to read this statement merely from within its immediate context, which is vv. 10-17, would be like interpreting a musical phrase in a symphony in isolation, without considering the movement in which it occurs, let alone the larger symphonic structure. This is not to say that the larger context provides a warrant for reading a passage in a way which does violence to its immediate context, but it does say that exegesis which analyzes the grammar and syntax of a sentence, or even a paragraph, in minute detail, without paying attention to the shaping influence of the larger context, is not complete exegesis.

What is the larger message of which Isa 7:14 is a part? Of course, to follow the metaphor described above, the largest message is to be found in the entire symphonic structure of the book of Isaiah. While a lengthy discussion of that topic is not warranted here, neither should it be overlooked, for like many of the Biblical books, there is substantial evidence for the conscious shaping of the whole, and that all which is included is included as a part of that whole.[21] If I were to express the overall theme in a sentence, it would be this: "The Holy One of Israel is the Sovereign of the Nations and the Redeemer of the World." The book is about God as Holy, Sovereign Savior.

---

19. For a highly detailed discussion of the possible literary forms involved, see Otto Kaiser, *Isaiah 1-12, a Commentary*, OTL (Philadelphia: Westminster, 1972). While it is certainly possible that someone may yet analyze these forms in still more detail, it is hard to imagine that anything but very diminished returns can come from it. Kaiser already seems to have gone far in that direction.

20. P. R. Ackroyd, "Isaiah 1-12, Presentation of a Prophet," in *Congress Volume: Göttingen, 1977*, VTSup 29 (Leiden: Brill, 1978) 16-48, has argued that chs. 1-5 should be included in the unit as well. Although he makes a good case, the argument that chaps.1-5 have a wider function in the book than this seems stronger.

21. For an extended treatment of this subject, see chapter 1 above.

Intertwined with that dominant theme is the issue of Israel's mission: will the chosen people bow down to the humanly-based gods of the nations or will they reveal the transcendent God to the nations? Thus, the move is from a people who, far from having light for others, grope about in a darkness of their own making (8:16–22) to a people upon whom the Lord has risen in such brightness that all the nations are drawn to the glory (60:1–3).[22]

Coupled with the question of mission is the whole issue of kingship: how will the Holy King whom Isaiah saw in the temple establish His dominion on the earth? How will He conquer pride, rebellion, and oppression? Will he do so with domination and aggressiveness, crushing his enemies beneath a mailed fist? No, he will come as a child would, harmless and weak (9:6; 11:3; 42:1–4; 49:7; 52:15–53:3).[23] Here is the power of God: to absorb all the evil of a hopelessly depraved world, and give back only boundless love and justice, free for the taking.

If that is what the larger movement is about, where do chapters 7–12 fit into that? What part does this movement play in the larger structure? In one sense they are introductory to the entire structure, in that they lay out the complete program. There is a sense in which, once Ahaz has made his fateful choice not to take the radical step of trusting God, the entire sequence of Israel's experience from that point on follows with a certain ineradicable logic. The justice of God (the cause and effect nature of existence) means that failure to trust him brings destruction and darkness upon his people (7:17–8:22). But the love of God decrees that they cannot be left in such a condition. In faithfulness to His promises to Abraham and David, He must deliver Israel (9:1–7) and that, not because the people have earned it, but as an expression of his free grace (10:20–27). How is such deliverance possible? Because Israel was brought down by God, not Assyria, and He who brought her down has the power to lift her up again (9:8–10:19; 10:27–34). The power which will characterize the coming King will be moral, not political or military (11:1–5). In the light of that universal kingdom (11:6–9), the truest values of the Exodus will be realized (11:10–12:6). Thus it may be said that the great themes of the rest of the book are contained in capsule form in this segment of the book.[24]

---

22. For a further discussion of Israel's mission, see chapters 7 and 8 above.

23. To be sure, there are statements of God's violent destruction of his enemies. Interestingly, all of those which occur in extended treatments are found after chap. 53 (59:15–19; 63:1–6; 66:15–16). Those who reject "the gently flowing waters of Shiloah" (cf. 8:6), will have to contend with rushing floodwaters.

24. In this light, it may be asked whether chaps. 1–12 are the introduction to the book, and not just chs 1–5(6), as suggested above. While good arguments can be mustered in favor of such a position (cf. Ackroyd, "Isaiah 1–12"), two important

The Significance of the ᶜalmah Prophecy

But there is another sense in which this unit fills a very specific place within the book. That is, it sets the stage for the particular teachings of chapters 13–39. What Ahaz had refused to believe was that God was with him, and his dynasty, and his people in any unique way. He had already made his own plans for extricating all of these from the threat of Pekah and Rezin to depose the Davidic monarch and place someone else on the throne (2 Kgs 16:5–9). Ahaz would trust Assyria, his worst enemy, before he would trust God. Far from trusting God and revealing him to the nations, Israel would trust the nations and, in so doing, deny God. As noted above, that decision would bring destruction, which would in turn bring redemption and the Messianic kingdom. But in the theological program of the book, this segment serves to introduce a question of major importance. Can God really be trusted? Chapters 13–35 provide the data to answer that question, and then chapters 36–39 show us another Davidic monarch who, in a much more serious situation, does trust God and has that trust vindicated in a marvelous way.

Thus, in a specific sense, chapters 7–12 have to do with the question of "immanu-el": is God really with us in any way that makes any difference? Isaiah's answer is that he is presently with us in the sense that we can depend on him to deliver us from the threats of Rezin and Pekah, but also that he will actually be with us as the Messiah. These two promises are inseparable and interdependent. If God was not truly with his people in the affairs of that moment, the lovely messianic promises are highly suspect. By the same token, if God can never be with his people in actuality, then there is reason to doubt that his transcendence can ever be truly overcome on our behalf.

What all of this says is that all the elements of this unit must be understood in light of the emphasis on divine trustworthiness and immanence on the people's behalf which characterizes the unit. This has a considerable bearing upon the correct understanding of 7:14. Whatever we might conclude from the paragraph alone, and this is hardly unambiguous, the larger context points us to an understanding which far surpasses Ahaz' own immediate experience. Just as his choice was to have far-reaching consequences for the kingdom of Judah, so we should expect the mysterious sign to have significance beyond the immediate historic context as well.

That the sign does have such significance is supported by the connection of children with both of the messianic prophecies. This is particularly

---

points weigh against it. First, chaps. 1–5(6) seem to be much more broadly stated and addressed than do chaps. 7–12. Chaps. 7–12 might be more aptly characterized as preparation for what follows. Second, careful examination of 7–12 in the light of 36–39 suggests that the two sections are part of an inclusio around chaps.13–35 showing that the whole segment (7–39) is about God's sovereignty and trustworthiness in the world. See chapters 1–3 of this volume above.

important with 9:2–7 where the Messiah's coming is as a child.[25] While the Messiah in 11:1–9 is not specifically called a child, the childlike qualities ascribed to him (11:3) and the repeated mention of children leading and playing among previously ravenous animals (11:6, 8) surely contributes to the same understanding. Can it be merely coincidence in a segment where the presence of God among his people is central that Immanuel is a child and the Messiah is a child? I think not.[26] In fact, there is every reason to believe that the language is intentional in order to guide the reader to make the association between the two.[27]

It should not be inferred from this argumentation that I believe the Immanuel prophecy refers solely to the Messiah. As I have stated elsewhere,[28] the statements in 7:15–16 surely point to a birth during the lifetime of Ahaz. What we know of Israelite and Syrian history confirms this, in that both Syria and Israel had been defeated and annexed by Assyria by 722 B.C., approximately 12 years after the most likely date of this prophecy.[29] Thus, it seems beyond question that the prediction was fulfilled, as intended, during Ahaz' lifetime. In addition, it seems very likely that it was fulfilled in Isaiah's own family through the birth of his son, Maher-shalal-hash-baz. This argument is supported by the recurrence of language in 7:14 and 8:3 ("she conceived and bore a son"), by the similarity of the signs,[30] and by the mention of Immanuel

---

25. Efforts to relate 9:6 to the birth of a son to Ahaz, perhaps even Hezekiah, have not met with any wide-spread agreement. The language is too expansive and cosmic to be applied to a human ruler. For a further discussion, see Oswalt, *Isaiah 1–39*, 246–47.

26. It may be objected that I have been selective in equating Immanuel with the Messiah and not either Shearjashub or Maher-Shalal-has-baz. But the reason for doing so is that there is absolutely no mystery about either of those two. They are clearly said to be the children of Isaiah and nothing more is to be said. But a great deal of mystery surrounds Immanuel. His mother is identified with a highly-ambiguous term; his father is not mentioned at all; and he is referred to as the owner, or at least, a notable inhabitant of the land of Judah. All of this says that he is the only likely candidate for association with the Messiah.

27. So for instance J. Skinner, *The Book of the Prophet Isaiah* (Cambridge: Cambridge, 1925) 83.

28. Oswalt, *Isaiah 1–39*, 206–14.

29. "Refuse the evil and choose the good" (v. 15) is taken by most commentators to refer to a child's attaining the age of accountability—12 years old.

30. Walton argues against this supposition on the grounds that the woman in 7:14 is already pregnant, whereas Isaiah's wife is just conceiving. In fact, the argument that the ʿ*almah* is already pregnant rests upon a misreading of the fem. ptcps. in Gen 16:11 and Judg 13:5. These two passages are clearly future and the fact that they are grammatically identical with Isa 7:14 argues that it too is future. He further argues that the signs are not the same since saying "mama" and "papa" occur long before the twelfth year. However, Damascus fell in 732 and Samaria paid heavy tribute at that same time. Clearly that date would be entirely in keeping with the sign. More importantly, both signs have

The Significance of the ᶜalmah Prophecy

on both sides of the mention of Maher-shalal-hash-baz.[31] One significance of this equation is that it clearly means that if the ultimate meaning of the Immanuel sign is that God will be with us in and through a son of David (9:7; 11:1), then the fulfillment in Ahaz' own time was not the ultimate one.

But even more importantly, it shows us that we should read 7:10–17 as part of a larger unit which extends at least as far as 9:7. The sequence of thought would be something like this: 1) The prophecy of Immanuel (7:10–17); 2) Expansions on the prophecy, showing that it is two-sided (God's presence with us is not a cause for happiness if we have rejected that presence) (7:18–23);[32] 3) Initial fulfillment of the prophecy in Maher-shalal-hash-baz (8:1–4); 4) Expansion of that prophecy with particular connection to Immanuel (again two-sided) (8:5–10); 5) Further reflection on the two-sidedness of God's presence, concluding that the ultimate significance of the signs was hidden at that time (8:11–22); revelation of the ultimate meaning of Immanuel in the child who would be born to sit forever on the throne of David (9:1–7). Thus it can be seen that a contextual reading not only supports the understanding that there was a fulfillment of the prophecy in Ahaz' own day, *but also* that that fulfillment was not the ultimate one.

But what about the specific wording of the promise in its context? John Walton has set forth some strongly worded arguments against reading ᶜalmah as "virgin" under any circumstances and has proposed an understanding of the historical setting which, while plausible, is also highly restrictive. What does the use of this word in this context imply? Of greatest significance is the air of mystery and ambiguity which surrounds the term. If, as Walton argues, the sign refers to one of Ahaz' concubines who is now pregnant and will shortly give birth, it is very hard to explain this language. Why not simply say "Your concubine has conceived and will bear a son to you. You shall call his name Immanuel. He will eat curds and . . ." Why not identify the father, particularly if it is the Ahaz to whom the oracle is addressed? Why not use the common term for concubine? Why not identify whose concubine it is?[33] In fact, the text gives no reason at all to associate

---

to do with something the child can or cannot do by a certain date.

31. See Herbert M. Wolf, "A Solution to the Immanuel Prophecy in Isaiah 7:14–8:22," *JBL*, 91 (1972) 449–56.

32. Note the recurrence of "curds and honey" in 7:15 and 22. This underscores the continuity of thought.

33. Walton's attempt to answer this question by reference to the definite article on ᶜalmah is very weak. He suggests that Ahaz would not have had so many concubines but that if one of them appeared to be pregnant there would have been some comment about the situation in the court and that by Isaiah's saying *the* ᶜalmah, his hearers would have known to whom he was referring. In the first place, there is no reason to associate ᶜalmah with a concubine at all. Perhaps the term could have been used to refer to a

this woman with the court, or with Ahaz. By its silence on these points it specifically points away from that possibility. Walton is grasping at straws in order to support his contention that the New Testament reading is simply a midrash on a misreading of the Old Testament.

But if the initial fulfillment of 7:14 is to be found in 8:1–4, as was contended above, why was that not stated explicitly in 7:14? That is just the point; it is an initial fulfillment only. If indeed Maher-shalal-hash-baz' conception, birth, and naming said all that the sign in 7:14 was to say, then it is very hard, if not impossible, to understand why 7:14 is not more explicit. Why not use a common term for "young woman" or even "your wife"? On the other hand, if the sign was intended to point to the birth of Christ, why not use the unambiguous *betulah*, "virgin"?

I believe that the answer to both questions lies in the double nature of the sign. It has two historic contexts: the immediate future when the evidence of God's presence would be the defeat of Syria and Israel and the ensuing attack of Assyria upon Judah, and the distant future when God would be physically present among his people either to purify or to judge (Mal 3:1–5). In the immediate future the virginity of the mother was not the issue, but in the distant future that was all-important. Thus an ambiguous word was used. Walton is certainly correct when he asserts that ʿ*almah* does not mean "virgin." But he is wrong when he goes on from that point to imply that the word can never connote virginity in a given setting. In fact, as he admits, the word seems to have to do with adolescence. If we are talking about an adolescent female in Hebrew society, there is *every* reason to think that this would be one of the chief connotations of the word. This supposition is only confirmed by the Septuagint's use of *parthenos*, "virgin," to translate ʿ*almah*.[34] In other words, the ambiguous term is used purposely so as to support both the immediate and distant occurrences of the sign.

---

concubine, but that is not the meaning of the term and it would not connote that meaning without some modifier. From that point the argument successively falls in upon itself, with each supposition being more questionable than the last.

34. Walton's attempt to devalue the significance of the LXX reading rests upon two pillars: an unpublished paper of Gleason L. Archer in which he is reported to have argued that the LXX translators of Isaiah often used equivalent terms and not exact ones, and the fact that *parthenos* does not always mean "virgin" in classical Greek. Neither of these will bear much weight. Whether *parthenos* is equivalent or exact, the question is why it was used at all, especially if, as Walton maintains, ʿ*almah* has nothing to do with virginity. Second, as is well-known, the Septuagint meanings are often at odds with classical usage. In fact, they must be defined by reference to the Hebrew word they are translating in many cases! Furthermore, NT meanings, and NT *parthenos* definitely means "virgin," are frequently dependent upon Septuagint meanings.

For this same reason the paternity of the child is left unidentified. All of this argues that no short-term fulfillment alone is in view here.

Added to this is the invitation to Ahaz to make the sign he asks be "as deep as Sheol or high as heaven." This hardly suggests something as insignificant as the naming of the child of an already pregnant concubine.[35] To be sure, Ahaz refused to ask, probably because he had already made his own plans. But that is all the more reason for God to make the sign even more stupendous as a final vindication of His trustworthiness.

In sum, I believe those who call Isaiah chapters 7–12 the book of Immanuel are correct. At this absolutely critical point in salvation history when North Israel was about to be expelled from the promised land and the Davidic monarch of Judah was displaying that breach of covenant which was to become calcified in his grandson Manasseh, and which would issue in the destruction of Judah, the complete outlines of the plan of God for His kingdom needed to be displayed. They are nowhere better done than in the book of Isaiah. And, as shown above, that display is prepared for in chapters 7–12. There God's trustworthiness is shown, not only in his ability to deliver from Syria and Ephraim, or even from the tool of Assyria brought on to punish them for their faithlessness, but ultimately and triumphantly from the unrighteousness and the wickedness which lie at the root of all this history. And how will this be accomplished? By the personal intervention of God in history. This has been the foundering point of all merely human philosophy. We have been terrified of the thought of transcendence. We need a god with us. The result has been the loss of any real transcendence, and the submerging of god into ourselves for the achievement of our transitory desires. The glory of the Bible in general and Isaiah in particular is that it is able to maintain God's transcendence by demonstrating that He can break into the world without becoming the world. He is able to be truly with us, in our midst, without being submerged into us. This is what "Immanuel" is made to point to in this segment, and this is what Jesus Christ means for the world. "God with us" is not merely a theological/historical construct; it is a spiritual/material actuality. The final confirmation that this segment is preeminently about the real presence of the Transcendent with us is found in the final verse of the segment, 12:6. "Shout, and sing for joy, O inhabitant of Zion, for great in your midst is the Holy One of Israel." To restrict the Immanuel prophecy to a banal event in Judean history, and to make the New Testament's appropriation of it an exercise in literary imagination is to miss the whole import of this segment, and indeed, of the book of Isaiah.

---

35. Note that the naming of the child is not even a command, as is that of Maher-shalal-hash-baz. Surely this would be a self-fulfilling prophecy and nothing more.

11

Isaiah 24–27
Songs in the Night[1]

[THE ORIGINAL ARTICLE IN which the following material appeared began with a lengthy discussion of the way in which chapters 1–39 are structured. For this information see especially chapters 1–3 above.]

Given the structure of chapters 1–39, how do chapters 24–27 function in these materials, particularly in chapters 7–39, which I have labeled "Trust, the Basis of Servanthood."? I suggest that they stand at the midpoint of a chiasm. Diagrammatically, it looks like this:

God's Triumph over the Nations
24–27

Don't Trust the Nations	Woe to Those Who Will not Trust
13–23	28–33 (34–35)
Trust God? No!	Trust God? Yes (but)
7–12	36–39

I am not arguing that the writer or the editors carefully plotted this all out in this fashion. They could have, and it is tempting to think they did. Why else are chapters 24–27, often called "The Little Apocalypse," located here and not at some other point in the book? But my interpretation does not depend on proving that point. What I am saying is that recognizing this

---

1. This material appeared as part of a larger article with this same title in the *Calvin Theological Journal* 40 (2005) 76–84 and appears here by permission.

relationship offers a helpful device for interpreting the function of chapters 24–27 in the present organization of the book.

The materials in chapters 24–27, in contrast to the materials on either side of them, are remarkably universalistic. Chapters 13–23 are addressed to very specific nations, while chapters 28–33 are dealing with a specific historic situation and are making very specific pronouncements about that situation. Chapters 24–27, on the other hand, move from microscope to telescope. In all of this challenge *not* to do this or *to* do that with respect to the nations, we are recalled to the larger issue again. At the center of the vision of the absolute superiority of Yahweh over all the nations in chapters 13–35 chapters 24–27 drag our eyes almost forcibly to the far horizons. They say to us that the discussion is not finally about the nations; it is finally about the God of all nations, and we need to be reminded of that. All of time and space are his.

These chapters, then, provide a way of reading the sections immediately before and after them. In the case of 13–23, we are reminded that God is not merely a "reactor" in history. It is not that the nations act and God then reacts to them. God is the sovereign actor on the stage of history. All that happens on earth is within his command. On the other hand, these chapters provide the true perspective for the waiting that is called for in chapters 28–33. If we will see God as he is: Lord of Time and Space, we will not be inclined to put a foolish trust in created things. If we cannot trust him, whom can we trust? Thus, it is hardly surprising to discover the following words near the physical center of chapters 24–27, and likewise near the center of the entire division which chapters 7–39 comprise: "Behold, this is our God; we waited for him and he delivered us. This is the Lord; we waited for him. Let us rejoice and be glad in his deliverance" (25:9); and "'The person whose imagination is settled, you will keep in complete peace(*shalom shalom*), because he trusts in you. Trust in Yahweh forever, because in Yah, Yahweh, is an eternal Rock" (26:3–4). The prophet is asserting that God can be trusted in all the particulars of life because all of life is in God's hands. Thus, chapters 24–27 offer us a fleshing out of what it means for Yahweh to be the all-holy One whose glory fills the earth (6:3).[2]

---

2. It seems to me that it is a misnomer to call these chapters "apocalyptic." They lack many of the features that are said to be the common properties of apocalyptic, such as fantastic imagery, symbolic numbers, and heavenly warfare. The feast portrayed in 25:6–9 might be said to have overtones of apocalyptic since it seems to portray an event at the end of time. However, to characterize the entire section on the basis of that one short segment is to go too far. To be sure, there is a universalistic sweep that transcends particular times and places, but that does not require the genre of apocalyptic. For a further discussion of apocalyptic and eschatology, see Oswalt, "Recent Studies in Old Testament Apocalyptic," in *The Face of Old Testament Study*, eds. D. Baker and B.

When we observe the materials in these chapters closely, we see the recurrence of several terms, or sets of terms. They are "city" (24:10, 12; 25:2, 3; 26:1; 27:10), "mountain" (24:23; 25:6, 7, 10; 27:13), "song, sing, singing" (24:9, 14, 16; 25:5; 26:1, 19; 27:2), "vineyard, wine" (24:7, 9, 11; 25:6; 27:2, 6), "Arrogant, exalted, ruthless" (24:4, 21; 25:3, 5, 11; 26:5), "Earth, world" (24:1, 3–6, 11, 17–21; 25:8; 26:9, 18, 19, 21; 27:6). Furthermore, when we examine these recurrences, we discover that they regularly appear in contrasting structures. Thus the worldwide destruction of chapter 24 stands in dramatic contrast to the feast of God on his holy mountain in chapter 25. The death which seems to reign supreme in 24 is replaced by the dramatic promise in 25 that God will remove the shroud of death from *all* faces. This is not a promise of universal salvation, but the promise that life will not only be available to Israel, but to all persons. Thus the songs of the ruthless (25:5) are replaced by the song of salvation (26:1) and the fading songs of the drunkards (24:7–11) are replaced by the song of the Lord's vineyard (27:3–6), a vineyard that will fill the whole of that earth (27:6) that had been destroyed by its own folly (24:1–6). The ruthless, arrogant city (26:5) which has been brought down to the ground (24:10, 12; 25:12; 26:5–6) is replaced by the city of God (26:1) whose walls are the deliverance of God. Finally, the ruthless nations (25:3) are contrasted with the righteous nation (26:1).

But there is even a larger contrast at work here, and this is between chapters 24–25 and chapters 26–27. The first pair focus on the destruction of Earth City and the ensuing Feast of God. That city is brought down and the Mountain of God is exalted to the place of supremacy (25:1–6). In chapter 25 all the earth is invited to a scene that is dramatically different from the one just observed in 24. There the vintage had failed and all joy had flown away (24:7–11). Nothing was to be found there but desolation and emptiness. Here the wine cellars are full to overflowing. There is no need to drink the raw new wine. There is plenty of well-aged wine available (25:6). There is abundance on every side. Here there is no stringy tough meat from starved animals; rather, the animals from which this meat has come were fat and well-fed.

When we see that chapter 25 is explicitly paired with chapter 24 in this way, we are helped to understand the final verses of chapter 25 in which Moab is used as a graphic illustration of the point being made (as Edom is also used in chapter 34). After the joyous feast and the promise of the final defeat of death, the gruesome depiction of God pushing the floundering Moab down into a manure pile seems inexplicable (25:10–12) and many commentators treat it as simply an unfortunate insertion expressive of a

---

Arnold (Grand Rapids: Baker, 1999) 369–90.

particularly repugnant form of Israelite chauvinism. But if we understand chapters 24 and 25 as a pair, this strophe becomes understandable. Throughout the book the author or editor is at pains never to allow a promise of the future to blur present realities. The good hope must not be allowed to cause the hearer to overlook present hard choices.[3] This is what is happening in 25:10–12. Does God wish to destroy the world in its sin? Not at all. As Ezekiel was to say, God takes no joy in the death of the wicked (Ezek. 18:23; 33:11). Thus, the announcement of the destruction of the earth (chap. 24) is followed by the promise that God is preparing a feast of new life for all nations (25:1–9). But what does that promise mean? Does it mean that humans can continue to exalt themselves, to build up their fortifications of pride, and to do it all with impunity, because God is going to make everything turn out well in the end. Not at all. Isaiah is at pains to remind us that Earth City *is* going to be destroyed, that its mighty walls are going to be leveled, and that only those who adopt a lifestyle that acknowledges Yahweh's sole Lordship are going to be participants at the Great Feast. God will exalt his mountain but "Your high-walled fortress he will throw down, lay low, bring it down to the earth, even to the dust" (25:12).

If chapters 24 and 25 are thus primarily about the destruction of Earth City and its aftermath, chapters 26 and 27 are primarily about the establishment of God City as a result of his ability alone. As in the first pairing, the second chapter is a reflection on the first. But in the case of chapter 27 it is not so much in contrast to its predecessor as it is a development of the preceding chapter's themes. Earth City was confident in itself and thus was destroyed. God City is the product of the delivering grace of God and can only continue to exist and be the city of God insofar as it trusts in him to give it life. Thus, chapter 26 has two main sections: verses 1–6 and 7–21. The first section lays out the foundation of trust in God upon which the city exists (vv. 1–4) as opposed to the self-sufficient arrogance upon which the "lofty city" had depended (vv. 5–6). Then the remainder of the chapter (vv. 7–21) is a meditation on what it means to be the people of God in the world. It in turn is also composed of two parts. In the first (vv. 7–18), the prophet seems to be speaking for the people, particularly the righteous element of the people, and is reflecting on the implications of what he has just

---

3. This feature appears as early as chapter 1 where the promises of vv. 24–27 are followed by a grim prediction of the fate of the unrepentant in vv. 28–31. On a larger plane this is what is happening in the entire section of chapters 1–5. As mentioned above, there are wonderful promises of future ministry (2:1–5) and future restoration to pure fellowship of God (4:2–6) contained here. But the section ends with chapter 5 and its stern announcement of the imminent destruction of God's vineyard. Isaiah is simply not going to allow his hearers to "dodge" the responsibility for their present choices

said. There are three components in the peoples' thought. First, God has established the way of righteousness, and his righteous people have been waiting for him to vindicate that way, while they walk upon it. Yet that vindication seems not to have happened; the wicked go right on (vv. 7–10). Second, the people do not attribute this failure to God. It is not his fault; his truth will triumph in the nations, and those who have arrogantly dominated his people have already been destroyed (vv. 11–15). Third, this victory is not in any sense the doing of the people themselves. They cannot deliver themselves, let alone the world (vv. 16–18). All of this provokes a response from God (vv. 19–21). He himself will accomplish his good purposes in them. He will deliver them from the power of death (v. 19) and will punish an arrogant earth which sought to enforce its dominance by wielding the power of death (vv. 20–21).

Chapter 27 fleshes out this response. It is composed of four segments: vv. 1–2; vv. 3–6; vv. 7–11; and vv. 12–13. They have in common the mighty, delivering power of Yahweh. The first expresses this power through an allusion to the Canaanite myth in which Baal was supposed to have subdued the god of the sea ("Leviathan") who is synonymous with chaos. Isaiah says that this victory was Yahweh's.[4]

In the second segment (vv. 3–6) Yahweh says that Israel is his vineyard and that he will go to great lengths to defend it so that someday it may spread out to cover the earth. One cannot help but contrast these statements with those in chapter 5 where the wild animals are called in to devour and trample the Lord's vineyard that can only produce bitter grapes. And that thought leads straight into the third segment. If God loves his "city," his vineyard, so much why has he allowed such terrible things to happen to it? In vv. 7–11 God protests that his own people have not been treated nearly as severely as those who have attacked them. Those nations that thought they were able to destroy Samaria and Jerusalem merely because of their superior strength and fighting ability were sadly mistaken. Jacob will respond to its punishment with repentance and a new absolute loyalty to Yahweh (11). But the "fortified city" of the oppressors, secure in its pride, will become a wasteland. For those arrogant and unrepentant nations, there will not be the grace and compassion that there would be for repentant Israel.

4. To say as some do that this points to an original Hebrew version of the widespread myth of cosmic origins seems very odd when we consider what book this statement occurs in. While all the Biblical books espouse a worldview that is diametrically opposed to the world view of paganism, the book of Isaiah is the most vociferous in its arguing for that view. To use the language of myth does not in any way argue for an adoption of the thought patterns behind it. For a modern person to say of a strong man, "He is a veritable Hercules" cannot be taken as evidence that the speaker is an exponent of Greek mythical thinking.

This thought leads to the final segment, vv. 12–13. The nations will be chaff on God's threshing floor, blown away on the wind. But Israel will fall back to earth like the good grain, and they "will come and worship the Lord on the holy mountain in Jerusalem."

When we come to sum up the message and content of these four chapters that have been here labeled "Songs in the Night," the modern classic *The Lord of the Rings*, now made even more popular by the successful movie series, comes to mind. There are the two cities, Minas Tirith and Cirith Ungol, facing each other across the valley of the Anduin. The first symbolizes all that is fair and hopeful in the world and the second all that is sinister and terrible. That is the picture here. There are two cities, cities that are different in their causes for joy, their causes for triumph, and their eventual outcomes. In this stark contrast the prophet is slicing through the complexities of life and calling us to face squarely which city we are a resident of. Where is our trust and where is the source of our songs? In Earth City joy springs from alcohol and dominion. If the alcohol dries up and the chance to dominate others disappears, there is nothing but gloom. In God City joy springs from the presence of God that guarantees deliverance and protection. And for the Christian that guarantee takes on new poignancy when we hear the Savior say, "I will never leave you nor forsake you."

In Earth City triumph is secured through assiduous self-exaltation and the application of ruthless power. In God City triumph is found in that self-denial which issues in a trust in divine grace and mercy. It lies in the admission that in ourselves we can neither defeat nor deliver the world and in the confidence that the Creator of the world can indeed break its power and save its life. Earth City has the power of death, but God City has the power of life. And because Earth City's only power is to kill, the only outcome it can look forward to is that of desolation, loss and death. God City, on the other hand, inhabited by the power of life, can offer endless abundance and everlasting life.

Thus, the prophet, here at the center of the long section on trust in God, has called his first hearers and every hearer since to step back and take a look at the central issues. Yes, it is true that all the nations are under the judgment of Israel's God (chaps. 13–23) and yes, it is true that to repose ones confidence in flesh and blood and military strength instead of God is simply folly (chaps. 28–35), but there are more foundational issues than even those. And those larger, deeper, wider issues are laid out for us here in chapters 24–27. What are they? The prophet has presented them in glaring contrasts. When we face the issues of life, our neediness, our fragility, the threats that are posed day after day, whether physical, psychological or spiritual, on what basis shall we decide what to do? Isaiah tells us we must always decide on these grounds:

The fallibility of creation and the infallibility of the Creator,

The untrustworthiness of humanity and the trustworthiness of the God revealed in Scripture,

The falsity of human pride and the truth of divine humility,

The joy of surrender and the bitterness of domination.

But there is something more, something that underlies even these. And that something more is revealed in the final verse of the unit: "[they] will come and worship [prostrate themselves before] the Lord in the holy mountain at Jerusalem" (27:13). Finally the life of trust can never be merely an intellectual exercise, one in which we coolly weigh the alternatives and calmly choose the better option. That is not possible for fallen humans. We will always be "blind-sided" by our instinctive hatred of everything and anything that smacks of submission. We will always find excellent reasons for doing what will exalt ourselves and seem to put us in control of our destiny. No, before the wisdom of trust can penetrate our cognitive faculties, something else will have to happen—we must be moved to worship. Until that happens, those faculties are notably capable of amazing folly. John Wesley said, "If a man will not believe the Bible, he will believe anything. Why, he may believe a man can be put into a quart bottle."[5] And G. K. Chesterton said, "It's the first effect of not believing in God that you lose your common sense, and can't see things as they are."[6] Both these men are reflecting the same truth the Apostle Paul expressed in Romans 1. It is because we as humans have refused to give God his rightful place of worship that we are unable to think straight about the meaning of life.

So Isaiah says that it is in prostrate worship that we can sing in the night. When we have come to the end of ourselves and know that there is no other hope for us or for our world (26:7–18), then there is reason to trust. And indeed, there is no other basis for song. All the others are based on what is temporary: substance abuse (24:7–13); human ability (25:10–12; 26:5–6); or creation (24:21–23). God alone has eternal strength (26:5). So the deliverance he offers has nothing of the temporary about it. He can bring not only temporal deliverance, he can bring eternal life, and that for people of every nation. Here is reason for song.

---

5. *The Works of John Wesley*, 3rd ed., 14 vols. (Grand Rapids: Baker, 1979) 13:407–8.

6. G. K. Chesterton, "The Oracle of the Dog," in *The Man Who Was Chesterton: The Best Essays, Stories, Poems and Other Writings of G. K. Chesterton*, ed. R. T. Bond (Freeport, NY: Books for Libraries Press, 1970) 331.

12

Isaiah 52:13—53:12
Servant of All[1]

IN EARLIER CHAPTERS I wrote at some length about the structure of the first 39 chapters of Isaiah. I do not propose to duplicate that here. However, for the purposes of this chapter let me recap two important points and recast them slightly. I have argued that chapter 6, the prophet's call, should be read together with chapters 1–5 as providing a solution to the dilemma that those chapters pose. That dilemma is that whereas 1:1–31; 2:6–4:1 and 5:1–30 depict Israel as corrupted, diseased, and hypocritical, 2:1–5 and 4:2–6 declare that the nation will become the pure light to the nations. How can this be? I suggest that the prophet presents his own experience as the paradigm for what could happen to the nation to enable them to become what is promised. Just as Isaiah became God's "servant" for Israel (cf. 20:3), so Israel can become God's servant for the nations. Although the term "servant" is not used in chapters 1–6 (indeed, it only appears 4 times in the first 39 chapters: 20:3; 22:20; 24:2; 37:35), I believe that in the light of the second part of the book, and that second part's use of "servant" in reference to Israel, it is appropriate to understand that what is taking place in chapters 1–6 is indeed a call to servanthood, both for the prophet (cf. 20:3) and for the nation.[2]

---

1. This material appeared in substantially the same form and under the same title in the *Calvin Theological Journal* 40 (2005) 85–94 and appears here with permission.

2. This fact that the second part of the book, so-called Second Isaiah, uses "servant" so regularly in reference to Israel while the first part (First Isaiah) does not seems to me to argue against H. G. M. Williamson's thesis that the author of Second Isaiah is really the author/editor of the first part as well (*The Book Called Isaiah* [Oxford: Clarendon, 1994]). It is difficult to believe that if this person exercised such a decisive role

As mentioned in the earlier chapter, what follows this call to servanthood is a reprise of 6:1–5 on a national scale. Israel is given a revelation of "The Holy One of Israel" and of itself that is analogous to the revelation that Isaiah experienced. In chapters 7–39 they are allowed to experience both the greatness and the goodness that comprise the holiness of God, and they are provoked to see how deep their own sinfulness goes. This revelation revolves around the concept of trust: the trustworthiness of God and their own sinful refusal to trust him in the face of the challenges to that trust. Not only do the specific terms related to trust appear at crucial points,[3] but even in the absence of the terms themselves, the issue is unmistakable. In the end, in chapters 36–39, it first seems that Hezekiah, facing a far worse crisis than his father had faced, has learned the lesson. He does trust God, and is delivered from Assyria (36–37). But when an opportunity occurs to declare God's grace and glory to the Babylonians, to begin to fulfill Israel's mission to the nations (2:1–5), Hezekiah fumbles that opportunity and instead takes it as an occasion to boast about his own accomplishments (38–39). In doing this, Hezekiah demonstrates two things: trust is not a one-time action, but must be a way of living, and the hope of Israel was not in any mere human, even if he were among the best examples of what humans could be. Because Judah as well would not learn these lessons, the exile became an inevitability.

Looked at from the perspective of servanthood, chapters 7–39 are dealing with the first prerequisite for any servant: trust. They are also a revelation of the transcendent holiness of God and the deep sinfulness of Israel. As Isaiah saw in the experience narrated in chapter 6, the only reasonable outcome of such a dramatic contrast is the destruction of the sinful one. But that was not God's intent for either Isaiah or Israel. Instead, he intended to use the fire of judgment to cleanse and purify his servants (6:7; cf. 4:4). That realization helps us to understand the function of chapters 40–55 in the present structure of the book. These chapters are addressed to the Judean exiles in Babylon in the years between the destruction of Jerusalem in 586 B.C. and the return to Judah in 539 or 538 B.C. They are answering two questions that Isaiah[4] knows will be uppermost in the exiles' minds. The

---

in the shaping and content of the book that this favorite concept of his would not have intruded itself into chapters 1–39. On the other hand, if the person who wrote the first part also wrote the second part, it is possible to explain the difference on the basis of an evolving understanding.

3 *baṭaḥ* 12:2; 26:3–4, 30:12; 31:1; 32:9, 10, 11; 36:4, 5, 6, 7, 9, 15; 37:10; *ḥakâ* 8:17; 30:18, 2t.; *qawâ* 8:17; 25:9; 26:8.

4.. I am convinced (with many others) that those who compiled the book as it now stands want us the readers to believe that all of the material in the book stems originally from the Isaiah ben-Amoz identified in 1:1 and 2:1. But is that a fact, or are we being misled? If we are being misled, on what basis can we maintain that the revelation of God

first is, "Have not the Babylonian gods defeated Yahweh?" or if not, then the second question arises, "Have not our sins defeated him?" If the answer to either question is "yes," then the exile spells the end for Israel and the end of the promises of God addressed to Israel.[5]

But these chapters are answering both questions with a resounding "no." Instead, they call upon the exiles not to lose faith, but to continue to trust in a gracious deliverance from the "fire" in which they would then find themselves. To retain that faith would not be easy, since, as far as the record goes, no one had ever returned home from exile before. Nevertheless, this is precisely what Isaiah promises. So chapters 40–48, utilizing a series of court cases in which God conclusively demonstrates his superiority over the Babylonian idol-gods, conclude that there is no reason why God could not deliver his people from the Babylonian grip. The striking thing about these several presentations of the case is that Jacob/Israel is said again and again to be the "chosen servants" of Yahweh who, far from being cast off for their sin, are to be the chief witnesses for Yahweh's unchallengeable superiority. What is being revealed here is the nearly incredible grace of God. And this grace becomes the motivation to engage in the trust called for in the preceding division (chaps. 7–39). This is analogous to Isaiah's experience when the recognition that he was not only alive, but possessed of clean lips led him to volunteer himself in service to God. He was motivated to entrust himself to God because of the evidence of God's grace.

But Israel's primary problem was not physical captivity. The much more serious problem was the alienation from God that their sin had produced. How could God, the Holy One, use sinful Israel as his servants? He could not simply ignore the fact of their sin and still be the just judge of the universe. If Israel were restored to the land, and yet were not restored to God that would be no solution to their problem at all. In other words, grace might be the motivation for sinful people to want to be the servants of God,

---

contained in this misleading document is true? On the other hand, if we are not being misled we are constrained to believe that Isaiah ben-Amoz spoke the words of chapters 40–66 to persons 150–200 years later than he lived. To many this seems preposterous. Thus Brevard S. Childs opines that to adopt such a view is to believe in "clairvoyance" (*Isaiah*, OTL [Louisville: Westminster John Knox, 2001] 3–4). But this is to take an insufficient account of the entire argument of chapters 41–48 which explicitly claim that what differentiates God from the gods is his ability to reveal the specifics of the future to his prophets (cf. 41:21–29; 43:8–13; etc.). What is being claimed is much more than a bit of clairvoyance. Furthermore, if we deny that God can do such a thing, what becomes of the argument for God's superiority?

5. Had the book ended with what is now chapter 39, the validity of the earlier revelations would have been called into question. "Yes, God could deliver from Assyria; but he couldn't deliver from Babylon, could he?" Thus in some sense the materials now in chaps. 40–66 were necessitated by the very breadth of the vision in chaps. 1–39.

but what would enable them to actually become such people? The answer to this question is the same as that to the former one: grace. Thus chapters 49–55 reveal a further dimension of God's grace; not only did his election love provide a motive for servanthood, it also provided the means. Thus the chapters no longer deal with the problem of captivity in Babylon. While deliverance language continues to be used, Babylon is never mentioned. Rather, the problem is how to restore the people to God. The answer is grace and the means of applying that grace is the Servant.

When we examine chapters 40–55 we discover that the term "servant" occurs with considerable frequency, 21 times in all.[6] Furthermore, when we examine these occurrences, we discover that two different servants are being spoken of. One of the servants is defined as blind, deaf, and rebellious. The major focus is upon the benefits this servant will receive from God. His only role is to be a witness to God's saving power. In all the places where this servant is identified, he is said to be Jacob/Israel. The second of the servants is described differently. He is responsive and obedient to God. Instead of the benefits accruing to him, the terrible price of his servanthood is detailed. Despite the fact that this servant is once named "Israel" (49:3), there is no question of this servant being the nation, because it is twice said that his role is to restore the nation to God (42:6; 49:6; cf. also 49:8–12).

When the references to these two servants are examined a striking fact emerges. In chapters 40–48 all the references except one (42:1) are to the first servant, the nation. In chapters 49–55 the situation is exactly reversed. Here all the references but one (54:17) are to the servant who suffers in order to bring Yahweh's people back to himself and bring his *mišpaṭ*, his justice, judgment, order, to the nations. This fact accords very well with the understanding of the two parts of the division being set forth here. In 40–48 God is trying to convince Israel that they are his chosen servants and that he is going to deliver them from captivity as he had promised through his prophets, thus becoming themselves the evidence of his sole Godhood. In chapters 49–55 God is dealing with the question that the promises in 40–48 raise, namely, how can a just and holy God use sinful Israel as his servants? The answer is that he will do so by means of an ideal Servant who will be the Israel that Israel had never yet been capable of being. This ideal Servant is introduced in chapter 42 simply so that the grace being promised in that section (they are not cast off, they are his servants, 41:8–9; 44:1–2, etc.) is made more explicable. Then in 54:17, the nation is reintroduced in that

---

6. 41:8, 9; 42:1, 19 (2 t.); 43:10; 44:1, 2, 21 (2 t.), 26; 45:4; 48:20; 49:3, 5, 6, 7; 50:10; 52:13; 53:11; 54:17.

section focusing on the Servant to remind the reader what the Servant's ministry is all in aid of.

When we look at the structure of chapters 49–55, there are pretty clearly three sub-sections. They are 49:1—52:12; 52:13—53:12; and 54:1—55:13. In the first subsection there is a movement from doubt to anticipation. The theme of "comfort" reappears from 40:1–2 for the first time in 49:13 in a song of praise which is clearly in response to the revelation of the Servant and his work in 49:1–12. How will the encouragement and strengthening promised to the people in chapter 40 be realized? It will be realized through the ministry of the Servant. But the reaction of the people is doubt: "But Zion said, 'The Lord has forsaken me; my Lord has forgotten me'" (49:14). The exiles will be convinced that God has rejected them and abandoned them because of their sin. But beginning in 49:15 God assures them again and again that this is not the case. Thus, from this point on until 52:12 the anticipation of restoration to God's favor steadily mounts. In various ways God assures them through the prophet that he has not rejected them. He says that he has not divorced their mother and has not sold them into slavery (50:1) and he urges them to listen to the voice of the Servant who is humbly obedient to God (50:10). Finally, they are ready to believe that God might take them back to himself, and call for the "arm of the Lord" to awake and bring the redeemed home (51:9–11). God responds by calling on Jerusalem/Zion to wake up herself (51:17; 52:1) and prepare for the spiritual deliverance that is coming. Finally, 52:9–10 seems to reach a joyous climax in which the work of God in restoration is seen as having been accomplished:

> Break forth together into singing,
>   you waste places of Jerusalem,
> for the Lord has comforted his people,
>   he has redeemed Jerusalem.
> The Lord has bared his holy arm,
>   before the eyes of all the nations,
> and all the ends of the earth
>   shall see the salvation of our God.

When we then look at chapters 54 and 55 we see recurring invitations to take part in this finished deliverance. People are called upon to avail themselves of all that God has done. They are invited to sing like a childless woman who discovers she is not childless at all (54:1–4), or a wife who thought she was abandoned and discovers it is not so (54:5–8). 54:10 says that God's *hesed* and compassion are theirs forever. Chapter 55 continues this note of invitation, where people are challenged not to hold back but to take advantage of everything God is making available to them, including the everlasting covenant of David. Clearly something pivotal has occurred to change the atmosphere from one of anticipation to one of invitation. What is that pivotal something? It is the material occurring between 52:12 and 54:1. That material, of course, is the last of four revelations of the character and work of the Servant. What makes it possible for God to offer free forgiveness and full restoration to a people who at the beginning of the book are described as diseased with sin and addicted to rebellion? Is it that they have bitterly repented and vowed to "clean up their act"? As a matter of fact there is hardly any of that in chapters 40–55. And if they had, what would that have accomplished? Whatever they might vow to do in the future, and supposing they did it without defect, the fact of their past sin could not simply be ignored by a God in whom justice is an inescapable facet of his holiness. In fact, what they are called upon to do is to receive by faith what God has done for them and not to succumb to the doubt and despair that would say that God can never be reconciled to them.

But how can God be reconciled to them? By what means can his justice be satisfied and the invitations of chapters 54 and 55 be issued? Clearly, that means is what the Servant has done or will do, as recorded in 52:13—53:12. It is this that makes free grace available to Israel and to the world. But who is this ideal Servant? If he is not Israel, since Israel can never restore itself to God, is it not the anonymous prophet (so-called "Second Isaiah") who supposedly spoke and wrote what are now chapters 40–55? Recently this idea has been promoted in the work of Whybray[7] and others. Thus, the prophet was unfairly punished for the very sins he accused his people of committing. Childs, who accepts the existence of "Second Isaiah," nonetheless comments that "this bland and even superficial understanding of the passage serves as a major indictment of [Whybray's] conclusions."[8]

Two elements in the text support Childs' conclusion that the text is not thinking of the prophet (or indeed any other human). First, in 52:13 the Servant is said to be "high and lifted up" (*yarûm wenissa'*). This combination of terms appears in two other places in the book: 6:1 and 57:15. In both places it is a description of the one holy God. To think that it is here applied to a human is insupportable. The second piece of evidence is that this person

---

7. R. N. Whybray, *Thanksgiving for a Liberated Prophet. An Interpretation of Isaiah Chapter 53*, JSOTSup 4 (Sheffield: JSOT Press, 1978).

8. Childs, *Isaiah*, 415. However, when Childs is asked who the prophet did have in mind, he is very difficult to pin down. Interestingly, he insists that "the servant of Second Isaiah is linked dogmatically to Jesus Christ primarily in terms of its ontology" (423), by which I take it that he means they are both serving the same function. In saying this in this way he seems to be attempting to avoid the charge that he thinks Isaiah 53 "predicts" Christ.

is called "the arm of the Lord" (53:1). As mentioned above, this phrase or its synonyms appears several times in 49:1–52:12 as a metaphor for God's mighty power to restore his people to himself (50:2; 51:5, 9, 16; 52:10). To equate a human who suffers unfairly with that mighty arm is unthinkable. Thus, whoever this person is, he is not merely a human. He is not suffering because Israel has sinned. He is suffering in order to deliver them from the consequences of their sin. He is suffering so that Israel (and the world, cf. 51:4–8) may be justified in God's sight and share his righteousness. This person will be, at one and the same time, a revelation of divine glory and of divine weakness, of divine grace and divine justice. Who else has ever filled that picture except Jesus Christ?

When we look at the structure of the poem we see five stanzas of three verses each. Each stanza reveals a different facet of the gem that is the Savior. In 52:13–15 he is exalted, but shocking; in 53:1–3 he is rejected and despised; in 53:4–6 he suffers for sinners ("us"); in 53:7–9 his ministry is unrecognized and he is treated unjustly; in 53:10–12 he is the sacrificial victor. In this regard we see the destiny of servanthood, the results of servanthood, the burden of servanthood, the outcome of servanthood and the goal of servanthood.

The destiny of the Servant is triumph. The segment opens (52:13) and closes (53:12) on that note. The Servant is sure to succeed[9]; there is no question of the final success of his ministry. He will triumph and will sit in the place of God. This of course accords exactly with what is said of Christ in Philippians 2:9–11 and in the Revelation 5:5–6. It is in striking contrast to the King of Babylon who sought in his arrogance to storm heaven and place himself on the throne of God (Isaiah 14:12–15). It is also in contrast to Lady Babylon who is told to get off the throne and sit in the dust (47:1). Likewise, after his rejection and his suffering, he "will divide the spoil with the strong" (53:12). That is, far from being vanquished, he will play the part of the victor. All of this is in confirmation of the counter-intuitive wisdom of the Bible: the way up is down.

Surely it was this consciousness of the ultimate success of his efforts that made it possible for the Servant to take the lowest place, to brave the scorn, and even worse, the dismissal of the very ones he came to serve. He knew who he was, he did not have to prove anything to himself, and thus he could lay aside the robes of royalty and assume the towel of a servant (John 13:3–5, 12–17). It is only those who do not know who they are and what their destiny is who must puff themselves up and lord it over others.

9. The Heb. verb *sakal* is often translated as "to be wise" or "to prosper." But behind both those meanings is the idea of being effective, or succeeding. That is surely the sense here in 52:13.

But that awareness will certainly be tested, as is immediately made apparent in both the first and last stanzas of the poem. The reader is left in no doubt that the Servant's exalted status is not the result of any of the things earth would build status upon. Above all, it is not based on appearance, for his appearance is not attractive but disgusting (52:14, see also 53:2b).[10] While there is probably a literal element here (Christians have typically referred it to the evidences of torture that Christ bore on the Cross), the main connotation is probably metaphorical. The Servant has none of the outward accoutrements of power, position, and success. People will not be attracted to him for superficial reasons. Instead, they will be shocked by his lack of all these things (52:15).[11] It is simply unheard of from a human perspective that strength should be achieved through weakness, or that victory should be achieved through being killed (53:12).

But not only is such a situation shocking, it is also off-putting. The person who adopts such a posture must expect not merely dismissal (53:3), but outright rejection. Humans do not want to ally themselves with someone they perceive to be a "loser." Everybody loves a winner, and we circle around them as though some of that aura might rub off on us. The incredible power of a beautiful girl in high school or college is the stuff of novels. She can have whatever she pleases because there will be a crowd of both boys and girls around her to do whatever she wants. On the other hand, the person in this poem is hardly to be noticed. He is like a tiny plant growing in dry soil. He does not call attention to himself by shooting up like the legendary bean-stalk. It is hard to tell if he is growing at all. Why should anyone take notice of him?

But it is not merely what his appearance does not have that is so astonishing. It is also what it does have. He is sickly and ill. Some interpreters imagine that the person being described is a leper.[12] But again, I suspect that the primary connotation is metaphorical. This Servant, as later verses will show, has taken on himself the sin-sickness of humanity. All the grief, all the sorrow, all the diseased relationships, all the disease that sin has brought to

---

10. 52:14 says that many were astonished at "you" and then that "his" appearance was marred. To resolve this apparent contradiction translators either emend the first to "him" (cf. NIV) or supply "my people" after "you" (cf. NASB). Neither is necessary; this kind of pronoun shifting occurs regularly in the prophets. Probably both pronouns refer here to the Servant. For a discussion of this problem in the poem as a whole, see D. J. A. Clines, *I, He, We, and They: A Literary Approach to Isaiah 53*, JSOTSup 1 (Sheffield: JSOT Press, 1976).

11. For a discussion of the probability that "startle" is the correct reading in 52:15 instead of "sprinkle," see Oswalt *The Book of Isaiah, Chapters 40–66*, NICOT (Grand Rapids: Eerdmans, 1998) 374 n. 56.

12. The thought goes as far back as the Talmud (*Sanhedrin* 98a).

the human race, as typified by Judah, he has taken into himself. Who wants to look at that? Who wants to ally himself with that? No, much better just to look the other way and hope the apparition will go away.

Added to this distaste for the appearance and demeanor of the Servant is the instinctive realization that his condition is actually ours. We would like to say that he has brought his troubles on himself. Perhaps he has not been careful enough, or not self-protective enough. Really, we imagine, he has brought it all on himself. Indeed, God has brought on him the consequences of his own foolish choices (53:4). But it will not do. He has not deserved what has befallen him. His burden is really our burden, and that makes us all the more unwilling to look at him or acknowledge him, because we know that it is because of us that he is in this condition. The hammering recurrence of the first person plural pronouns throughout verses 4–6 leaves no doubt on this score. And it is not just that he is suffering because we have sinned. He is suffering *for* our sin; he is *carrying* our sins (cf. 2 Cor. 5:21, "He made Him who knew no sin to be sin on our behalf, that we might become the righteousness of God in Him." [NASB]). There is a shocking causal sequence here: we sinned–he was beaten–we were healed. In other words, the suffering of the Servant is the effective cause of our restoration to favor with God. Brevard Childs has said it well, "What occurred was not some unfortunate tragedy of human history but actually formed the center of the divine plan for the redemption of his people and indeed of the world."[13]

The contrasting comparison to sheep is instructive in this regard (6–7). Both "we" and the Servant are compared to sheep, but the characteristics of sheep that the two parties manifest are radically different. In "us" it is that stubborn, short-sighted determination to eat the next clump of grass without regard to where we have come from or where we are going. In him it is that mild, defenseless, utterly collapsed surrender to the shearer. We are of the same nature and yet in him that nature is transformed into something almost utterly different from anything we know. Not only has he taken what we were upon himself, he has also shown us the way to what we might become.

If the destiny of the Servant is triumph while the immediate results are astonishment and rejection, and if the burden of the Servant is the sins and sorrows of others, what is the outcome of his Servanthood? In the short term, the outcome of Servanthood is not pleasant, and all those who would follow in his footsteps must prepare themselves for the same (cf. John 15:18–21). Those outcomes are detailed in verses 7–9. They include oppression and affliction (7). They also include (unjust) judgment (8). But much

---

13. Childs, *Isaiah*, 415.

more seriously, verse 8 seems to suggest that he was killed when he had no children. Particularly in the Near East, this would be the worst possible outcome; it was to be as if you had never lived.[14] This would be the crowning injustice. But to add insult to injustice, the Servant is not even permitted to be buried with the humble poor whom he loved. Instead, he is buried with the wicked rich. This might be the greatest irony of all.[15] What this says is that no one should adopt the stance of servanthood because of its short-term outcomes. Given the nature of humanity, no one should think that if he lays his life down for others he will not be walked on. If we expect to be honored for our servitude, we will be sorely disappointed. That is exactly the point Jesus was trying to make in the passage from John 15 cited above. The disciples expected that being "servants" of the King would mean wealth, honor, and power. But in this world those are not the outcomes of service to this King. But how was it possible for the Servant to do this, and how is it possible for the servants of the Servant to do it? It was possible because he left the ultimate outcome of his service in the hands of his Father, and so we must do as well.

And what is this service all about? Already in verse 5 above it has been intimated what the goal is. But verses 10–12 underline it with a force that makes it unmistakable. The goal of the Servant's ministry is nothing other than the justification of the unrighteous (11). And he will accomplish that goal by *bearing* their iniquities (11) and their sins (12). He is not suffering *for* them; he is suffering *as* them. This explains what is surely one of the most terrible verses in all of Scripture. That is verse 10. Many of us are familiar enough with it that we do not see its horror. Literally, the opening line says, "Crushing him made the Lord happy." What? Are we to think that the Creator of the Universe is a sadist? Would any but a deranged parent be glad to see his child crushed under the wheels of a hurtling tractor-trailer? What is going on here? The point is found in the rest of the verse. What is procured because the Servant has been crushed? Suppose ones son or daughter had died in the successful effort to break the door down so a hundred school children could escape from a burning building. Would that be a source of legitimate gladness for a parent even in the midst of wracking grief? Of course it would. And so it is here. "When you make his soul an offering for sin, he

---

14. For a discussion of the numerous interpretive problems in this verse, see Oswalt, *Isaiah, Chapters 40–66*, 392–96.

15. The attempts of various commentators and translators to keep this passage from being a judgment on the rich are misguided (cf. NASB). The OT is very ambivalent about riches. If one has them as a gift from God, then they are a blessing. But most riches are not from God at all; they are simply the result of oppression and injustice. For the two points of view, see Prov 22:4 and 16.

will see seed and prolong days, and the gladness of the Lord will be realized at his hand." If humans will appropriate his offering of himself for their sins,[16] then he *will* have children and he *will* know the blessing of long life and he *will* achieve what the Lord was hoping for from his ministry. Verse 11 suggests an analogy with a woman who has delivered a whole and healthy baby. Was the process of giving birth arduous and painful? No woman who has done so will say it was not! Was it something no one would choose to go through for itself? Of course! But was it worth it? It is hard to imagine any woman saying otherwise. So it is with the Lord and his Servant. If the pain, the suffering, the dismissal, the rejection and even the death would result in justification for the iniquitous and forgiveness for the transgressors, that result would mean victory had been achieved and both would say, "It was worth it all."

In this chapter I have tried to root the fourth of the so-called "Suffering Servant" songs decisively in its context in the book of Isaiah. Too often interpreters on both the right and the left have treated it as a "sport," something unique, emerging from nowhere, and disappearing again without making a recognizable difference in its surroundings. But that is decidedly not the case. Isaiah 52:13—53:12 is an intrinsic part of what is being said in chapters 40–55, but equally so in the book as a whole. How can God use sinful Israel to be a light to the nations? He cannot unless some way can be found to purge them from their sins. But if they suffer for their own sins as they deserve, they will all die and disappear and their mission will die with them, for "the soul that sins shall die" (Ezek. 16:20). So obviously some other way must be found; God must bare his mighty arm on their behalf and do for them what they cannot do for themselves. That is what this wonderful and mysterious chapter is about. It is about the Servant who in a way not fully explained here is able to take all the death of not merely Judah and Jerusalem, but of all the race upon himself and set us free. Glory to his name!

---

16. Because of a possible Pelagian taint to the phrase "If you [my hearers] make his soul an offering for sin," commentators and translators have struggled to make the phrase say something else. The NIV reads "If" as "Though" and emends "you" to "the Lord," but without ms. evidence. NASB has "If He would render Himself as a guilt offering" but again without ms. evidence. NKJV capitalizes "You" to make it refer to God. But if it were not for the theological discomfort raised by the plain sense of the passage, none of these alternatives would suggest themselves. In fact, there need be no discomfort. This is no different than St. Paul's statement, "If you confess with your mouth, 'Jesus is Lord' and believe in your heart that God raised him from the dead, you shall be saved" (Rom. 10:9). All that is being said in both passages is that there must be a human response to the divine initiative (it being understood that even that response is enabled by God).

13

Isaiah 60–62
The Glory of the Lord[1]

IN THE TWO PRECEDING chapters (as well as chapters 1 and 2) I have suggested that Isaiah presented his experience as recorded in chapter 6 of his book as the paradigm for his people. Just as the man of unclean lips was enabled to speak the Lord's message to his nation, so the nation of unclean lips would be enabled to speak his message to the nations. In chapters 7–39 the nation is given a vision of the Lord and of his holiness, particularly as evidenced in his trustworthiness. At the same time the nation is given a vision of itself, a nation that seems chronically unable to trust God and is instead seduced by the glory of the nations into trusting them. An example of this fact is given in chapters 38–39 where Hezekiah, after having been miraculously healed by God, misses an opportunity to give glory to God (cf. 6:3) and instead uses the occasion to boast of his accomplishments to the Babylonians.

So what will motivate the people to trust God, and even further, enable them to actually become the servants of God he says they are? Strangely enough, the exile was to be that motivation and means as God's grace was manifested to them through it and in spite of it. Just as Isaiah had experienced the fiery grace of God when the coal touched his lips, so the nation of Israel would experience the grace of God in the fires of the exile (cf. 4:4–6). In chapters 40–48 God establishes that the exile is not a sign either of his rejection of Israel or of his defeat by the Babylonian gods. Instead, he will

---

1. This material appeared in substantially the same form and with the same title in the *Calvin Theological Journal* 40 (2005) 95–103, and appears here with permission.

use Israel as the evidence that he alone is God. He will do this by means of predictive prophecy. First of all, he will graciously use Israel, in spite of their previous sin, as his witnesses that he had long before specifically predicted not only the exile, but also the return from exile. This was something none of the idol gods, being merely personified cosmic forces, could do. The first part of the prophecy having occurred, God would then carry out the second part and do something that had never occurred before; he would graciously deliver his people from their captivity, using a Persian emperor whom he had had the audacity to name in advance, as his appointed servant. Surely grace like this should motivate a people to entrust themselves to God as his servants.

However, there is still a problem. What about the sins of the past that landed Israel in exile? Will God simply ignore them, acting as though they had never happened? How can the love between Yahweh the groom and Israel the bride be restored, when all those offenses stand between them? Can a just God who has made a world of cause and effect simply suspend cause and effect on a whim?[2] As we stated at length in the previous chapter, the way to that reconciliation, to the satisfaction of divine justice is the Servant, the One who would give his life to carry away the sins of the world. It is for this reason that chapters 54 and 55 are full of the invitation to take advantage of the gracious provision that we are assured God has given and will never withdraw (55:10–11). It is no wonder then that chapter 55 closes on a note of lyrical delight:

> You will go out in joy
>   and be led forth in peace;
> the mountains and hills
>   will burst into song before you,
> and all the trees of the field
>   will clap their hands.
> Instead of the thornbush will grow the pine tree,
>   and instead of briers the myrtle will grow.

---

2. Might it not be said, as Harry M. Orlinsky did (*Studies on the Second Part of the Book of Isaiah: The So-Called "Servant of the Lord" and "Suffering Servant" in Second Isaiah*, VTSup 14 [Leiden: Brill, 1967] 3–133), that these questions do not actually arise, since Israel had fully paid for its sins in the exile itself (cf. 40:1–2)? In fact, Israel did not fully pay for its sins in the exile. The exile was one result of their sinning, but the only complete effect of sin is death. Thus Israel should have gone into exile and simply disappeared from the face of the earth as a distinct people. The nation should have died, as should we all, as a result of our persistent self-alienation from the only source of life. That it did not do so was a result of God's grace. But the question still remains, what makes that grace possible?

> This will be for the LORD's renown,
>   for an everlasting sign,
>   which will not be destroyed." (Isa 55:12–13 NIV)

But all of this raises a problem. Why does the book not end at this point? What more is there to say after the revelation of the Servant who makes it possible for Israel, and indeed all persons, to become the servants of the Lord, or even better than that, his friends (John 15:13–15)? In fact there is much more to say, just as there is more to say after Isaiah's glad offering of himself for service in 6:9.[3] Those further things are contained in chapters 56–66, which seem to be addressed to the returned exiles in years after 539 or 538 B.C.[4] What we have in this final division of the book is a synthesis of the viewpoint of the two previous divisions (7–39; 40–55). If each of those divisions is read by itself, it could be seen as contradicting the other. One example of this feature may be seen in their contrasting uses of the concept of righteousness (ṣedaqâ).[5] In chapters 7–39 (indeed, in 1–39) righteousness is almost exclusively viewed as a kind of human behavior that is demanded by a righteous God (1:21; 26:2, etc.). And in general Israel fails to live in this manner. But in 40–55 the term is almost as exclusively used to describe God's character as deliverer (46:13; 51:5, etc.). It is an expression of God's "rightness" that he will not leave his covenant partner to suffer shame and disgrace. This is of course much more than legal "rightness." Viewed simply from the point of view of legality, the *only* right thing to do with a partner who had repeatedly broken the covenant as Israel had was to leave them in such a state. But as Moses had discovered (Exod 32:11–13; 34:6–7),

---

3. It is only very rarely that a sermon on Isaiah 6 in fact treats the whole chapter. Is it that we do not want to believe that a loving Father might call us to service that would not be pleasant and immediately rewarding?

4. There is little unanimity among higher critics as to the authorship and composition of these chapters. Among those who advocate multiple authorship of the book, many see chaps. 40–55 being the work of a single author, but there are few today who would see 56–66 in the same light. The proposal of Duhm that they were the work of "Third Isaiah" has now been largely rejected. Most today would agree with Paul Hanson that it is a composite from several sources collected over a period of time after the return (*The Dawn of Apocalyptic* [Philadelphia: Fortress, 1975]). Fewer would adopt his idea that the work represents the struggle between the the elitist followers of Ezekiel and the visionary marginalized followers of "Second Isaiah." This article will attempt to show in passing that there is every reason to see it as an integral part of the book and that as such it could stem from the mind, if not the hand, of the Isaiah who is responsible for the whole book. For treatments of these issues at greater length, see Oswalt, *The Book of Isaiah, Chapters 40–66* (Grand Rapids: Eerdmans, 1998) 10–16; and Oswalt, "Recent Studies in Old Testament Apocalyptic," in *The Face of Old Testament Studies: A Survey of Contemporary Approaches* (Grand Rapids: Baker, 1999) 369–89.

5. For a more detailed treatment of this issue see chapter 5 above.

this God is more than just. Thus, the right thing for him to do is always to act in grace. This means that "righteousness" is often used synonymously with "deliverance" in this part of the book (e.g., 46:13).

On the surface, at least, it would appear that the two divisions are in conflict. Are humans righteous because of their adherence to some divine standard of righteousness, or are they simply given a relationship with God (on the basis of their birthright) through the righteousness of God? Is "servant of the Lord" only a matter of relationship or is it a matter of character and behavior? Had the book ended at 55:13 that question would have been unresolved. But chapters 56–66 seem to have as one of their purposes the resolution of the problem. Here justice (*mišpāṭ*) and righteousness as demonstrated in concrete human behavior are called for. But at the same time it is God's righteousness that is seen as making such a thing possible.[6] This synthesis emerges immediately in 56:1:

> Keep justice and do righteousness,
> For my salvation is about to come,
>   And my righteousness to be revealed.

In other words, the demand of the first part of the book is to be met through the grace revealed in the second part. There is to be a real change in the behavior of God's servants, but that behavioral change is the result of appropriation of divine grace and not the result of human effort. I am aware that this assertion has a distinctly New Testament flavor, but I believe it is supported by the data without appeal to the New Testament.

Some of this data is found in recurring themes throughout the division. They are:

Gentiles coming to God	56:1–8; 66:18–23
The people corrupt, idolatrous	56:9–57:14; 66:3–4
Redemption for the contrite	57:15–21; 66:1–2
The people corrupt, idolatrous	58:1–59:8; 65:1–16
Confession of helplessness	59:9–15; 63:7–64:12
Divine Warrior	59:15–21; 63:1–6
Glory of Restored Zion	60:1–22; 61:4–62:12

When the occurrences of these themes are examined an interesting pattern emerges. The first recurrence is at the extreme ends of the segment;

---

6. The occurrences of the terms are as follows: Justice 56:1; 58:2; 59:4, 9, 11, 14, 15; 61:8; Righteousness 56:1(2 t.); 57:1(2 t.), 12; 58:2, 8; 59:9, 14, 16, 17; 60:21; 61:3, 10, 11; 62:1, 2; 63:1; 64:5, 6. Another term having to do with behavior that recurs frequently in this division is iniquity 57:17; 59:2, 3, 4, 6, 7, 12; 64:6, 7, 9; 65:7 (2 t.). This term occurs 14 times in 1–39, and 4 times in 40–55.

the next is one step inward, etc. When the recurrences are plotted graphically, the following pattern emerges:

    Gentiles coming to God 56:1–8
        The people corrupt, idolatrous 56:9–57:14
            Redemption for the contrite 57:15–21
                The people corrupt, idolatrous 58:1–59:8
                    Confession of helplessness 59:9–15
                        Divine Warrior 59:15–21
                            Glory of restored Zion 60:1:22
                              The anointed one 61:1–3
                            Glory of restored Zion 61:4–62:12
                        Divine Warrior 63:1–6
                  Confession of helplessness 63:7–64:12
              The people corrupt, idolatrous 65:1–16
            Redemption for the contrite 66:1–2
        The people corrupt, idolatrous 66:3–4 (17)
    Gentiles coming to God 66:18–23

There thus appears a clear chiastic structure in the segment.[7] The recognition of this structure answers a question many students of the book have when they come to this final division. They feel that the climax of the book is chapters 60–62 and that chapters 63–66 are an anti-climax. But when we recognize the chiastic structure we can see that the final four chapters are not anti-climactic at all. Rather, they are reinforcing the point made leading up to chapters 60–62. That point is that from God's perspective birthright has nothing to do with the glorious hope that beckons us all. Neither does "position" considered merely as a religious fiction. God is determined to have changed character in his servants, all the more so because he has himself provided the means for that change of character to take place. This divine determination is illustrated almost shockingly in the opening and closing segments. God is more pleased with foreigners and eunuchs who keep his covenant than he is with pure-bred Jews who do not.[8] But the shocking truth is that the people called to be God's chosen servants not only do not keep his covenant, but seem helpless to do so. They are proud and arrogant about being the chosen of God, and yet live lives that are an

---

    7. For further discussion of this structure, see Oswalt, *The Book of Isaiah, Chapters 40–66*, 461–65.

    8. This should not be taken to be an anti-Semitic remark. The same might be said in other terms: "God is more pleased with liberals who keep his covenant than with 'born-again' evangelicals who do not." The intent to gain attention by shock-effect is apparent.

offense to him, that call into question his very nature. What must take place? They must be delivered. The "arm of the Lord" that was bared on their (and our) behalf in chapters 49–53 must be bared again.[9] But what deliverance is being talked of here? What enemy is it that must be destroyed? What Edom is it whose blood stains the garments of the Warrior?

If scholars are correct, as seems likely, that these chapters are addressed to those who will have returned from exile, then the deliverance the Divine Warrior offers is not from Babylon. Nor is Edom, having been wiped out by the Babylonians 50 years earlier, the enemy to be destroyed. The enemy to be destroyed is persistent sinning, and the deliverance that is graciously promised is a deliverance from that kind of behavior that is a reproach to the Holy One of Israel. Thus it will be that the light of God can shine out of the lamp of Zion and draw all nations to himself (60:1–3). The servants have been endowed with the very righteousness of God. The placement of the Divine Warrior segments (59:15b–21; 63:1–6) on either side of the Glory of the Lord segments (60:1–22; 61:4–62:12) seems to me to make this point inescapable. There *is* glorious hope, but it is only for those who humbly admit their helplessness to live godly lives, who detest their persistent sinning, and who avail themselves of the grace of God through the Savior to live lives that witness to his delivering power (cf. Ezek. 36:20–26).

But there are three elements in chapters 56–66 that have no parallel member, as can be seen by the blanks in the graphic layout above. They are 61:1–3; 65:17–25; and 66:5–16. The latter two, occurring in the second part of the chiasm, reflect the impact of the revelation of the dawn of the Glory of the Lord in chapters 60–62. Pointing back to those promises while reiterating the present detriments to their realization (the sinful behavior of "you"), there is still the assurance that that bright future does indeed lie in the future for those who are truly his servants. Thus, in chapter 65, after a rather caustic contrast between those who *are* the Lord's servants and those who are not (65:11–16), there is a promise of the new heavens and earth God is preparing for his servants (65:17–25). Likewise, in chapter 66, after the denunciation of those who trust in ritual holiness, there is the promise to those "who tremble at his word" (66:5) that Zion will be filled with rejoicing as God rewards his servants and destroys their enemies (66:5–16). Thus the chiasm is not a static one but reflects the future reality that was portrayed at the center of the structure.

But the third element that does not recur is perhaps the most interesting. This is found at the very center of the chiastic structure, in 61:1–3. By definition, the center element of a chiasm is the most important, the one the

---

9. See the discussion on "the arm of the Lord" in the preceding chapter.

entire structure is pointing to. But what is the center here? Is it the dawning of the Glory of the Lord as recorded in all of chapters 60–62, with 61:1–3 merely being the central element in the center? If we were to conclude that the referent in those verses is merely a human speaker, the prophet or a member of the prophetic community, as many recent commentators do,[10] we should probably conclude that. However, not only is the placement of the material suggestive of something more important, so is the material itself. Hanson admits that the language is that applied to the Servant of the Lord in 42:1, and Childs agrees that there is a connection again to 48:16, with its reference to the Spirit. What Childs does not want to permit is that there is also a connection with 11:1–4 where the Messiah is endowed with the Spirit of God.[11] But even more important than these intertextual references is the function of these statements in their present context. What are they doing here? On either side are prophetic predictions of the dawn of the Glory of the Lord upon Israel, that his righteousness will flower in his people and that all the nations will stream to Zion in homage to Zion's God. This person is not merely going to tell of the divine grace that will enable all of this (61:1–2). He is going to *be* that grace *so that* "they may be called trees of *righteousness* [italics mine], the planting of the Lord that he may be glorified" (2–3). In 59:16 and 63:5 the Divine Warrior is the "arm of the Lord" who will make it possible for God's people to manifest his righteousness. Thus, this person is to be identified with that person, the Lord himself. That being so, this is a further revelation of the Messiah that the book has been pointing to throughout, and this segment is indeed the center of the chiasm in 56–66.[12]

When we see 61:1–3 in this way, it makes it easier to see how 60:1–22 and 61:4–62:12 parallel each other. If we look at 60:1–62:12 as some sort of a unit, it is very difficult to see any kind of structure in it. It seems miscellaneous in character.[13] On the other hand, when the two blocks of material

---

10. So Paul D. Hanson, *Isaiah 40–66*, Interpretation (Louisville: Westminster John Knox, 1995) 223–24.

11. Brevard S. Childs, *Isaiah*, OTL (Louisville: Westminster John Knox, 2001) 504–5.

12. When 61:1–3 is looked at in connection with 59:15–21 and 63:1–6, we perhaps see again the two poles of the Messianic person that have posed such problems for interpreters and theologians over the years. Is the Messiah the Davidic king coming in royal power, or is he the Child who will not break a bent reed? The answer to both questions is "yes." For further discussion of this polarity and others in the book, see chapters 1–3 above.

13. See the comments of R. E. Clements on chapter 60 in "'Arise, Shine for Your Light has Come': A Basic Theme of the Isaianic Tradition," in *Writing and Reading in the Scroll of Isaiah*, eds. C. Broyles and C. Evans (Leiden: Brill, 1997) 1:441–54.

on either side of 61:1–3 are compared with each other, we see commonalities and differences that are instructive. First of all, while this is certainly not determinative, the two blocks of material are almost exactly the same size, with 22 verses in the first and 20 in the second. Second, both discuss the righteousness of God having been realized in the behavior of his people (60:17, 21; 61:10, 11; 62:1, 2). Third, both make the appearance of the divine righteousness (God's glory) in the lives of God's servants the reason for the coming of earth's nations to Jerusalem (60:3; 61:11; 62:2). Fourth, this coming of the nations is the chief theme of both blocks of material.

However, the two blocks are not merely repetitive. They look at these common themes from slightly different perspectives, as might be expected if they are not indeed part of the same unit, but are separated by the restatement of the cause of all this in 61:1–3. In chapter 60 four segments can be identified. The first is introductory (vv. 1–3). Here the basic point is made: the glory of God will now be seen in the very nation that only one chapter previously had confessed that there was only darkness and evil resident in it (59:1–15a). And to that light of God, all the nations will be drawn. The second and third segments expand on verse three as they speak of the nations coming to the light. In the second segment (vv. 4–9) it is said that the nations will come bringing Zion's children back to her, but also bringing their gold to beautify the Lord's house. Verse 9 confirms the statement of 51:5 that the ends of the earth ("the islands") will put their trust in ("wait for") Zion's God. The third segment (vv. 10–16) might seem at first glance to contradict what was just said. Here the foreigners serve Zion and if they will not, they will be destroyed (v. 12). This hardly sounds like partners in worship! But the overall point of the segment is to focus upon the amazing reversal that God is going to orchestrate for his people. Once foreigners came to destroy Judah and Jerusalem. Now they come to build it up. Once the city gates were fast shut to keep the looting nations out. Now the gates stand open to allow the eager nations to come in with their gifts. Once Israel was forced to bow down in oppressive servitude to the nations. Now the nations will serve Israel. Thus, the point is not so much to make some final statement about the nations as it is to underline the completely reversed relationship between the past and the future. When the second and third segments are read together, as they should be, and not in opposition, a more wholistic picture emerges. The nations may join with Zion in worship, but if they will not, they will be compelled to servitude and if not to that, then to destruction.[14] The fourth and final segment (vv. 17–22) expands on verses 1 and 2, that is, the nature of the glory that will be seen in Zion. There will be

---

14. For further discussion, see chapter 8 above.

no question that it will be a reflected glory. It will be God's light that shines out of the nation (vv. 19–20); it will be his righteousness that is reproduced in the nation (vv. 17, 21). The reference to the nation as a plantation of trees is interesting because while the same word occurs in 61:3, and also in the context of righteousness, trees are used throughout the book, both to represent a life that is blessed of God and a life that is lived in arrogant defiance of God.[15] In short, what this segment portrays is the kind of reversal that God had promised in 1:25–27: from dross to gold, particularly on the ethical level. It seems very significant to me that the next material the reader encounters is the final revelation (after 59:15b-21 and 63:1–6) of the means whereby that reversal can occur, namely the Messiah, in 61:1–3.

How then does 61:4–62:12 function as a chiastic partner of 60:1–22? A similar collection of themes is to be found: Israel's reflected glory drawing the nations to Jerusalem (61:8–9, 11; 62:2, 10); the nations that had destroyed Zion becoming the ones to rebuild it (61:4–5); God's city being a place of beauty and delight rather than horror and derision (61:7; 62:4, 12). But the way in which these themes are presented is rather different from the way they are presented in the first occurrence of the pair, and I would contend that this is because of the occurrence of 61:1–3 between them. Here in 61:4–62:12 the focus is more on the change in Israel itself and less on the change in its circumstances. And that change has primarily to do with Israel's relation with God. Here the previously discussed issues of "salvation" and "righteousness" come together in explicit ways. Here also the issue of Israel's alienation from God is addressed. Israel sees itself as "delivered" or "saved," and that means that God's righteousness is seen in her. This is not merely the fact that he has righteously delivered her from her sinfulness, but that his actual righteous character is displayed in her.[16] This is the truest evidence that she is "no longer forsaken" (62:4, 12), and it is this evidence that becomes the attraction of Jerusalem for the nations (61:8–62:2).

In fact, this thought that Israel's character is the attraction for the nations forms the entire core of the unit. Verses 4–7 recap the previous thought of the oppressor nations now rebuilding the city and nation, so that its former shame is replaced with glory. But why is this so? 61:8 begins with the causal conjunction *kî* which indicates that what follows is the

---

15. 1:29; 2:13; 10:33–34; 37:24; 44:23; 55:12; 57:5; 65:22. On a related note it is surely significant that "gardens" (of trees) appears in the first and last chapters of the book, both in connection with pagan worship (1:29, 30; 66:17; cf. also 65:3). By contrast, Israel is God's garden (see 61:11).

16. The tendency of modern translations to translate *ṣedaqâ* with "[your] vindication" instead of "[your] righteousness" in these segments is very unfortunate because it obscures the point that is being made in this entire division of the book.

substantiation for what preceded. God will have restored glory to his people because he wants to display his ethical character in them. God will display this righteousness in his people before all the nations.

> For I, the Lord, love justice,
> > hating robbery in place of burnt offering.
> I will make their work true,
> > and will cut an everlasting covenant with them.
> Their descendants will be known among the nations,
> > and their offspring in the midst of the peoples.
> Everyone who sees them will acknowledge them,
> > because they are the posterity the Lord has blessed. (61:8–9)

In one sense this thought continues steadily onward right to the end of chapter 62, with 62:10–12 being a kind of climactic conclusion. Thus 62:10 can speak of raising up a signal flag to call the nations home to Zion. "Signal flag" is used throughout the book, normally as a call to assembly.[17] Both the first and the last occurrences (5:26 and 62:10) use it in this way but to very different effect. In the first the nations are called to come and destroy God's vineyard. In this last occurrence, they are called to come and see what God's vineyard looks like when he has redeemed them and made it possible for the life of his Torah ("the everlasting covenant" 61:8) to be realized in them. But along the way are two other occurrences that are of unmistakable importance. They are 11:10, 12 and 49:22. What is this signal flag that calls the nations to their Lord? It is the Messiah who will himself be the flag to call the nations to himself (11:10) and who will be the sign for the nations to restore the captives to God's city (11:12; 49:22).

Thus the chiastic pair (60:1–22 and 61:4–62:12) complement each other as they speak of the fulfillment of the picture that was first painted in 2:1–5 and 4:2–6. A nation that has been made pure and clean, from which God is no longer alienated, but in whom he has taken up his residence, becomes such a manifestation of the validity of the Torah, that the nations come streaming to learn it and to conform their lives to it. This reality is no glory to the nation, any more than Isaiah's ministry was a testimony to him. Just as was the case with the prophet, so the ministry of the nation would be a testimony to the glorious grace of God, a grace made available supremely and solely through the Messiah. In this light, chapters 60–62 do indeed form the climax of the book, but more than that, they express the climax of history, when God's saving purposes will have finally been realized and "all flesh will come to worship before me" (66:22).

---

17. 5:26; 11:10, 12; 13:2; 18:3; 30:17; 31:9; 33:23; 49:22

www.ingramcontent.com/pod-product-compliance
Lightning Source LLC
Chambersburg PA
CBHW030858170426
43193CB00009BA/650